Ephesians
Commentary

Written by Bob Warren

Thanks to the following saints who devoted countless
hours to the production of this work:

Trey Alley
Brent Armstrong
Kylie Barron
Myra Cleaver
Jhonda Johnston

Published by The Hill Publishing, LLC
PO Box 13
Hardin, KY 42048
www.lifeonthehill.org

ISBN: 978-1-62727-070-0

All scripture, unless otherwise noted, is from the
New American Standard Bible.

Table Of Contents

Introduction

Welcome to an in-depth analysis of Paul's letter to the Ephesians. If you have studied our *Romans 1-8* series, you will find those truths mesh perfectly with Paul's words to the church at Ephesus. Thus, Paul's epistle to the Romans is the perfect backdrop for what he records here. I perceive *Romans 1-8* as a delicious cheeseburger—Ephesians as a T-bone steak. Much "chewing" is required to digest the grandeur of this epistle, so enjoy every tasty morsel!

Paul wrote this epistle between 60 and 62 A.D. during his first imprisonment in Rome (Ephesians 3:1). Some theologians perceive Ephesians as a letter read by multiple churches in Asia Minor. More than likely Paul wrote it to believers in the region of Ephesus, where he spent at least three years (Acts 20:31), two of which he taught at the school of Tyrannus (Acts 19:9-10). However, the phrase, *"at Ephesus"* (Ephesians 1:1), is not included in some of the most ancient manuscripts. Paul dictated this letter to Tychicus who delivered it from Rome (Ephesians 6:21-22).

Since Paul had spent considerable time with the recipients of this letter, he could go into greater depth with his readers. Consequently, this letter is filled with the "deeper things of Christ." In fact, chapters 1-3 are inundated with these "deeper things" while chapters 4-6 teach practical ways to "live out" these wonderful truths. Expect to be encouraged as we begin our journey. It should be much fun.

Note: Words and phrases are sometimes underlined in verses for emphasis. Words are also inserted within brackets in particular passages for clarity.

Ephesians 1

Ephesians 1:1—Paul, an apostle of Christ Jesus by the will of God, to the saints who are at Ephesus, and who are faithful in Christ Jesus:

Paul not only addresses his apostolic authority, but also the fact that these believers are saints and faithful. We will break down this verse, as well as all of the verses in this epistle, and deal with them phrase-by-phrase.

Paul, an apostle of Christ Jesus, (1:1a)

Paul was an apostle of Jesus Christ to the Gentiles (Romans 11:13). The apostles were messengers of God sent by *"Jesus Christ, and God the Father"* (Galatians 1:1) to lay the foundation of the gospel of Christ. Their teaching was the final authority in the early church (they had *"seen"* Christ—1Corinthians 9:1) and was confirmed by signs and wonders and miracles (2Corinthians 12:12). Hence, when the believers at Ephesus received this letter, they likely took every word to be absolute truth. Because Paul met Christ after the resurrection (Acts 9:1-30), he was *"untimely born"* (1Corinthians 15:8). He, however, was not inferior to even *"the most eminent apostles"* (2Corinthians 12:11-12).

by the will of God, (1:1b)

God's *"will,"* not Paul's, determined that Paul would become an apostle. Thus, sitting under Gamaliel (Acts 5:34; Acts 22:3), a great teacher of the Law, failed to qualify him. His overwhelming apostolic authority came from receiving his gospel through a revelation of Jesus Christ (Galatians 1:11-17). He actually saw Christ (Acts 9:1-9), a prerequisite for the original twelve (1Corinthians 9:1).

to the saints who are at Ephesus, (1:1c)

Paul wrote this epistle to *"the saints"* (holy ones) at Ephesus, believers with whom he had spent much time during his missionary journeys. As we discussed earlier, he taught at Ephesus for a prolonged season while on his third missionary journey (Acts 19:1-10). Therefore, Paul's readers would have likely understood exactly what he meant by *"saints"* (or holy ones). Also, Paul writes in several other epistles that all New Testament believers are saints (Romans 1:7, Romans 8:27, 1Corinthians 14:33, 2Corinthians 13:13, Ephesians 1:18, and Philippians 1:1). He taught that God makes New Testament believers holy and blameless at the point of salvation/justification (Romans 3:20; Romans 5:1; 1Corinthians 1:2; Galatians

3:24; Ephesians 2:8-9; Ephesians 1:4; Titus 3:5). Because this truth was the foundation of Paul's gospel, these readers would have understood his message. Note: A saint is <u>not</u> a person who lives void of sin. A saint is an individual who has, at the point of salvation, been made holy in his person (in his soul and spirit) but whose behavior is progressively increasing in holiness.

and who are faithful in Christ Jesus: (1:1d)

Paul also states that these *"saints"* were *"faithful in Christ Jesus."* This phrase can be viewed from a couple of perspectives.

The first perspective stems from the fact that these believers could not quit the race—quit being Christians. The God Who had begun a good work in them would see it to completion (Philippians 1:6). Hence, God is responsible for completing the believer's salvation—not the believer (Hebrews 7:25).

The second perspective is influenced by the environment surrounding these believers. Wuest, in his commentary on the book of Ephesians, writes:

> There were two kinds of saints (*hagios*) in Ephesus, those who were devotees of the pagan religions, and those who were devotees of Christianity. The Greek word was taken by Paul from the Greek mystery religions and transplanted into Christianity. It, therefore, needed careful definition. It was the saints who were believers in Christ Jesus to whom Paul was writing, not the 'saints' in the pagan religions. (Wuest, 1989, p. 20)[1]

This insight supports Paul's words, *"to the saints who are at Ephesus, and who are faithful in Christ Jesus,"* confirming that his readers were believers in Jesus Christ—not unbelievers who followed the pagan religions of Paul's day.

Ephesians 1:2—Grace to you and peace from God our Father and the Lord Jesus Christ.

"Grace to you and peace from God our Father and the Lord Jesus Christ" is one of Paul's favorite statements. He also employs it in Romans 1:7, 1Corinthians 1:3, 2Corinthians 1:2, Galatians 1:3, Philippians 1:2, Colossians 1:2, 1Thessalonians 1:1, 2Thessalonians 1:2, 1Timothy 1:2, 2Timothy 1:2, Titus 1:4, and Philemon 1:3.

Grace to you and peace (1:2a)

In 2Corinthians 9:8, Paul states that *"God is able to make all grace abound to you, that always having all sufficiency in everything, you may have an abundance for every good deed."* Abundant grace is available for every need in the believer's life. Peace, which results from accepting God's grace, is a *"fruit of the Spirit"* (Galatians 5:22).

Grace can be defined as "unmerited favor" as well as "the power to do God's will." Paul realized that accepting God's grace is a prerequisite for peace to inhabit the soul. Paul is not only dealing with saving grace here, he is also referencing the grace accessible to the believer as he faces life's challenges. When this grace is accepted, peace results and the believer is energized with God's authority and power. When it is rejected, turmoil and confusion are inevitable and the believer walks in defeat.

God's grace is sufficient for any situation the believer faces (2Corinthians 12:9). Paul urges Timothy to *"be strong in the grace that is in Christ Jesus"* (2Timothy 2:1), and the writer of Hebrews revealed that this grace is found by boldly approaching God's throne (Hebrews 4:16). Peter also states that grace is *"multiplied"* to the believer as his knowledge of God and Jesus Christ increases (2Peter 1:2), and that the believer is to *"grow in the grace and knowledge of our Lord and Savior Jesus Christ"* (2Peter 3:18).

from God our Father and the Lord Jesus Christ. (1:2b)

This phrase confirms that God the Father and Jesus provide grace and peace. Because the Father and the Son are members of the same Godhead, Jesus is Deity just as the Father is Deity (Colossians 2:9). Thus, both grace and peace are *"from God our Father and the Lord Jesus Christ."* (The Holy Spirit, the third Person of the Godhead, also provides *"peace"* based on Galatians 5:22.)

Ephesians 1:3—Blessed be the God and Father of our Lord Jesus Christ, who has blessed us with every spiritual blessing in the heavenly places in Christ,

What a powerful verse! We could camp out in verses 3-14 the remainder of our days and fail to exhaust the depths of their significance. Therefore, even the short time allotted to them in this study should be extremely enlightening. If we can grasp even a portion of what Paul is communicating, all doubt, worry, and fear—anything that might steal our joy—will be given to the Father to rectify, rather than remain a deterrent to our spiritual wellbeing. We have all eternity to bask in the greatness of these Scriptures, so be encouraged.

Verses 3-14 comprise one sentence in the Greek language. As he begins verse 3, Paul seems to become so enthralled in the wonder of these truths that he can hardly contain himself. He almost seems out of breath by the end of verse 14. My prayer is that these truths might stimulate the same wonder, gratitude, and awe in us as well!

Blessed be the God and Father of our Lord Jesus Christ, (1:3a)

Paul begins by blessing (praising) *"the God and Father of our Lord Jesus Christ,"* the Source of all blessings—including those listed in verses 3-14. Blessing (praising) God comes naturally once one has a proper view of God's blessings. Blessing, praise, and adoration are natural byproducts of understanding the heart of God and His provision for man. If faith is to work *"by love"* (Galatians 5:6), and if love is the only legitimate motivator for the believer (2Corinthians 5:14), what better way to begin establishing a deeper love and faith than to understand His blessings? But we must be very careful. Paul praised (blessed) God not only for the blessings he had received through Christ, but also because he had come to understand God's heart and His ultimate plan and purpose in the gospel.

As long as the believer walks with and worships God solely for what he (the believer) receives through the cross, he lives in shallowness and immaturity— which was the case with me. I initially submitted to Christ for the benefits I received, never considering what the Father, Son, and Holy Spirit might have received (and continue to receive) through Christ's selfless submission to the cross. After all, I was delivered from hell (John 3:16), God would supply all my needs (Philippians 4:19), He would work all things for my good (Romans 8:28), I would reign with Christ (Revelation 20:4), and on and on. In other words, my gospel was a man-centered gospel. I submitted to Christ for what "I" received through the cross. But eventually, as I matured in the faith, I began comprehending what God the Father received through Jesus' sacrifice, what the Son received through the same, and what the Person of the Spirit received as well. This new insight allowed me to begin, and I emphasize "begin," to comprehend how the three Persons of the Trinity—God the Father, God the Son, and God the Holy Spirit—relate to one another. In essence, the heart of the Triune God, as well as His ultimate plan for man, was revealed in such a new and exciting way that every aspect of my Christian experience was totally revolutionized.

Have you ever wondered why God the Father would subject Himself to the pain of having His Son die on a cross? When I think of having my son Benjamin put to death for any reason, especially by way of crucifixion, I realize my agony would greatly surpass his. The Father's pain must have been excruciating! But consider that the Father suffered this heartache for the sake of the Son, so the Son might receive a body (the body of Christ, the church—which began in Acts 2) through which to express Himself to the universe (Ephesians 5:23, 29-30; Romans 12:4-5; 1Corinthians 10:17; 1Corinthians 12:12-27). The Father suffered also that the Holy Spirit might receive a temple in which to dwell (Ephesians 2:19-22). (We will discuss this temple at greater length when we study Ephesians chapters two and five.) The Father submitted Himself to such agony solely for the benefit of the other two Persons of the Trinity, the Son and the Spirit. Also consider that the Son went to Calvary, not for what He would receive through the cross, but for what the Father and Spirit would receive. Jesus' statements in John 7:18, John 8:50, 54, and John 14:13 confirm that Jesus never sought His own glory, but desired that through His obedience the Father might be glorified. Through the cross, the Father received a family (John 1:12) that increases numerically as individuals submit to Christ— and, again, the Spirit received a temple that enlarges as believers accept Jesus during the church age (Ephesians 2:19-22). But what is the Spirit's mindset? The Spirit glorifies the Son by revealing what Christ accomplished through the cross and His subsequent resurrection (John 15:26; 16:13-15). Hence, the Spirit's choices are never for the betterment of Himself, but for the benefit of the Son. If anyone knows the Son, he knows the Father also (John 14:9). Therefore, as the Spirit glorifies the Son, He glorifies the Father also. Thus the Spirit's actions are for the benefit of the other two Persons of the Trinity—as was the case with the Father and Son. No selfishness is involved in these relationships!

We, in our lives today, are to love the Father not just for what we receive from the relationship, but to bring joy to Him through being His offspring (John 1:12). After all, we *"exist for Him"* (1Corinthians 8:6). The same principle applies with the Son. We are privileged to be brothers with Christ, not just for what we gain through the relationship, but because we, as His body (Ephesians 5:23, 29-30), can serve as a vehicle through which He expresses Himself to the world. As for our relationship with the Spirit, we are being fitted together into a temple, a temple that serves as a *"dwelling of God in the Spirit"* (Ephesians 2:20-22). Because each member of the Triune Godhead lives for the Others' good, the individual members of the body of Christ, having *"the mind of Christ"* (1Corinthians 2:16), should display selfless living in all relationships, including those with the Godhead.

As we begin to understand God's heart and live as He lives, "self" is taken out of the equation. Only then can we enter into meaningful, fulfilling, and lasting relationships that benefit others. The transformation in our families, churches, workplaces, schools, in fact, in every facet of our lives, would be beyond belief should this type of love be the norm?

We must begin to perceive the cross from a selfless point of reference if we are to properly understand the heart of God and His ultimate plan. Therefore, as we speak with others concerning Christ, we must present a God-centered gospel—never one so shallow as to be man-centered.

You will understand very little from this point forward if your view of the cross remains self-centered—that Jesus died solely to get you out of hell and into heaven, leaving you to flounder on planet earth until He takes you home. Are you willing to allow the Lord to deepen your understanding of the death, burial, and resurrection of Christ? If so, Paul's epistle to the Ephesians should provide insight into the awesomeness of God, which, in turn, will result in praise. Just wait and see!

Overall, a deep passion for God's heart is lacking in believers today. Is it any wonder that Christ's body knows so little about praise? The solution is not better voices, better songs, better lyrics, or a new style of worship. The answer lies in understanding God's heart and the awesomeness of the selfless sacrifice of His Son.

God doesn't possess an ego that needs to be stroked. His desire for praise is not linked to such immature reasoning. Praise brings us into His presence (Psalm 100:4) so we can begin to know Him (Philippians 3:10) and, in turn, allow His Spirit to lead us in the way of truth (Romans 8:14; 2Corinthians 3:18). But some believers perceive God as incapable of functioning without their encouragement, so they praise Him out of duty rather than love. This mindset could not be more misguided. Only adoration from a heart filled with gratitude and awe will fulfill God's ultimate purpose in praise—that the one doing the praising will, in the end, benefit the most.

Verse 3 conclusively settles the matter of Christ's relationship to the Father. Jesus is God the Father's offspring, regardless of who teaches otherwise. If not, Joseph would have been Jesus' father, and Jesus would have been born with a sin nature (Adamic nature or dead spirit)—the Adamic nature is inherited by all descendants of Adam (Romans 5:12-19). Ephesians 2:3 reveals that man's sin *"nature"* (Adamic *"nature"*), not the sins he commits as an unbeliever, makes him a child *"of wrath"*:

> *Among them we too all formerly lived in the lusts of our flesh, indulging the desires of the flesh and of the mind, and were by nature children of wrath, even as the rest.* (Ephesians 2:3)

Thus, had Joseph been Jesus' father, Jesus could not be Savior—even having lived a sinless life. His sin nature would have made Him a child *"of wrath"* (Ephesians 2:3). Hence, He had to be God the Father's Son. The *Romans 1-8* course produced and distributed by this ministry includes a section (Romans 5:12 through Romans

6:6) that addresses this subject, which would be beneficial to reference should you possess that resource.

Matthew includes Joseph's lineage in Matthew 1:1-16 to prove that had Jesus been Joseph's son, He could never prosper as King over Israel because Jeconiah (Matthew 1:11) was part of Joseph's lineage. According to Jeremiah 22:24-30, Coniah, the same person as Jehoiachin, or Jeconiah, could have no descendant prosper while sitting on David's throne. Thus, had Jesus been Joseph's son, Jesus could never rule as *"KING OF KINGS, AND LORD OF LORDS"* as required by Revelation 19:16. Thank you, Matthew, for helping confirm the virgin birth.

who has blessed us with every spiritual blessing in the heavenly places in Christ. (1:3b)

God's idea of a good time is blessing His people. As early as the days of Abraham, God was preparing to bless mankind through Abraham's offspring (Genesis 12:3), the *"seed"* of Genesis 3:15. This *"seed,"* Who is Christ (Galatians 3:16), a descendant of Abraham, would *"bruise"* the serpent's (Satan's) *"head"* (Genesis 3:15). Through this avenue Abraham would bless the world (Genesis 12:3). Therefore, Christ was sent to bless all men who choose to accept Him as Savior (John 3:16-17).

Paul blessed *"the God and Father of our Lord Jesus Christ"* (Ephesians 1:3a) because He *"has blessed"* New Testament believers *"with every spiritual blessing in the heavenly places in Christ"* (Ephesians 1:3b). Can we even begin to comprehend the scope of this astounding truth? God the Father not only sent His Son to offer salvation to fallen man, but to bless repentant sinners *"with every spiritual blessing"* the moment they repent and believe. These blessings mean that the instant we were saved (justified—Romans 5:1), God gave us everything we needed to live life abundantly. In fact, all we will be doing until the Lord takes us home is digging through that huge treasure chest of spiritual blessings we received the moment we accepted Christ. For this reason (and an abundance of others) we should pursue spiritual maturity, for only then can we begin to comprehend all that is already ours. Many church saints, due to immaturity, are "doing" to try to attain what is already theirs. Defeat and despair result—a big smile and very sad eyes.

God blessed us with these spiritual blessings *"in the heavenly places in Christ"* (Ephesians 1:3b). Because Christ is now at the right hand of the Father (Hebrews 8:1-2; 9:24), to be placed into Christ means that we were taken into the realm of the heavenlies. As a result, Paul's words, *"who has blessed us with every spiritual blessing in the heavenly places in Christ"* (Ephesians 1:3b), mean that when we repented of our sin and accepted Christ through faith, He, through the avenue of the

Holy Spirit (1Corinthians 12:13), placed us into Christ. I don't even pretend to understand all the positive ramifications here, but one thing is certain. We who believe during the church age (an age which began in Acts 2) are *"in Christ"* (2Corinthians 5:17) and have been blessed with every spiritual blessing required for victorious living (Ephesians 1:3b). So, if you are God's child, give up on trying to perform well enough to obtain more spiritual blessings. They are already yours. So, *"rest"* dear friend (Hebrews 4:9-10) while enjoying the view from above.

As we continue, key on the phrases *"in Christ"* and *"in Him."* To omit these phrases would drastically change the meaning of this epistle; in fact, removing them from the New Testament would birth utter chaos. On the other hand, through viewing our walk from this perspective we realize that whatever we are or possess is *"in Christ."* Our battles are His battles, for we fight *"in the strength of His might"* (Ephesians 6:10). We also wear His armor (Ephesians 6:11 and 13). *"In Christ"* we: have *"redemption"* (Romans 3:24), are *"alive to God"* (Romans 6:11), have *"eternal life"* (Romans 6:23), are *"saints"* (1Corinthians 1:2), have received *"the grace of God"* (1Corinthians 1:4), are lead *"to triumph"* (2Corinthians 2:14), are made into a *"new"* creation (2Corinthians 5:17), have *"liberty"* (Galatians 2:4), have received *"the blessing of Abraham"* (Galatians 3:14), have been *"seated"* with Christ in the heavenlies (Ephesians 2:6), *"have been brought near"* to God *"by the blood of Christ"* (Ephesians 2:13), have been *"forgiven"* (Ephesians 4:32), have all of our *"needs"* supplied (Philippians 4:19), are *"complete"* (Colossians 1:28). *"In Him"* we: are *"enriched"* in *"everything"* (1Corinthians 1:5), have *"become the righteousness of God"* (2Corinthians 5:21), *"have redemption"* and *"forgiveness"* (Ephesians 1:7), were *"sealed...with the Holy Spirit"* (Ephesians 1:13), *"have been made complete"* (Colossians 2:10), were *"circumcised with a circumcision made without hands"* (Colossians 2:11). And this is only a partial listing of the blessings received as a result of being *"in Christ"* or *"in Him."*

Scripture also speaks of Christ living in the New Testament believer. Passages such as Galatians 2:20 and Colossians 1:27 confirm that Jesus lives in all church saints. But Scripture communicates more about us being in Christ than it speaks of Christ dwelling in us. Therefore, from what vantage point would the Lord have us live? From the heavenly vantage point, of course!

Ephesians 1:4—just as He chose us in Him before the foundation of the world, that we should be holy and blameless before Him. In love

New Testament believers were chosen in Christ *"before the foundation of the world"* (Ephesians 1:4a). This phrase must be handled with care, for many strange doctrines have evolved from misconstruing Paul's intent.

just as He chose us in Him before the foundation of the world, (1:4a)

God chose us, but understanding <u>where</u> He chose us is of utmost importance if the passage is to be interpreted in context. We were chosen by God in Christ (*"in Him"*—1:4a). Thus, we were <u>not</u> chosen to be placed in Him. We were chosen once we were *"in Him."* The Scriptures teach as well that we were not placed in Christ and made new until we chose (in our depravity) to receive Him as Savior (John 1:12; 1Corinthians 12:13; 2Corinthians 5:17). Let's allow the full counsel of God's Word to reveal how these truths are to be perceived.

We learned earlier that we, like the church at Ephesus, were *"blessed...with every spiritual blessing in the heavenly places in Christ"* (Ephesians 1:3b). Hence, having been placed *"in Christ"* we are *"blessed...with every spiritual blessing"*— one of which is sharing in Jesus' chosenness. Let me explain.

Christ, according to Luke 9:35, was *"chosen"*:

> ... *"This is My Son, <u>My Chosen One;</u> listen to Him!"* (Luke 9:35)

Isaiah 42:1 also speaks of Christ's chosenness:

> *"Behold, My Servant, whom I uphold; <u>My chosen one</u> in whom My soul delights. I have put My Spirit upon Him; He will bring forth justice to the nations.* (Isaiah 42:1)

God the Father chose Jesus to be the Savior of the world, further confirmed by Luke 23:35, 1Peter 2:4, and 1Peter 2:6. His chosenness, however, had nothing to do with His eternal destiny, for He was in heaven when the Father chose Him. Nor was He chosen, obviously, to spend eternity in hell. He was chosen to serve as Savior.

We must be careful not to equate Jesus' chosenness with selection. Christ was not "selected" from a group of candidates qualified to function in the "office" of Messiah. No one but the eternal Son was capable of paying man's sin debt. Therefore, His chosenness had nothing to do with selection.

But you may ask, "Were not the twelve disciples chosen?" The twelve apostles were chosen, but not for salvation. They were chosen to be apostles—to fulfill a particular function within the body of Christ—an office they could accept or reject. In John 6:70 Jesus states:

> ... *"Did I Myself not choose you, the twelve, and yet one of you is a devil?"* (John 6:70)

Had they been chosen for salvation, why was Judas, who died unsaved (John 17:12), included in the twelve? The disciples' chosenness is also mentioned in passages such as Luke 6:13, John 13:18, John 15:16 and 19, Acts 1:2 and 24-25, some of which reference all twelve apostles while others speak of only eleven (the twelve minus Judas). The apostles were chosen to office, an office Judas chose to reject.

God even chose the nation of Israel (Deuteronomy 7:7-8; Isaiah 44:1; 45:4; Acts 13:17; Romans 9:11; Romans 11:28), but not for salvation. She was chosen to bring the Messiah into the world and to take the message of His coming to the Gentiles, but God has saved only those Jews who have exercised faith in the *"seed"* of Genesis 3:15. This *"seed,"* of course, *"is, Christ"* (Galatians 3:16). Consider as well that since the beginning of the church age in Acts 2, all who have chosen in their depravity to receive Christ (both Jews and Gentiles) have been placed into Christ (after believing) and entered into His chosenness. For this reason Paul can say, *"Just as He chose us in Him"* (Ephesians 1:4a). We were chosen *"in Him"* (and entered into His chosenness) because we were placed *"in Him"* after we exercised repentance and faith while depraved. Thus, we were not chosen (or selected) to be placed into Christ, but were chosen once we were *"in Him."*

Ephesians 1:4a states that we were chosen in Him *"before the foundation of the world."* Paul is not teaching that God *"chose"* (selected) us before we were born (or from eternity past) to be placed into Christ, rather he is communicating that when we accepted Christ we were placed into Christ (2Corinthians 5:17; 1Corinthians 12:13) and entered into His chosenness. We also received Christ's kind of life, eternal life, having no beginning and no end. Therefore, once we were placed into Christ and received eternal life, the Father saw us as having always been in Christ. This rock-solid truth allows us to have been in Him before the foundation of the world, even though our entry point into Christ occurred almost two thousand years after the cross. Are you beginning to see the necessity of living from the view above—from the heavenlies where you are "in Christ"? Without this view our vision is extremely limited.

We must not overlook the fact that *"elect"* and *"chosen"* are synonymous, and thus interchangeable, as evidenced by 1Peter 1:1-2 in the NASB (*"chosen"*) and the KJV (*"elect"*):

> *Peter, an apostle of Jesus Christ, to the strangers scattered*
> *throughout Pontus, Galatia, Cappadocia, Asia, and Bithynia, Elect*

according to the foreknowledge of God the Father, through
sanctification of the Spirit, unto obedience and sprinkling of the
blood of Jesus Christ: Grace unto you, and peace, be multiplied.
(1Peter 1:1-2 KJV)

Peter, an apostle of Jesus Christ, to those who reside as aliens,
scattered throughout Pontus, Galatia, Cappadocia, Asia, and
Bithynia, who are chosen according to the foreknowledge of God
the Father, by the sanctifying work of the Spirit, that you may obey
Jesus Christ and be sprinkled with His blood: May grace and
peace be yours in fullest measure. *(1Peter 1:1-2 NASB)*

The following truth confirms that a New Testament believer is chosen/elected to office when he is placed in Christ through the power of the Holy Spirit after repenting and believing while depraved—not chosen/elected to salvation from eternity past.

1Peter 1:1-2 states that New Testament believers, church saints, are *"chosen* [elected] *according to the foreknowledge of God." "Foreknowledge"* means "to know beforehand." We will verify shortly that the Scriptures require God's *"foreknowledge"* to precede that time when a New Testament believer is *"chosen"* (elected). Thus, church saints could not have been *"chosen"* (elected) to salvation from eternity past by means of an eternal decree. Nothing, not even God's eternal foreknowledge, can precede what has always existed. (If this statement is somewhat confusing, Diagrams 1, 2, 3, 7 and 8 in the Reference Section should bring clarification.) Consequently, church saints are chosen/elected once they are placed in Christ through God's Spirit (1Corinthians 12:13) after repenting and believing while depraved, leaving ample room for God's foreknowledge to precede such an arrangement.

The Scriptures teach, beyond doubt, that Christ is the Father's *"chosen one"* (Luke 9:35; Isaiah 42:1):

... *"This is My Son, My Chosen One; listen to Him!"* (Luke 9:35)

"Behold, My Servant, whom I uphold; My chosen one in whom My
soul delights. I have put My Spirit upon Him; He will bring forth
justice to the nations. (Isaiah 42:1)

As confirmed earlier, Jesus was chosen by the Father, not to salvation, but to the office of Messiah. Hence, when we were placed in Christ subsequent to repenting and believing while depraved, we were placed in the *"chosen one"* of Luke 9:35

and Isaiah 42:1, Jesus Himself. To what were we chosen once we were placed in Him? We were chosen to office, for all New Testament believers receive a special gift (office) in conjunction with being placed in the Father's *"chosen one"*:

> *As each one has received a special gift, employ it in serving one another, as good stewards of the manifold grace of God.* (1Peter 4:10)

This special gift is similar to the disciples' chosenness. The disciples were <u>not</u> chosen to salvation, but rather to apostleship (John 6:70)—an office that could be accepted or rejected, as shown by Judas' betrayal (John 6:70).

Conclusion: All New Testament believers are chosen to office (to a special position, or gifting, within Christ's body—1Peter 4:10) after repenting and believing while depraved.

Would you agree that election (the New Testament believer's chosenness) is relatively easy to comprehend? It becomes complicated only when branches of Calvinism redefine "foreknowledge" as "foreordination" or "predestination," a subject addressed in *God's Heart as it Relates to Foreknowledge/Predestination*—a resource produced and distributed by this ministry.

We can be certain that God's foreknowledge must precede the New Testament believer's election/chosenness because the action or entity that follows the words *"according to"* in any verse in God's Word (such as in 1Peter 1:1-2) must occur (or exist) <u>before</u> the action or entity that precedes the words *"according to."* Stated differently:

If A is <u>according to</u> B

Then B <u>precedes</u> A

For instance, God *"commanded"* Noah to act in a certain way before Noah responded in obedience:

> *Thus Noah did; <u>according to</u> all that God had commanded him, so he did.* (Genesis 6:22)

This truth applies in every instance (all 790 in the NASB and 725 in the KJV) where *"according to"* is implemented in the Scriptures. Consequently, the election of New Testament believers cannot occur in situations where God's foreknowledge cannot apply; for the election of church saints is *"according to"* His *"foreknowledge"* (1Peter 1:2 KJV).

> *Elect <u>according to</u> the foreknowledge of God the Father,...* (1Peter 1:2 KJV)

Peter confirms that believers could not have been elected/chosen to salvation by means of an eternal decree, for such an arrangement would leave no room for God's foreknowledge to precede the New Testament believer's election/chosenness. God can't foreknow what has always existed (refer to Diagram 2 in the Reference Section). Election, therefore, cannot point to God selecting (decreeing) certain individuals to salvation from eternity past by means of an eternal decree. To what then does election point in passages such as 1Peter 1:2? It points to an individual (during the church age) being placed in the *"chosen* [elected] *one"* (Isaiah 42:1 NASB), Jesus Christ (1Corinthians 12:13), subsequent to repenting and believing while depraved. Only then is the New Testament believer chosen (elected)—elected to a special office (position) within the body of Christ. This, however, is not the end of the story. Once New Testament believers are chosen (elected), through being placed in God's chosen (elected) Son (subsequent to repenting and believing while depraved), they are perceived by the Father as having always been elected/chosen (Ephesians 1:4—*"before the foundation of the world"*). Why? The Son possesses eternal life, life with no beginning or end—the same *"life"* received by New Testament believers once placed in the eternal Son (John 3:16; John 10:28; Colossians 3:4; 1John 1:4) <u>after</u> repenting and believing while depraved. What a sovereign, wise, intelligent, and loving God we serve! Our *God's Heart as it Relates to Foreknowledge/Predestination* study explains in more detail why God's foreknowledge must <u>precede</u> His decrees, thus refuting all forms of Calvinism, including Reformed Theology.

Christ was chosen to be Messiah; and we, due to our having been placed into Him after having exercised repentance and faith while depraved, entered into His chosenness. But we by no means, having been chosen in Him, became little Messiahs. We became *"holy and blameless"* saints, as the remainder of the verse confirms.

that we should be holy and blameless before Him. (1:4b)

We who are in Christ are *"holy and blameless."* We are not worthless sinners saved by grace, but *"holy and blameless"* saints who sometimes commit acts of sin (Ephesians 1:1, 4b). In fact, when we are presented *"before Him"* (Ephesians 1:4b) after physical death, we will *"stand in the presence of His glory blameless with great joy"* (Jude 24). How so? We, based on what Jesus has done, have been made *"the righteousness of God"* (2Corinthians 5:21). We are also *"forgiven"* (Ephesians 4:32; Colossians 2:13), a fact also addressed in Ephesians 1:7. We are *"justified"* (Romans 5:1), *"glorified"* (in soul and spirit—Romans 8:30), never to be condemned by God (Romans 8:1), *"complete"* (Colossians 2:10), and much more—all because God *"crucified"* and eradicated everything He couldn't stomach about us (Romans 6:6) and made us into *"new"* creations in Christ (2Corinthians 5:17). Thus, Paul has every right to say, *"just as He chose us in Him before the foundation of the world, that we should be holy and blameless before Him"* (Ephesians 1:4a-b).

In love (1:4c)

Much debate exists as to where the phrase, *"in love,"* should be attached. Some think it belongs at the end of the previous phrase, *"that we should be holy and blameless before Him."* Others view it as relating to the first phrase of verse 5, *"He predestined us to adoption as sons through Jesus Christ to Himself."* The debate exists because verses 3-14 are one unending sentence in the Greek. The New American Standard Version attaches *"in love"* to the beginning of verse 5, so we will study it from this vantage point. Actually, it makes little difference, for all that God does, since His very nature is *"love"* (1John 4:8, 16), is done in unconditional, agape love.

In love (1:4c) He predestined us to adoption as sons through Jesus Christ to Himself, according to the kind intention of His will, (Ephesians 1:5)

Ephesians 1:5 contains *"predestined,"* an intriguing term indeed. Does God predetermine, through a selection process, who will go to heaven and who will go to hell; or is the individual allowed to choose his own destiny? Let's look at this passage phrase-by-phrase and try to determine Paul's intent.

In love He predestined us to adoption as sons through Jesus Christ to Himself, (1:4c, 5a)

One thing is certain. We were *"predestined...in love"* (1:4c)—unconditional, agape *"love."* So with proper motives and tremendous compassion God predestines His people. But what does Paul mean by the phrase, *"He predestined us"*? Is he saying that God predetermined (from eternity past, by means of an eternal decree) that a portion of mankind would be saved and the remainder condemned? This conclusion doesn't seem to agree with 1Timothy 2:4, 2Peter 3:9, and other similar passages. Is Paul teaching that man has no choice in where he will spend eternity? Should this be the case, it seems that God could have created Himself a family of robots and saved His Son the pain of the cross. For God to have "selected" (from eternity past) those who will receive salvation, never allow the remainder to believe, and follow by sending His Son to Calvary makes absolutely no sense! Why? The cross grants man a choice as to where he will spend eternity.

The Scriptures teach that the cross represents man's prerogative to make a choice. In fact, God's Word verifies that two trees in the history of man represent man's freedom to choose his destiny: *"the tree of the knowledge of good and evil"* (Genesis 2:17) and the cross, or *"tree"* of Christ (Galatians 3:13). Predestination, therefore, may point to something other than God selecting from eternity past who will be lost or saved. Let's examine this word in its Scriptural context.

"Predestined" is used only six times in Scripture (Acts 4:28; Romans 8:29; Romans 8:30; 1Corinthians 2:7; Ephesians 1:5; Ephesians 1:11), four of which refer to the church (Romans 8:29; Romans 8:30; Ephesians 1:5; Ephesians 1:11). These passages, examined in context, reveal that God did not predestine us to become believers, but rather that as believers we have received a glorious future destiny. Therefore, predestination has nothing to do with who will become believers, but relates to the destiny granted to an individual in conjunction with being made *"new"* (2Corinthians 5:17). Thus, New Testament believers are predestined in association with being saved. Consider the following, noticing that I repeat myself quite often, saying the same thing in different ways. I have found repetition to be a profitable tool when communicating truths that are somewhat controversial.

The phrase, *"predestined us to adoption as sons"* (Ephesians 1:5a), along with Romans 8:23, prove that a person is not predestined until he receives Christ. *"Us,"* the first word after *"predestined"* in Ephesians 1:5a, confirms this truth. Because Ephesians was written to believers, *"us"* refers to believers. Consequently, only believers are predestined—not prospective believers who will later be saved. To what are believers predestined? They are *"predestined...to adoption as sons"* (Ephesians 1:5). When do they receive this adoption? Romans 8:23 provides the answer:

> *And not only this, but also we ourselves, having the first fruits of the Spirit, even we ourselves groan within ourselves, waiting eagerly for our adoption as sons, the redemption of our body.* (Romans 8:23)

The *"adoption as sons"* occurs when the New Testament believer receives a new body, an event that transpires long after spiritual regeneration/salvation—except in the case of those who are saved (born-again) shortly before the Rapture of the church. Thus, we were predestined when we were placed into Christ <u>after</u> believing Him for salvation. Hence, we were <u>not</u> predestined to "be saved," but rather were predestined to *"adoption as sons"* in conjunction with being made new. Even Paul has not yet received the *"adoption as sons"* to which he was predestined when he believed, an event that will transpire when all church saints receive their resurrected bodies in accordance with 1Thessalonians 4:13-18 and 1Corinthians 15:35-58— verses which deal with the Rapture of the church.

Romans 8:29 states:

> *For whom He foreknew, He also predestined to become conformed to the image of His Son, that He might be the first-born among many brethren;* (Romans 8:29)

Long before time began, God looked ahead (by means of His eternal foreknowledge) and saw that many people would put their trust in Christ during the church age. *"In love"* (Ephesians 1:4c) He decided that these individuals, once they chose to receive Christ and were placed in Christ (1Corinthians 12:13; 2Corinthians 5:17), would be given a glorious future destiny (Romans 8:29; Ephesians 1:5)—that of receiving a resurrected body at the Rapture of the church. Therefore, in association with choosing to accept Christ, they would be predestined *"to become conformed to the image of His Son"* (Romans 8:29), or predestined *"to adoption as sons"* (Ephesians 1:5)—pointing to that day when their glorified souls and spirits will be joined to their glorified bodies—a body like Christ possessed once He was resurrected.

It should be apparent by now that the members of the body of Christ are not adopted as sons in the most extreme sense until they receive their resurrected bodies at the Rapture of the church. Romans 8:23 states:

> *And not only this, but also we ourselves, having the first fruits of the Spirit, even we ourselves groan within ourselves, waiting eagerly for our adoption as sons, the redemption of our body.* (Romans 8:23)

Believers now have *"the first fruits of the Spirit"* (Romans 8:23), a *"spirit of adoption as sons,"* for Romans 8:15 states:

> *For you have not received a spirit of slavery leading to fear again, but you have received a spirit of adoption as sons by which we cry*

out, "Abba! Father!" (Romans 8:15)

New Testament believers, having received a *"spirit of adoption"* (Romans 8:15), are *"sons"* (Romans 8:15; Galatians 4:6-7) who are *"led by the Spirit of God"* (Romans 8:14). As a result of possessing the Holy Spirit (John 14:16-17), they have already received the down payment (first fruits, or earnest) of what is to come (Romans 8:23). But only when their bodies are resurrected (1Thessalonians 4:13-18) will they lay hold of, in the fullest sense, all that this sonship involves.

Taking what we have discovered, we can draw the following conclusions: Believers today, not yet having received their resurrected bodies, have received *"a spirit of adoption as sons"* (Romans 8:15). They are holy, blameless, complete, justified, glorified, forgiven, children of God who are presently being taught and trained by the Spirit, Son, and Father. One day they will receive their new bodies, at which time they will receive that for which they were predestined when they were made new in Christ—the *"adoption as sons"* (Ephesians 1:5; Romans 8:23). They will have been holy and blameless in their person (in soul and spirit) since the day they were saved and entered into God's family (Ephesians 1:4), but after their bodies are resurrected they will be holy and blameless in soul, spirit, and body. Hence, for the first time while living in a body, every aspect of their behavior will be totally perfected. Why? The power of sin, which lived in their unredeemed bodies (Romans 7:23), will not reside in their resurrected bodies. Also, their brains, which stored their unrighteous habit patterns, will be replaced with brains free of such patterns. As a result of the training received while in their earthly bodies (through the Son and the Spirit—in fact, the entire Godhead), and because of their new resurrected bodies (along with having seen the Godhead after physical death), they will be mature saints who can be trusted with the responsibility and authority given them while reigning with Christ during His one-thousand-year reign on the earth (Revelation 20:4). But even after receiving their redeemed (resurrected) bodies and later reigning with Christ, they will be no more holy and blameless in their souls and spirits, and no more a part of God's family, than when God saved them subsequent to their repenting and believing while depraved.

Yes, we were made holy, blameless, righteous, and glorified children of God (in soul and spirit) the moment we were born again (saved/justified). But the Godhead is now growing us up, preparing us for the day when we will reign with Christ. Only when we receive *"our adoption as sons"* (Romans 8:23; Ephesians 1:5), through the *"mortal"* putting *"on immortality"* (1Corinthians 15:51-53) at the Rapture of the church (through church saints receiving resurrected bodies), will we be fully ready and prepared to reign with Christ.

In Galatians 4:6, Paul states:

> *And because you are sons, God has sent forth the Spirit of His Son into our hearts, crying, "Abba! Father!"* (Galatians 4:6)

Did you hear that? The Holy Spirit entered your spirit crying, *"Abba! Father!"* In other words, He (the Spirit) makes us mindful of the fact that Jehovah God is our Father. In crying, *"Abba! Father!,"* the Holy Spirit brings an awareness that salvation includes much more than getting out of hell and into heaven. He allows the believer to see that one day all church saints will be, in the fullest sense, adopted as *"sons"*—receive the *"adoption as sons"* that Paul addresses in Romans 8:23 and Ephesians 1:5. Galatians 4:5 states:

> *in order that He might redeem those who were under the Law, that we might receive the adoption as sons.* (Galatians 4:5)

God not only redeemed us (Galatians 4:5) and gave us *"a spirit of adoption as sons"* (Romans 8:15), but also granted us the privilege of one day being fully adopted *"as sons"* (Galatians 4:5) through the resurrection of our bodies (Romans 8:23). Also, in 2Corinthians 3:18, we find that our behavior is transformed as we choose to pursue God's heart. Consequently, one of the Spirit's main purposes is to assist in bringing God's sons to a place of maturity so they can experience all that sonship entails.

Certainly, when Paul stated that *"He predestined us to adoption as sons"* (Ephesians 1:5a), he realized that becoming an adopted son in the truest sense would be a future event for him and his readers. This event occurs in the future for us as well. Therefore, to be predestined to adoption as sons does not mean that we were predestined from eternity past to be saved. Rather, it communicates that in conjunction with a New Testament believer being saved/justified, he is predestined to be adopted as a son in fullest measure (Ephesians 1:5a) at the Rapture of the church. Only then will he be *"conformed to the image of"* Christ in every respect (Romans 8:29)—spirit, soul, <u>and body</u>. We must be mindful, however, of the following truth.

At the point of salvation/justification, the New Testament believer is made into a finished product in his soul and spirit (in his person). He is as *"holy and blameless"* (Ephesians 1:4), *"justified"* (Romans 5:1), *"righteous"* (2Corinthians 5:21), *"forgiven"* (Ephesians 4:32; Colossians 2:13), *"complete"* (Colossians 2:10), and *"glorified"* (Romans 8:30) <u>in his person</u> (soul and spirit) as he will ever be. But only at the resurrection does he receive an immortal body (1Corinthians 15:53)—a body like Jesus' resurrected body. Hence, the resurrection is the piece of the puzzle that allows our bodies *"to be conformed to the image of God's Son"* (Romans 8:29). To this we were predestined (Romans 8:29) <u>when</u> we accepted

Christ—not beforehand. Thus, all individuals who adhere to the idea that God predestined the "elect" to salvation from eternity past by means of an eternal decree are in error.

Jesus was not only *"the first-born from the dead"* (Colossians 1:18; Revelation 1:5), but *"the first-born among many brethren"* (Romans 8:29). In fact, even though Jesus has always been the eternal Son of God (Romans 8:58), only through His resurrection was He *"declared the Son of God with power"* (Romans 1:4). Therefore, when we receive our resurrected bodies we will be sons in the fullest sense. To this resurrection we have been predestined, and we were predestined when—not before—we became believers.

Paul, in Romans 8:30, gives us further insight as to "when" we were predestined:

> *and whom He predestined, these He also called; and whom He called, these He also justified; and whom He justified, these He also glorified.* (Romans 8:30)

"Predestined," "called," "justified," and *"glorified"* are all in the aorist tense, pointing to past, completed action. Consequently, the entirety of the action contained in Romans 8:30 would have been applied to all the believers in Rome by the time they received Paul's epistle. Why? They were believers—not potential believers. This same truth applies to all New Testament believers, for they are *"predestined," "called," "justified,"* and *"glorified"* by God the instant they repent and believe while depraved.

Romans 8:30 does not, as some theologians have erroneously assumed, provide the chronological order of events in the life of a believer. In other words, the passage does not teach that God first predestined the elect to be saved from eternity past, then called them when it was time for them to be saved, then justified them, and will, in the future, glorify them. This arrangement is impossible since all of these verbs are in the past tense. Yet, Arminianism and all forms of Calvinism (including Reformed Theology) perceive Romans 8:30 as teaching that all believers (past, present, and future) were predestined to salvation from eternity past by means of an eternal decree. Such a view, however, would allow Romans 8:30 to teach that the *"predestined"* of Arminianism and Calvinism who are not yet in existence are presently *"called," "justified,"* and *"glorified"*—since *"predestined," "called," "justified,"* and *"glorified"* are all in the past tense. Stated differently, had future believers been *"predestined"* to salvation from eternity past, they would presently be *"called," "justified,"* and *"glorified."* This arrangement would cause them to be *"justified"* and *"glorified"* prior to existing as well as *"justified"* and *"glorified"* at physical birth. Therefore, passages such as Ephesians 2:3 discredit both Arminianism and all forms of Calvinism (including Reformed Theology), for all persons arrive on the earth *"children of wrath."*

> *Among them we too all formerly lived in the lusts of our flesh,*
> *indulging the desires of the flesh and of the mind, and were by*
> *nature children of wrath, even as the rest.* (Ephesians 2:3)

If you are a believer, the entirety of the action included in Romans 8:30 has already transpired. Let's dig even deeper into this subject matter.

We will first deal with what it means to be *"called"* (Romans 8:30). Greek words such as *kletos, kaleo, kaleomai,* and *klesis* are normally translated "called" or "calling" and point to two different scenarios in Scripture: (1) that we have been invited by God to receive Christ (2) that the New Testament believer receives a specific office (gifting or purpose) once placed in Christ—after repenting and believing while depraved. Let's examine these two scenarios in more detail.

Paul, in 1Corinthians 1:9, states:

> *God is faithful, through whom you were called into fellowship with*
> *His Son, Jesus Christ our Lord.* (1Corinthians 1:9)

Unquestionably, we were *"called* (invited) *into fellowship with"* Christ. However, God did not force, elect, or predestine us to be saved.

The most common use of "called" or "calling" in Scripture is in relation to the New Testament believer's office, gifting, or purpose. Paul was *"called as an apostle"* (Romans 1:1), a special office (gifting, purpose) indeed. Paul encouraged the church at Ephesus by saying:

> *...walk in a manner worthy of the calling with which you have been*
> *called,* (Ephesians 4:1).

Evaluating Ephesians 4:1 in context with Ephesians 4:1-16, we discover that Paul is addressing the different callings, giftings, or offices within the body of Christ. The believers at Ephesus were to *"walk in a manner worthy of"* their *"calling,"* office, or gifting (Ephesians 4:1). Paul, in Colossians 3:15, states that the believers at Colosse *"were called in one body,"* meaning they were called to office (given a special spiritual gift) when placed into the *"body"* of Christ—after repenting and believing while depraved. They were all called to allow *"the peace of Christ"* to *"rule in"* their *"hearts"* (Colossians 3:15) while serving in their particular individual gifting—a wonderful purpose indeed. Coupling what we have gleaned with Ephesians 4:1, the *"calling and choosing"* described in 2Peter 1:10 took place in conjunction with our being made new in Christ:

> *Therefore, brethren, be all the more diligent to make certain about*
> *His calling and choosing you; for as long as you practice these*
> *things, you will never stumble;* (2Peter 1:10)

Consider as well that we were *"called as saints"* (Romans 1:7) the moment we were placed *"in Christ"* (1Corinthians 1:2) through the power of the Holy Spirit (1Corinthians 12:13) after repenting and believing while depraved. What a noble purpose—to live, through Christ's strength, as a *"saint"* should live. Consequently, the fact that the New Testament believer is *"called"* can point to something other than being called or invited to be saved. New Testament believers, in conjunction with being saved, are *"called"* to a particular gifting, office, or purpose within the body of Christ. Paul seems to be referencing this calling in Romans 8:30:

> *and whom He predestined, these He also called; and whom He*
> *called, these He also justified; and whom He justified, these He*
> *also glorified.* (Romans 8:30)

God also justifies New Testament believers once they exercise *"faith"* in Christ—*"justified"* (Romans 8:30; Romans 5:1) meaning "to be made righteous." This just standing before God was granted the instant we became children of God. But when were we *"glorified"* in soul and spirit (Romans 8:30)? We were *"glorified"* at the same time we were *"justified"*—when we became children of God and were made new (2Corinthians 5:17). Our new man is a *"holy"* (Ephesians 1;4), *"blameless"* (Ephesians 1:4), *"complete"* (Colossians 2:10), *"sanctified"* (Hebrews 10:10), *"perfect"* (Hebrews 10:14), *"glorified"* (Romans 8:30) *"saint"* (Ephesians 1:1)—and more. Therefore, according to Romans 8:30, a New Testament believer is not only called (receives a special office, gifting, or purpose) and justified (made righteous and is totally forgiven) at the point of salvation/justification, but is also glorified (made into a holy, blameless, perfect, glorified saint). Could the New Testament believer also be *"predestined"* at the same time? Absolutely, and Romans 8:30 makes it even more certain (placing *"predestined,"* *"called,"* *"justified,"* and *"glorified"* in the past tense in regard to church saints), proving that Paul and his readers (who were believers) had already been *"predestined,"* *"called,"* *"justified,"* and *"glorified."* Remember: The New Testament believer receives a glorified body through resurrection at the Rapture of the church (1Corinthians 15:35-58). Only then will we be like Christ in <u>body</u>, which will house our previously glorified soul and spirit.

Conclusively, Scriptural predestination does not include the idea that God predetermined (from eternity past) where individuals will spend eternity. Rather, a New Testament believer is *"predestined"* by God at the same time that he is *"called"* (given a special office, gifting, or purpose within the body of Christ), *"justified"* (made righteous by God after repenting and believing), and *"glorified"* (in soul and spirit). All of this action occurs at the same time—when the New Testament believer is placed in Christ and made new after repenting and believing while depraved. His future destiny is that of being *"conformed to the image of"* God's *"Son"* (Romans 8:29) and to be fully adopted as a son (Romans 8:23; Ephesians 1:5) when he receives his redeemed (resurrected) body (Romans 8:23). Note: Paul probably places *"predestined"* before *"called,"* *"justified,"* and *"glorified"* in Romans 8:30 because predestination is mentioned in the preceding verse (Romans 8:29). Consequently, Romans 8:30, by no stretch of the imagination, describes the chronological order of events in the life of a believer. How could it do so when all the action transpires the moment a New Testament believer is placed in Christ after repenting and believing while depraved?

We were *"predestined...to adoption as sons through Jesus Christ to Himself"* (Ephesians 1:5a). If we were *"predestined...through Jesus,"* and if we were not placed in Him until we repented of our sins and accepted Him as Savior, we could not have been predestined until we were placed in Him through the power of the Holy Spirit (1Corinthians 12:13) after repenting and believing. So again Paul confirms that believers were not predestined to salvation from eternity past as Arminianism and all forms of Calvinism (including Reformed Theology) suppose. Paul will verify this same truth in Ephesians 1:6, for tying verse 5 in with verse 6 confirms that we did not receive the grace to be predestined until we were *"in the Beloved."* We will deal with this phrase in more depth shortly.

according to the kind intention of His will. (1:5b)

God gave us our glorious future destiny (that of becoming full-fledged sons of God conformed to His image—Ephesians 1:5a; Romans 8:29) *"according to the kind intention of His will"* (Ephesians 1:5b). These passages abolish the falsehood that God is an angry tyrant who gains much pleasure in punishing His people. God's intentions are *"kind"* toward those who are His. Remember: God's relationships are based on what others receive, as is the case within the Trinity. Once we understand this principle, we can better comprehend why *"faith"* works *"through love"* (Galatians 5:6), and why only *"the love of Christ"*—not law, duty, or wrath—will keep us motivated to the end (2Corinthians 5:14). If you have viewed God differently than He is portrayed here, won't you ask Him to enlighten *"the eyes of your heart"* (Ephesians 1:18)?

Ephesians 1:6—to the praise of the glory of His grace, which He freely bestowed on us in the Beloved.

Let's first observe the phrase:

to the praise of the glory of His grace, (1:6a)

To discover what Paul is addressing here, we first need to examine the phrase, *"the glory of His grace."* Because God possesses flawless character, He possesses glory. He is holy, perfect, all wise, sinless, without error, just, forgiving, a God of grace, and much, much more. In other words, God's character is so perfect and all-encompassing that when He shows up, glory is manifested (read Exodus 3:1-5 and Exodus 19:16-18). One of God's most prevalent character qualities is His grace. In fact, Peter refers to Him as *"the God of all grace"* in 1Peter 5:10. Thus, God's glory is an avenue through which His grace manifests itself, for all aspects of God's flawless character are displayed through His glory. God's grace is the subject in Ephesians 1:6; therefore, Paul says, *"the glory of His grace."* Jesus possesses *"glory"* (John 1:14); so, He was correct in saying to Philip that in seeing Him he had seen the Father (John 14:9). In fact, Jesus was, and is, *"the image of the invisible God"* (Colossians 1:15). As J.B. Phillips states in his translation, *"Now Christ is the visible expression of the invisible God"* (Colossians 1:15).[2] Remember this input for future reference.

God *"predestined us to adoption as sons through Jesus Christ to Himself"* (Ephesians 1:5a) *"to the praise of the glory of His grace"* (Ephesians 1:6a). *"To the praise of the glory of His grace"* is an exceptionally captivating phrase, for praise and adoration should be man's most natural response to God's glory. Hence, when Moses entered the tent of meeting, and God's cloud of glory would stand at its entrance, *"the people would arise and worship"* (Exodus 33:7-11). We, one day, will return with Christ (Revelation 19:11-16) as His glorified body (Ephesians 5:30; Colossians 3:4)—as individuals conformed to His image (Romans 8:29). Christ's Second Coming will result in the defeat of the Antichrist and his armies during the campaign of Armageddon, after which the Millennium will be established and the creation restored to a place of abundant blessing (Romans 8:19-22). Worship, praise, and adoration will naturally follow.

Jesus was a visible expression of the Father's glory during His First Coming (John 1:14; 14:9; Colossians 1:15). Because the majority rejected His Messiahship, they missed the awesome privilege of having the Spirit reveal the Father through the Son. Had the world only known Christ's origin and purpose, *"they would not have crucified the Lord of glory"* (1Corinthians 2:8). A day will come, however, when the Son will be revealed to an even greater degree. This revelation will occur when

He returns with His body, the church, in all her glory (Colossians 3:4)—having been conformed to His image (Romans 8:29). Even the cursed earth waits eagerly for that day (Romans 8:19-22), the day when church saints, clothed in their new bodies (Romans 8:23), return with Christ (Revelation 19:11-16). What unmatched glory and light will be manifested on that day! If Jesus' desire during His First Coming was to reveal the Father (Matthew 11:27; Luke 10:22), just think of the degree to which the Father will be revealed when the Son returns with His body, the church, made up of many sons conformed to His image (Romans 8:29) and brought to glory (Hebrews 2:10). Thus, Paul realized that after the church receives that to which she was predestined (Ephesians 1:5a), she will bring great praise to the Father's glory (Ephesians 1:6a). How could such an event not do so!

All that we receive through the Father's flawless plan for the church also brings glory to His Son. Why should it be any other way? Only He, the Creator, Who possesses all wisdom, sovereignty, power, and grace, could generate such a perfect strategy. In fact, what could be more glorifying to the Son than to return as head over all church saints, each of whom possess and reflect His glory? Paul states:

> *For momentary, light affliction is producing for us an eternal weight of glory far beyond all comparison,* (2Corinthians 4:17)

He also writes:

> *and if children, heirs also, heirs of God and joint heirs with Christ, if indeed we suffer with Him in order that we may also be glorified with Him.* (Romans 8:17)

And again:

> *For I consider that the sufferings of this present time are not worthy to be compared with the glory that is to be revealed to us.* (Romans 8:18)

Paul also communicates in Colossians 1:27:

> *...Christ in you, the hope of glory.* (Colossians 1:27)

The writer of Hebrews records:

> *For it was fitting for Him, for whom are all things, and through whom are all things, in bringing many sons to glory, to perfect the author of their salvation through sufferings.* (Hebrews 2:10)

Yes, *"many sons"* will be brought *"to glory"* through God's sovereign plan for man, and God is glorified through the Son. Therefore, the glory addressed in Ephesians 1:6 is the type of glory that enhances both God and man but is accomplished through the Son. Hence, through Christ, and to the Father's glory, we are conformed to the image of the Father's Son (Romans 8:29) and receive the adoption as sons (Ephesians 1:5)—that to which we were predestined when we believed on Christ. How do these remarkable events glorify God? Once we receive that to which we were predestined, we will live in sinless perfection in a glorified body—pursuing a lifestyle of total submission to the Father, the lifestyle that Christ experienced and demonstrated during His First Coming. Wow!

which He freely bestowed on us in the Beloved. (1:6b)

Be sure to follow as closely as possible as we progress. In fact, this section may require more than one reading.

"Which" (Ephesians 1:6b) refers to *"grace"* (Ephesians 1:6a), the grace that allowed God to predestine us *"to adoption as sons"* (Ephesians 1:5a). *"Beloved"* (Ephesians 1:6b) refers to Jesus, in Whom believers receive this grace. Combining these factors and considering that through having been placed *"in the Beloved"* (after repenting and believing while depraved) we were saved/justified (2Corinthians 5:17; 1Corinthians 12:13), we can conclude that we were not predestined until we were placed *"in the Beloved."*

The New Testament believer needs more grace than that supplied for predestination. In fact, he needs continual grace (on a daily basis) to experience everything made available through Christ (2Corinthians 12:9; 1Corinthians 15:10; Ephesians 1:2). Paul seems in Ephesians 1:6b, however, to address that particular grace which allows God to predestine New Testament believers to adoption as sons in conjunction with making them new. Should this be the case, we have further confirmation that a New Testament believer is predestined <u>when</u> he is saved/justified once placed in Christ—not beforehand. If you have difficulty accepting this line of thinking, consider that no person receives grace outside of Jesus Christ. Note: *"Beloved"* is a perfect tense participle, meaning that the Father, Who is *"love"* (1John 4:8), has always loved Jesus (*"the Beloved"*) with a permanent and enduring love (also read Matthew 3:17 and Colossians 1:13). Because we are in Jesus, *"the Beloved,"* we too are *"beloved of God"* (Romans 1:7). What a magnificent thought!

Ephesians 1:7—In Him we have redemption through His blood, the forgiveness of our trespasses, according to the riches of His grace,

In Him we have redemption through His blood, (1:7a)

The blood of Christ redeemed us from our sins (Ephesians 1:7a; 1Peter 1:18-19; Romans 3:24; Galatians 3:13). Stated differently, Jesus' blood paid our sin debt and liberated us from sin's grip (Galatians 5:1). Redemption, therefore, can be defined as paying a ransom for the purpose of liberating or freeing an individual from bondage. Some might say, "I think I will submit to Christ so I can go to heaven and, while on earth, bask in a lifestyle of sin." To this person I would say, "You have never met Christ." The liberation brought about through true redemption results in a zeal for obedience—not an excuse for an undisciplined, sinful existence (Titus 2:14).

After Adam and Eve disobeyed in the Garden, man, in his lost condition, was temporarily locked in sin. The only remedy was a Redeemer, a perfect God-man Who would die for the sin of man. Jesus is that perfect God-man Who said, while on the cross, *"it is finished"* (John 19:30). In dealing with the topic of redemption, Paul states in Colossians 2:13-14:

> *And when you were dead in your transgressions and the uncircumcision of your flesh, He made you alive together with Him, having forgiven us all our transgressions, having canceled out the certificate of debt consisting of decrees against us and which was hostile to us; and He has taken it out of the way, having nailed it to the cross.* (Colossians 2:13-14)

Jesus' blood was the payment required to cancel our sin debt and release us from sin's grasp. Yet His blood was also a symbol of the fact that a death had occurred. His death made the difference, for a syringe filled with His blood and applied to the cross would have been insufficient. He had to die for redemption to be made accessible to lost mankind (Hebrews 2:14-15; 9:15).

I had something happen a few years back that relates well to our subject matter. A man named Robert came to my pastor and asked for assistance. He hadn't eaten for some time and needed food and shelter. He told my pastor that he knew how to work, and that he desired to work on a farm. I was in the process of planting my crops, so my pastor called and asked if I needed help. I told him I did, so Robert moved in my home and worked with me for quite some time. A few months had passed when I sensed he was becoming restless. One morning I awoke and Robert was gone—and he had not departed empty handed. He had stolen my truck, shotgun, and a few other odds and ends. I called the local sheriff, and two days later Robert was found in northern Florida. The authorities locked him up and impounded my truck, but my shotgun was nowhere to be found.

Given my circumstances, I had two options—either press charges and have him convicted of auto theft, or send the authorities in Florida the remuneration required to have him released. I chose the second option and had him drive my stolen truck home. To describe how this set of events enhanced our relationship is impossible. He was a broken man when he returned, willing to do anything within reason for me. In fact, soon after this incident he began calling me "brother." Why? I had redeemed him from his physical bondage and forgiven his misdeed. What had it cost me? The price was approximately two hundred dollars. Jesus, to a much greater degree, paid our sin debt: *"In Him we have redemption through His blood"* (Ephesians 1:7a). Only *"in Him"* and *"through His blood"* is redemption granted—after repentance and faith are exercised by the depraved seeking salvation.

the forgiveness of our trespasses (1:7b),

All New Testament believers experience God's forgiveness, for through Christ's perfect sacrifice we have *"the forgiveness of our trespasses"* (Ephesians 1:7b).

The issue of forgiveness is one of the most important, yet misunderstood, doctrines in all of Christendom. Hence, many followers of Christ have a distorted view of the finality of Jesus' sacrifice. They believe that Christ's blood brought forgiveness for the sins committed from the time they were born until the time they were born again/saved, but that the sins committed after salvation are forgiven only through seeking God's forgiveness. If that were the case, since *"without shedding of blood there is no forgiveness"* (Hebrews 9:22), Christ would need to be crucified each time a believer confessed sin. Christ died <u>once</u> for all sin (Hebrews 10:12), meaning He can never die again. Therefore, every sin committed both before and after a New Testament believer accepts Christ must be forgiven when he (the believer) is placed *"In Him"* (Ephesians 1:7a). The church saint is required to confess and repent of sins committed after salvation—not to receive forgiveness, but to have communication restored with the Father. Why should we seek something we already have?

The moment we were placed into Christ, God forgave all our past, present, and future sins (Ephesians 1:7b). Passages like Ephesians 4:32, Colossians 2:13, and 1John 2:12 confirm this truth. However, 1John 1:9 appears to teach otherwise:

> *If we confess our sins, He is faithful and righteous to forgive us our sins and to cleanse us from all unrighteousness.* (1John 1:9)

1John 1:9 seems to imply (on the surface at least) that sins committed subsequent to becoming a child of God are forgiven through seeking God's forgiveness once they are committed. But when examined in the Greek (the original language of the New Testament), it becomes obvious that any such use of this passage is out of context and invalid. The structure of the verbs *"forgive"* and *"cleanse"* will not allow such an interpretation. Also, should 1John 1:9 teach that sins committed subsequent to becoming a child of God must be confessed to receive forgiveness, the passage contradicts Ephesians 4:32, Colossians 2:13, and 1John 2:12—which place forgiveness in the past, coupled with completed action. New Testament believers confess sin after salvation, but not for the purpose of receiving forgiveness. They do so to have fellowship restored with the Father. (The *Romans 1-8* course produced and distributed by this ministry has much more to say regarding the subject.)

Another verse that <u>seems</u> to indicate that New Testament <u>believers</u> are to seek forgiveness on an ongoing basis is Matthew 6:12. This passage is extremely familiar due to being included in the Lord's prayer. Here Jesus said, *"And forgive us our debts as we also have forgiven our debtors."* On the surface, the Lord appears to be instructing New Testament believers to ask for forgiveness when sin is committed. The question that must be answered is: "Did Jesus make this statement before or after the cross?" He made it <u>before</u> His crucifixion. Also consider that none of the Old Testament sacrifices took away sin, for they only covered sin until Jesus could die (Hebrews 10:4, 11). Since we must always interpret Scripture from its proper context, we should keep this truth in mind while assessing Matthew 6:12. Jesus was addressing individuals who lived before the cross; their forgiveness was yet future. Therefore, for them to seek forgiveness was proper. Things changed once Jesus died, for all sin (past, present, and future) is removed for the New Testament believer. Please don't hear me saying that the teachings of Jesus are outdated or irrelevant. I am simply communicating that all Scripture must be interpreted in context, even the teachings of Jesus.

Nothing outside of the cross will remove man's sin. The Old Testament sacrifices couldn't do so (Hebrews 10:4, 11), for they only <u>covered</u> the worshiper's sins (the cross <u>removed</u> them). Neither can we, after becoming members of Christ's body, receive forgiveness by asking God to forgive us. Why should we seek something we already have? The cross removed all our sin for all time (once we repented and believed while depraved), so may we forever enjoy the fullness of the redemption and forgiveness made available through Jesus.

according to the riches of His grace (1:7c),

God's grace is limitless. His *"grace"* not only permitted Him to predestine us *"to adoption as sons"* (Ephesians 1:5a-6b) once we repented and believed while depraved, but allowed Him to grant us redemption and forgiveness (Ephesians

1:7a-c) through our accepting His Son as Savior. His grace, like His love, holiness, wisdom, sovereignty, power, and other impeccable qualities, knows no bounds. Thus, Paul uses *"according to"* instead of "out of." Should the wealthy give "out of" their wealth, they could offer a small gift and fulfill their obligation. However, to give *"according to"* their wealth would require a substantial contribution. Because God is rich in grace, and forgave us *"according to the riches of His grace,"* we need not be concerned that our disobedience surpass it.

Ephesians 1:8—which He lavished upon us. In all wisdom and insight

which He lavished upon us. (1:8a)

A believer can't commit enough sins to surpass God's gracious forgiveness because His grace is *"lavished upon us"* (Ephesians 1:8a)—made abundant toward us. On the other hand, a true born-again believer will detest sin—no longer enjoy sin. He will sin at least to some degree while inhabiting an earthly body, but will despise even the slightest indication of disobedience.

Because the phrase, *"In all wisdom and insight"* (Ephesians 1:8b), ties in with verse 9, we will study this section of Scripture as a solid block.

In all wisdom and insight (1:8b) He made known to us the mystery of His will, according to His kind intention which He purposed in Him (1:9)

In all wisdom and insight (1:8b).

God bestows additional blessings to the redeemed and forgiven (Ephesians 1:7)—(*sophia*) *"wisdom"* and (*phronesis*) *"insight"* (Ephesians 1:8b).

Vine's Expository Dictionary defines *"wisdom"* (*sophia*) as, "The insight into the true nature of things." I perceive wisdom as the ability to view life from God's perspective. Only believers possess wisdom (Proverbs 9:10), wisdom being revealed through the Person of the Holy Spirit (1Corinthians 2:6-12). Due to the abundant wisdom accessible to the New Testament saint, Paul is even free to proclaim: *"We have the mind of Christ"* (1Corinthians 2:16).

Insight (*phronesis*), according to *Vine's*, is "understanding, prudence in the management of affairs." *Vine's* also contrasts wisdom (*sophia*) to insight (*phronesis*): "While *sophia* is the insight into the true nature of things, *phronesis* is the ability to discern modes of action with a view to their results; while *sophia* is theoretical, *phronesis* is practical."[3]   Therefore, wisdom (*sophia*) allows the believer to begin to determine the true nature of the character of God, the will of God, God's plan for man, God's overall strategy in history, the cross, hell, heaven, etc. Insight (*phronesis*) is more practical, helping the saints understand how to apply the theoretical to daily living. Thus, *"wisdom"* allows the believer to determine God's will, while *"insight"* links His will to the practicalities of everyday living.

He made known to us the mystery of His will, (1:9a)

Let's apply what we have gleaned to verses 8 and 9. *"In all wisdom and insight"* (Ephesians 1:8b) *"He made known to us the mystery of His will"* (Ephesians 1:9a). Only through wisdom (theoretical understanding) and insight (practical application) can God make known to His people *"the mystery of His will."* Hence, God makes known *"the mystery of His will"* to His people; we never make known *"the mystery of His will"* to ourselves. Everything the believer learns regarding the Godhead and His strategy results from God's revelation of Himself (Romans 1:17; Ephesians 1:9a; 15-19; 3:3; etc.). What, then, is *"the mystery of His will"*? *"The mystery of His will"* is what He is accomplishing through His overall strategy in human history. God has a plan. He gives man the freedom to choose as he desires; yet regardless of man's response, nothing can thwart His overall strategy. *"The mystery of His will"* is understood only by the born again/justified saint of God. This reality does not negate the fact that the depraved/lost have access to ample truth to repent and believe, for Adam was convicted of his wrongdoing as soon as he partook of the forbidden fruit and became depraved (Genesis 3:6-20)—before God made a covering for he and Eve in Genesis 3:21. Thus, God later gave the Law to Israel to convict the depraved (lost) of sin (Galatians 3:24; 1Timothy 1:9-10), confirming that the depraved are capable of understanding truth prior to spiritual regeneration.

God's *"mystery,"* a subject addressed in verse 10, can be understood by the New Testament believer (Romans 11:25; 16:25; 1Corinthians 2:7; 15:51; Ephesians 1:9; 3:3-4; 6:19; Colossians 1:26-27; 2:2; 4:3; etc.). Because Christ is *"the wisdom of God"* (1Corinthians 1:24), New Testament believers possess wisdom due to having been placed *"in Christ"* (2Corinthians 5:17; 1Corinthians 12:13). Comprehending God's strategy for man through the wisdom and insight granted in Christ (Ephesians 1:8-9), we can many times discern how present-day events fit into God's overall plan. Therefore, only the redeemed can properly interpret the evening news. These events, broadcast to the masses, must be extremely unnerving to those void of insight into God's strategy. Realizing that the free will of man can never thwart God's overall plan, believers bask in the confidence that God wins in the end! To Him be the glory!

This portion of our study should be enormously encouraging since God uses the "bad things" in life for the believer's good. So long as we are *"fixing our eyes on Jesus, the author and perfecter of faith"* (Hebrews 12:2), we will learn that pain is healthy for the soul. Jesus, *"who for the joy set before Him endured the cross, despising the shame, and has sat down at the right hand of the throne of God"* (Hebrews 12:2), knew well that "hardship" yields spiritual maturity within the wise. When Jesus was crucified, the disciples were ill equipped to deal with adversity. In fact, they viewed Christ's crucifixion as the death of their dreams. Because they followed His teachings, their physical wellbeing was also in jeopardy. What could they possibly do to make life normal again? Only after receiving the Holy Spirit in Acts 2 (which transformed Jesus' words from information to revelation subsequent to their believing on Christ) did they comprehend the depth of the significance of the cross. Hence, God's instruction manual for Kingdom living (the truth of the Scriptures) differs greatly from Satan's *"lies"* (John 8:44) that so permeate his sphere of influence (2Corinthians 4:4).

For example, Jesus said:

> *"For whoever wishes to save his life shall lose it; but whoever loses his life for My sake and the gospel's shall save it.* (Mark 8:35)

He also said:

> *and whoever wishes to be first among you shall be your slave;* (Matthew 20:27)

What radical proclamations! Yet, once the depraved believe and are made new (the depraved comprehend enough truth to choose to be saved—as verified on several occasions in this study), a wealth of wisdom is granted so they might understand the deeper things of God (Ephesians 1:8b, 9). They realize, for instance, that one day the slain Lamb of God will rule as *"King of Kings, and Lord of Lords"* (Philippians 2:10; Revelation 5:12; 19:16). What will be the characteristics of His Kingdom? Brokenness, gentleness, meekness, and selfless love will permeate this unprecedented environment. Satan, meanwhile, who rules by brute force, pride, and arrogance, will be removed from the premises (Revelation 20:2). Good always overcomes evil (Romans 12:21; 1Thessalonians 5:15), for wisdom and insight consistently defeat error before the eyes of the wise.

Jesus was glorified through His resurrection. In fact, He was *"taken up in glory"* (1Timothy 3:16). But Jesus seems to indicate that He was glorified through His crucifixion (read John 12:23-25, 27-28; 13:31-33). The glory of Jesus, as we have touched on briefly, is centered around His being *"the Lamb that was slain"* (Revelation 5:9, 12, and 13). He conquered his enemies by dying as a grain of wheat for the purpose of giving life (John 12:24) to those who accept Him as Savior. Clearly, His glory differs from the "glory" of those who rule based on the values of the world system, the "might-makes-right" mindset.

The church will reign *"with Christ for a thousand years"* (Revelation 20:4). Thus, a slain Lamb will ultimately rule over creation (Revelation 5:13), the church (Christ's body—Romans 12:5) ruling with Him (Revelation 5:9-10; 20:4). The church must possess the character qualities that will permeate the Kingdom (brokenness, gentleness, meekness, and selfless love) to properly rule. How does one own such characteristics? By: (1) allowing the Spirit of God to work in our lives as we gaze at Christ (2Corinthians 3:18) through His Word (2) living through difficult circumstances known as "adversity." Yes, in many cases, pain is used of the Lord to transform information into revelation.

In the midst of our trials, we must continually remind ourselves that life comes through death, that true power is gained through brokenness, and that selfless love, rather than self-centeredness, always wins in the end. We will never learn these transforming truths from the world system, which consistently rejects truth while endorsing self-centered living. We learn them by focusing on the Lamb Who was slain, Who will lead us into a deeper understanding of His heart as we face the "variables" of our day. No wonder Paul viewed pain as his friend (2Corinthians 12:10). Through his struggles he discovered the "deeper life" accessible only to believers. Not all of the redeemed will experience this "deeper life" due to rejecting the mindset of the Lamb. They refuse to say, "Whatever it takes Lord, whatever I need to experience to know the depths of the cross, so be it." They refuse, in other words, to place a blank check on God's desk and say, "Fill it out, Father, however You like."

Paul had learned to live in any state and be *"content"* (Philippians 4:11-13) by understanding how his "circumstances" related to the mystery of God's will (Ephesians 1:8-9). He had learned, in other words, that pain carries purpose. Paul's sufferings as an apostle (not having been orchestrated by God, but used by God for Paul's good) were preparing him to reign with Christ—thus fulfilling God's sovereignly ordained plan orchestrated before time began. Circumstances transpiring around Paul were no "mystery" to him, for his wisdom allowed pain to become his friend. So, Paul had every right to say, *"He made known to us the mystery of His will"* (Ephesians 1:9a). He possessed the authority to say as well:

> *For to you it has been granted for Christ's sake, not only to believe in Him, but also to suffer for His sake,* (Philippians 1:29).

according to His kind intention which He purposed in Him (1:9b)

This phrase can actually be interpreted *"according to His good pleasure which He purposed in Him."* Consequently, the mystery of God's will is made known to believers *"according to His good pleasure which He purposed in Him."* Be sure to notice that this mystery is only understood *"in Him"* (in Christ). Paul may have emphasized this truth to refute the Gnostics—who taught that a deeper "knowledge" of the universe is revealed to a select few, and that "knowledge" is superior to faith. The Gnostics also believed that Deity could not inhabit humanity—totally contrary to Paul's gospel which advocated that the fullness of Deity resided in Christ (Colossians 1:19; 2:9), and that Christ dwelt in every New Testament believer (Galatians 2:20). The apostle taught that a person must be *"in Him"* (2Corinthians 5:17; 1Corinthians 1:30; Ephesians 1:9b) before he can know the mystery of His will and interpret how the events of daily living fit into God's overall strategy.

The *wisdom* and *insight* granted the New Testament believer *"in Him"* (in Christ) brings understanding concerning Who God is and how He, in a practical sense, is fulfilling His overall sovereign plan. The plan that God has devised is clearly revealed in verse 10.

Note: Some versions translate the last phrase of Ephesians 1:9, *"according to the kind intention which He purposed in Him"* (the *"in Him"* pointing to Christ), as *"according to the kind intention which He purposed in Himself"* (the *"in Himself"* pointing to the Father). Either translation is fine, for in both instances the wisdom and insight required to understand the mystery of God's will is unattainable outside the Godhead—the Godhead consisting of God the Father, God the Son, and God the Holy Spirit.

Ephesians 1:10—with a view to an administration suitable to the fullness of the times, that is, the summing up of all things in Christ, things in the heavens and things upon the earth. In Him

with a view to an administration suitable to the fullness of the times, (1:10a)

Because *"administration"* can be interpreted "plan," *"fullness"* interpreted "completion," and *"times"* interpreted "seasons," Ephesians 1:10a can be rendered: *"with a view to a plan suitable to the completion of the seasons."* The *"seasons"* are the cycles of history that have transpired throughout the ages; discord has abounded in some *"seasons,"* and peace in others. All of these seasons have been working toward a final season, *"the completion of the seasons,"* when God's ultimate plan comes to full fruition. The next phrase of verse 10 describes this plan.

that is, the summing up of all things in Christ, things in the heavens and things upon the earth. (1:10b)

"All things...in the heavens and...upon the earth" will eventually be summed up *"in Christ"* (Ephesians 1:10b) and reconciled to God (Colossians 1:20). The phrase, *"the summing up of"* (from the Greek *anakephalaioo*—Ephesians 1:10), can actually be interpreted, *"to bring together several things under one."* Wuest's commentary states:

> the compound preposition *ana* signifies *again*, pointing back to a previous condition where no separation existed. God contemplates a regathering, a restoration to that former condition when all things were in perfect unity, and normally combined to serve God's ends. This unity was broken by sin. The mystery of God's will includes the restoration of this unity in and through Christ.[4]

God's will is that the created realm bask in the unity present before the fall. This state of affairs will be brought about through His holy Son, the Savior of the world (John 3:16).

We must not overlook the fact that all things were created not only *"by Him"* (by Christ), but *"for Him"* (Colossians 1:16). Therefore, "in" and "through" Christ this regathering will occur—*"the summing up of all things in Christ"* (Ephesians 1:10b). Only those *"things in the heavens"* and *"the earth"* will be involved—not the things in hell. Paul is in no way teaching universal salvation. Those who have rejected Christ (while on earth) will one day *"bow"* before Him (Philippians 2:10), but will spend eternity in *"the lake of fire"* (Revelation 20:15).

Christ will reign in the Millennium until *"He has put all His enemies under His feet"* (1Corinthians 15:25). At the end of the Millennium, after Satan has been cast into the lake of fire (Revelation 20:7-10) along with all the unredeemed (Revelation 20:11-15), *"death,"* the final *"enemy,"* will be destroyed (1Corinthians 15:26). (Death cannot be annihilated until the author of death, Satan, has been abolished.) At this time, or this season, God's plan of *"summing up...all things in Christ, things in the heavens and things upon the earth,"* will be fulfilled (Ephesians 1:10b). The old creation, as we have known it, will be destroyed and replaced with the new (Revelation 21:1). All that remains will be totally holy. When all things are subject to Christ, *"then the Son Himself also will be subjected to the One who subjected all things to Him, that God may be all in all"* (1Corinthians 15:28). What a marvelous strategy!

The Father will sum up *"all things"* in the Son (Ephesians 1:10). The Son, in the process, dedicates Himself to the Father so as to reveal (Matthew 11:27; Luke 10:22), glorify (John 7:18; 17:1; 21:19), and please (obey—John 4:34; 5:30; 6:38) the Father. After all things are subjected to the Son through the Father, the Son will reign over the entire universe. Once seated in this prominent position of power, the Son will turn everything over to the Father (1Corinthians 15:28). Why? The Son is in relationship with the Father for what the Father receives, never for what He (the Son) receives—and vice versa. Even the Spirit does not glorify Himself, but the Son (John 16:13-14)—meaning that the Person of the Spirit lives with the same selfless mindset as the Father and the Son. God would have us operate from this same perspective, placing the interests of the Godhead and others above our own. Paul functioned in this manner, for he states:

> *For if we are beside ourselves, it is for God; if we are of sound mind, it is for you.* (2Corinthians 5:13)

Paul served without regard to self, always placing God's interests and the interests of others first—the attitude of all who have progressed from self-centeredness to God-centeredness.

The principle of the cross (selfless love), which has eternally existed in each member of the Trinity, was displayed in time by the Son and explained by the Spirit (John 16:13-14). Thus the principle of the cross, which demonstrates selfless love, must control our decisions if we are to embrace God's way of living. Only when man fails to apply this principle is a cross needed in time—Christ's cross at Calvary. Had Adam and Eve laid aside their own desires (lived by the principle of the cross), they would have lived by the tree of life (by God's very life) and matured into individuals who consistently put God's interests above their own. (An excellent book that addresses this topic is *The Ultimate Intention* by DeVerne Fromke—Sure Foundation.)

Paul said it well:

> *For we who live are constantly being delivered over to death for Jesus' sake, that the life of Jesus also may be manifested in our mortal flesh.* (2Corinthians 4:11)

Paul lived by the principle of the cross (by viewing adversity as an opportunity to bring glory to God), which meant that the cross as a principle was continually manifested through his life as he suffered for the cause of the gospel. He experienced great joy in the midst of his trials by realizing that difficult circumstances, coupled with God's incredible grace, served to remind others that as Christ died, He was also raised. The hearts of the redeemed were empowered by Paul's lifestyle, for he states, *"So death works in us, but life in you"* (2Corinthians 4:12).

In Him (1:10c)

The two words, *"In Him,"* tie in with the first statement of verse 11.

Ephesians 1:11—also we have obtained an inheritance, having been predestined according to His purpose who works all things after the counsel of His will,

In Him (1:10c) also we have obtained an inheritance, (1:11a)

In the Greek, the phrase, *"we have obtained an inheritance,"* can also be interpreted *"we have been made a heritage,"* or, *"we were made an inheritance."* Regardless of which rendering we choose, the passage does not contradict what is taught elsewhere in Scripture. Certainly, in Christ we have an inheritance (Acts 20:32; Ephesians 1:13-14; Ephesians 5:5; Colossians 1:12; Colossians 3:23-24; Hebrews 9:15; 1Peter 1:3-4). In fact, we are *"fellow heirs with Christ"*—which means that what He owns we own as well (Romans 8:16-17). He is also, at the same time, our inheritance in the sense of being our very *"life"* (Colossians 3:4)—a rich inheritance indeed.

"In Him" we were also made God's inheritance, causing many scholars to render Ephesians 1:11a as, *"we were made an inheritance."* Ephesians 1:18 verifies this interpretation:

> *I pray that the eyes of your heart may be enlightened, so that you*
> *may know what is the hope of His calling, what are the riches of*
> *the glory of His inheritance in the saints,* (Ephesians 1:18)

How could you have been placed into Christ (after repenting and believing while depraved), Christ being God's Son, and not be the Father's inheritance? Jesus, on many occasions, spoke of the Father gifting believers to Himself—to Jesus (John 6:37, 39; 10:29; etc.). These believers, of course, were gifted to the Son after they repented and believe while depraved.

Just think what this means! We are valued so highly in God's eyes that He views us as His very own *"inheritance."* I don't know about you, but when I think *"inheritance"* I think "special." In fact, an inheritance is something to be cherished. God views us in this manner (as something very special—beings possessing great value) because we are sons. Why then should we consider ourselves as worthless sinners saved by grace, who are less than second-class citizens of the Kingdom? If we do so, we have bought a lie. God, through Paul, says we are His *"inheritance"* (Ephesians 1:11), *"holy and blameless before Him"* (Ephesians 1:4). Let's bask in the joy and freedom of this truth and never look back!

having been predestined according to His purpose (1:11b)

We discovered in Ephesians 1:5-6 that once God placed us *"in the Beloved"* (after we exercised personal repentance and faith while depraved) we were *"predestined to adoption as sons."* We were given this future destiny of one day receiving a new *"body"* (Romans 8:23) and being conformed to the image of God's Son (Romans 8:29—in body) in conjunction with being born again/saved. Therefore, New Testament believers are predestined <u>when</u> they are saved/justified—<u>not beforehand from eternity past.</u> All that we discussed in Ephesians 1:5 concerning predestination is reaffirmed in verses 11-12, for in verse 11b Paul states that the New Testament believer has *"been predestined according to His purpose."* Verse 12 states that purpose. We will tie Ephesians 1:11b in with Ephesians 1:12 shortly, but before doing so we must deal with the phrase:

who works all things after the counsel of His will, (1:11c)

Ephesians 1:11c does not teach that all events are determined by God's will. *"Works,"* from the root word *energeo* (to be at work, to work, to do), can also be interpreted "energizes." Thus, God *"energizes all things after the counsel of his will."* In Colossians 1:29 we read:

> *And for this purpose also I labor, striving according to His power, which mightily works within me.* (Colossians 1:29)

"Works" in this case is *energeo*, so we can view the verse as:

> *And for this purpose also I labor, striving according to His power, which mightily energizes within me.*

This energizing is from God. Even in Philippians 2:13 and 1Corinthians 12:6 (along with other passages), Paul teaches that God works in (energizes) those who are His. But does all "energizing" come from God? Not according to

2Thessalonians 2:9:

> *that is, the one whose coming is in accord with the activity of*
> *Satan, with all power and signs and false wonders,*
> (2Thessalonians 2:9)

"Activity" in 2Thessalonians 2:9 can be viewed as an energizing, being derived from the Greek *energeia*, meaning "operative power." Hence, Satan energizes whomever he can in an attempt to thwart God's ultimate plan (the plan described in verse 10). Also read Ephesians 2:1-2, realizing that *"working"* is from the Greek *energeo*. Since both God and Satan are in the business of energizing mankind, the believer must plug himself into the proper energy source by yielding to God's indwelling presence (Romans 6:13).

We next need to consider the words *"all things"* in the phrase, *"who works all things after the counsel of His will."* The *"all things"* here cannot mean all events or all that transpires, for Luke 7:30 states:

> *For the Pharisees and the lawyers rejected God's purpose for*
> *themselves, not having been baptized by John.* (Luke 7:30)

We learn here that God's ultimate plan and purpose for the universe will stand even though some, on an individual basis, refuse to participate. Yet God desires that no individual perish:

> *The Lord is not slow about His promise, as some count slowness,*
> *but is patient toward you, not wishing for any to perish but for all*
> *to come to repentance.* (2Peter 3:9)

Clearly, if a man perishes, he perishes as a result of his own choice. God would relish the idea of having all mankind accept His Son and be a part of *"the summing up of all things in Christ"* (addressed in Ephesians 1:9-10) and the breathtaking events that follow.

Salvation involves a choice on the believer's part, which leads to another interesting topic—the *"will"* of God addressed in Ephesians 1:11c: *"who works all things after the counsel of His will."*

God may will something for an individual only to see that individual reject His will for his own. Jesus substantiates this truth in Matthew 23:37 by stating:

> *"Oh, Jerusalem, Jerusalem, who kills the prophets and stones*

those who are sent to her! How often I wanted to gather your children together, the way a hen gathers her chicks under her wings, and you were <u>unwilling</u>. (Matthew 23:37)

Man possesses a free will to choose as he desires (read Isaiah 65:12 for further confirmation). But regardless of how few choose to obey, God's sovereign will cannot be thwarted—that of *"summing up...all things in Christ"* (Ephesians 1:9-10). Thus the phrase, *"who works all things after the counsel of His will"* (Ephesians 1:11c) refers to the fulfillment of God's ultimate will and plan—that of *"summing up...all things in Christ"* (Ephesians 1:10). Paul is in no way communicating that men are robots, unable to accept or reject God's will and purpose for themselves. Let's tie this truth to the profoundness of Ephesians 1:12.

Ephesians 1:12—to the end that we who were the first to hope in Christ should be to the praise of His glory.

The Phillips translation interprets the last phrase of this verse as *"may bring praise to His glory."* No doubt, those who have become God's *"inheritance"* (Ephesians 1:11a), and are *"predestined"* (Ephesians 1:11b) *"to adoption as sons"* (Ephesians 1:5a), will bring *"praise to His glory"* (Ephesians 1:12). What else could result if, after we receive our resurrected bodies (that to which we were predestined once we were placed in Christ after repenting and believing—Ephesians 1:5-6; Romans 8:23), we return with Christ as His holy body and bride? As we discussed earlier, if Christ glorified the Father at His First Coming, just imagine how the Father will be glorified when Christ returns with His glorified body made up of believers conformed to His image (Romans 8:29). Hence, the Son's return brings glory to the Father, reaffirming the Son's commitment to benefiting the Father, the Spirit, and others in all His ways.

Ephesians 1:13—In Him, you also, after listening to the message of truth, the gospel of your salvation— having also believed, you were sealed in Him with the Holy Spirit of promise,

In Him, you also, after listening to the message of truth, the gospel of your salvation—having also believed, (1:13a)

"The message of truth" (Ephesians 1:13a) is *"the gospel of your salvation"* (Ephesians 1:13a). Because *"the gospel"* is the account of Jesus, the Source of *"truth"* (John 14:6), the gospel is unadulterated truth. Truth is astounding in that it, without fail, exposes error. Thus Jesus, *"the truth"* (John 14:6), Who is also

"light" (John 8:12; 9:5), stated:

> *"For everyone who does evil hates the light, and does not come to the light, lest his deeds should be exposed. "But he who practices the truth comes to the light, that his deeds may be manifested as having been wrought in God."* (John 3:20-21)

Truth reveals things as they really are—without bias, prejudice, or partiality. Therefore, so long as we walk in truth, we perceive life as the Creator perceives life—the definition of wisdom. What an awesome privilege!

For truth to impact our lives, we must "listen" to what it communicates. Many people "hear" truth but fail to "listen" to what they have heard, as was the case in my own life for several years. I began *"listening"* only when my problems exceeded my ability to resolve them. Thank God that He is proficient at "allowing" difficulties to cross our paths that cause truth, which previously may have been dull or mundane, to become remarkably captivating. He knows that "obedience" (acting upon what has been heard) naturally follows *"listening"* (Ephesians 1:13a).

Where are you in regard to truth this day? Do you passionately desire to know and understand God's Word? If you doubt what truth can accomplish in the soul of man, read Psalm 119—every word of it.

A word of warning: Salvation consists of more than just believing the gospel. God, Who established the gospel, bestows salvation only when the depraved exercise personal repentance and faith and the Holy Spirit places them *"in Christ"* (1Corinthians 12:13; 2Corinthians 5:17). Only through being placed *"In Him"* (Ephesians 1:13a) do we become members of God's family. Consequently, we are to view our Christian experience as an intimate friendship with the Creator—not an intellectual exercise in what He lived and taught.

you were sealed in Him with the Holy Spirit of promise, (1:13b)

Once a person repents and believes on Christ, he is *"sealed in Him with the Holy Spirit of promise"* (Ephesians 1:13b). The fact that we are *"sealed"* in the Lord should convey incredible comfort.

In ancient times, individuals sealed objects (such as letters) with wax and stamped the wax with an identifying image—such as a *"signet ring"* (Daniel 6:17). Once the letter or object was sealed, the impression on the wax identified the owner of the letter or the authenticity of the document.

A seal was used for a variety of purposes, such as confirming the completion of a transaction (Jeremiah 32:9-10). Thus, the fact that we are *"sealed in Him"* (in Christ) validates a finished, nonnegotiable transaction.

A seal also validated ownership in situations such as Jeremiah 32:11-12, where a sealed deed confirmed the ownership of property. Because we are God's *"inheritance"* (Ephesians 1:11a), and *"have been bought with a price"* (1Corinthians 6:20), we belong to Him (2Timothy 2:19). Magnificent!

A seal also pointed to approval. In 1Kings 21:5-16, Jezebel *"wrote letters in Ahab's name and sealed them with his seal"* (1Kings 21:8). The seal indicated that Ahab had approved the letters' content even though he probably never saw them. Also, in Esther 3:10-13, anything that Haman approved indicated King Ahasuerus' approval, for Haman was given the king's signet ring. Therefore, having been sealed in Christ by the Holy Spirit, after repenting and believing while depraved, New Testament believers are approved by God. We are welcomed members of God's family, with all the privileges that Sonship entails—both in the present and throughout eternity. Wow!

To be sealed in Christ by the Holy Spirit also means that New Testament believers are secure in Christ. Once Haman's evil decree was sealed with King Ahasuerus' signet ring (Esther 3:10-15), revocation was impossible (Esther 8:8). An additional decree was required, sealed with the same ring, allowing the Jews to defend themselves (Esther 8:9-14) against the decree of Esther 3:10-15. Daniel 6:17 and Matthew 27:66 also confirm that a sealed object is not to be disturbed. New Testament believers are *"sealed"* in Christ (2Corinthians 1:21-22), *"sealed for the day of redemption"* (Ephesians 4:30)—*"sealed"* for that day when they will receive their glorified bodies. God sees to it that we are *"kept"* (Jude 1) secure in Him (John 10:28-29). As a result, we are in Christ, and Christ is in the Father (John 14:20), Who will finish the work He has begun in us (Philippians 1:6).

Paul mentions both *"truth"* and *"the Holy Spirit"* in Ephesians 1:13. We received the Holy Spirit the moment we accepted Christ (Romans 8:9), but we can't live on truth alone or the Holy Spirit alone once we become believers. A combination of both is necessary. Those who learn truth as an end in itself, without seeking the revelation of the Holy Spirit, become intellectually stagnant. Those who seek the Holy Spirit's revelation, void of a steady diet of truth, end up deceived. Only truth revealed through the Holy Spirit results in positive change (read 1Corinthians 2:4-5; 4:19). When the Spirit reveals truth, we know it (read Luke 24:32)!

Ephesians 1:14—who is given as a pledge of our inheritance, with a view to the

redemption of God's own possession, to the praise of His glory.

who is given as a pledge of our inheritance, (1:14a)

The Spirit of God is *"given as a pledge* [earnest, or down payment] *of our inheritance,"* meaning that He (among other things) serves as a guarantee that the remainder is sure to come. Hence, the Holy Spirit is given to Christ's future bride, the church, for the purpose of assuring her of His eternal acceptance (2Corinthians 1:22; 5:5). Some theologians even perceive the Holy Spirit as a divine engagement ring, sealing the bride's relationship with her Husband, Jesus.

The Holy Spirit serves several different functions as the New Testament believer walks with God. So not only are we sealed in Christ by means of the Spirit, but having Him as a down payment confirms that more is to come—part of which is addressed in the next phrase of Ephesians 1:14:

with a view to the redemption of God's own possession, (1:14b)

The Holy Spirit *"is given as a pledge of our inheritance"* (Ephesians 1:14a) *"with a view to the redemption of God's own possession"* (Ephesians 1:14b). Because the Father created all things through Christ (Colossians 1:15-16), He desires to rescue what is rightfully His (that which came under the control of Satan, *"the god of this world,"* when Adam sinned—2Corinthians 4:4). This restoration will come to fruition when our bodies are resurrected (1Thessalonians 4:13-18) and we later return with Christ (Revelation 19:11-20:3; Romans 8:19-23).

to the praise of His glory. (1:14c)

After our bodies are resurrected, we later (at the Second Coming) return with Christ *"to the praise of God's glory."* What could bring more *"glory"* to the Father than to have many sons (church saints), conformed to Christ's image (Romans 8:29), who reflect His glory? When we return with Christ (Revelation 19), as Christ's body (Romans 12:5; Ephesians 5:23; Colossians 1:18), the creation will be released from its bondage into the freedom of the glory of the sons of God (Romans 8:19-21).

Ephesians 1:15—For this reason I too, having heard of the faith in the Lord Jesus which exists among you, and your love for all the saints,

When Paul says, *"For this reason,"* he is referencing all the blessings he has outlined in verses 3-14. These believers had been blessed *"with every spiritual blessing...in Christ"* (Ephesians 1:3), chosen in Christ (Ephesians 1:4), *"predestined...in the Beloved"* (Ephesians 1:5-6), redeemed and forgiven *"in Him"* (Ephesians 1:7), received in Him *"wisdom and insight"* to know God's ultimate plan (Ephesians 1:8-10), made an inheritance *"in Him"* (Ephesians 1:10-11), and *"sealed in Him with the Holy Spirit"* (Ephesians 1:13-14). Paul, writing from prison in Rome, had heard of their *"faith in the Lord Jesus"* and their *"love for all the saints"* (Ephesians 1:15). But some time (around four years) had passed since he had seen them. This news of their obedience had to greatly encourage Paul, especially since he had instructed them in the ways of the Lord as early as his third missionary journey (Acts 19:8-10). *"Love"* in verse 15 is *agape*, meaning unconditional love, a *"fruit of the Spirit"* (Galatians 5:23). Thus, Paul's readers loved God's people unconditionally. Ephesians 1:15 also reconfirms that New Testament believers are *"saints"* who sometimes sin, not lowly sinners saved by grace.

To know that these saints walked in faith and loved one another unconditionally must have brought joy beyond measure to this seasoned missionary. Sadly, however, the apostle John, some years later, described these same believers as having *"left"* their *"first love"* (Revelation 2:1-5). Paul realized the need for the truths of Ephesians 1:3-14 to be transformed from intellectual stimulation to spiritual revelation. Therefore, he prayed for the church at Ephesus, the subject of Ephesians 1:16.

Ephesians 1:16—do not cease giving thanks for you, while making mention of you in my prayers;

In Colossians 1:9 Paul states:

> *For this reason also, since the day we heard of it, we have not ceased to pray for you and to ask that you may be filled with the knowledge of His will in all spiritual wisdom and understanding,* (Colossians 1:9)

Paul was a man of prayer. No wonder he prayed for the believers at Ephesus (Ephesians 1:16)! They were people of *"faith"* (Ephesians 1:15)—individuals who applied what they believed. Because of their faithfulness, Paul gave thanks for them on a regular basis.

I can't begin to express the encouragement I receive while thanking the Lord for the faithful. As I do so, I am privileged to remember how these individuals have impacted my life and the lives of countless others. If you aren't in the habit of thankfully praying for the faithful, I highly recommend that you begin. In fact, you might bow right now and thank the Lord for those saints who have encouraged you in the faith. You might even mail them a letter. A friend of mine has a ministry in this area, and his hand-written notes I always read in full.

God honored Paul's prayers, for the Ephesian church walked in faith and love while Paul interceded on their behalf. But something happened between the date of this epistle and John's God-inspired writing of the book of Revelation. The church at Ephesus had *"left"* her *"first love"* (Revelation 2:4).

Conclusion: Regardless of the effectiveness of the teacher, or the depth of the subject matter, the student will not experience a sustained obedience unless the Holy Spirit is allowed to consistently transform information to revelation.

As a new believer, I had to learn that the "good feelings" experienced from studying God's Word must never be mistaken for spiritual growth, for I can experience an emotional "high" on information alone. Hence, information by itself never brings about change. Only revealed truth makes a difference in the lives of God's people.

Ephesians 1:17—that the God of our Lord Jesus Christ, the Father of glory, may give to you a spirit of wisdom and of revelation in the knowledge of Him.

This passage records Paul's method of praying for the church at Ephesus. First, he mentions *"the God of our Lord Jesus Christ, the Father of glory."* Because *"the Father of glory"* is Jesus' Father (also review Ephesians 1:3), Paul again confirms that Jesus is the Father's Son through the *"virgin"* of Isaiah 7:14. The phrase, *"the Father of glory,"* also points to the Father's flawless character, which results in manifested glory each time He reveals Himself. It also confirms His worthiness to receive the glory we ascribe to Him. (The manifestation of God's glory throughout the Old and New Testaments is recorded in the following verses: Exodus 3:2-4; Exodus 19:16-18; Exodus 20:18-19; Exodus 40:34-38; 2Chronicles 5:13-14; 2Chronicles 7:2-3; Ezekiel 11:22-25; Luke 2:8-9; John 1:14; Acts 1:9-12; Acts 2:1-3; Colossians 1:27). Notice that Paul refers to Jesus as *"Lord"* for the second time in three verses (review verse 15).

Paul prayed that *"the God of our Lord Jesus Christ, the Father of glory"* would impart to these believers *"a spirit of wisdom and of revelation in the knowledge of Him."* Wuest writes in his commentary on Ephesians:

> What Paul is praying for is that God might so work in the lives of

the Ephesian saints that they will have the spiritual wisdom and a
revelation from Him that is the result of the Holy Spirit's work of
energizing their human spirit. This spiritual wisdom and revelation
is "in the knowledge of Him." [5]

Paul basically states that the wisdom and revelation he desires for these believers is
to be found in a deeper knowledge of God Himself. Paul's approach makes sense,
for his personal goal was not activity, but to know intimately the heart of Christ
(Philippians 3:10). He understood well that to know the Son was to know the
Father (John 14:9). He also realized that in knowing the Son, and falling deeply in
love with Him, meant that his faith would always support the activity that God
prescribed. In fact, Paul, in pursuing Christ's heart above all else, learned to live by
Christ's very life (Colossians 3:4; Romans 5:10; Philippians 1:21).

"The fear of the Lord is the beginning of wisdom" (Proverbs 9:10), but God imparts
additional wisdom as the believer progresses *"in the knowledge of Him"*
(Ephesians 1:17). Thus, the *"fathers"* (the spiritually mature) of the faith possess
enhanced wisdom due to knowing *"Him who has been from the beginning"* (1John
2:13-14). The principle of the cross is consistently manifested in their
relationships, for they live for the benefit of others—never themselves. The
Godhead receives much glory from such individuals.

Note that Paul writes *"a spirit of wisdom"* in Ephesians 1:17 rather than "the spirit
of wisdom." The lack of a definite article verifies that Paul is not referencing the
Holy Spirit, although through the Holy Spirit this *"spirit of wisdom"* is received.
Ray Stedman, in his commentary on Ephesians, writes:

> So he is not praying that they will be given the Holy Spirit. He is
> praying for a special ministry of the Holy Spirit. In the book of
> Isaiah, the prophet speaks of the seven spirits of God—the spirit of
> wisdom, the spirit of understanding, the spirit of counsel, the spirit
> of knowledge, etc. (Isaiah 11:2). He doesn't mean that there are
> seven Holy Spirits; he means that there is one Holy Spirit who has
> a seven-fold ministry of illuminating and enlightening the heart. [6]

These believers already possessed *"everything pertaining to life and godliness"*
(2Peter 1:3). Their problem was not a deficiency of provision but a lack of
application. For this reason Paul prayed for *"wisdom"* and *"revelation"* on their
behalf.

"Wisdom" and *"revelation"* are somewhat synonymous: *"revelation"*—the
illumination of truth; *"wisdom"*—an understanding of how truth applies to God and

His plan for man. We must never forget that *"wisdom"* and *"revelation"* are only attained through *"the knowledge of Him"*—through a deeper understanding of Who God is. No amount of Christian activity and busyness will result in an impartation of wisdom. Only time alone in His presence will suffice.

Ephesians 1:18—I pray that the eyes of your heart may be enlightened, so that you may know what is the hope of His calling, what are the riches of the glory of His inheritance in the saints,

I pray that the eyes of your heart may be enlightened, (1:18a)

"Heart" is not referencing the physical pump that circulates blood throughout our bodies. *"Heart"* is from the Greek *kardia*, which is interpreted *"heart"* in a majority of cases in the New Testament. But *kardia* is rendered *"mind"* in passages such as Luke 1:66 and Acts 7:23, and *"minds"* in Luke 21:14. So the *"heart"* (Ephesians 1:18) is the believer's innermost being—totally separate from anything physical.

Paul prayed that the *"eyes"* of these believer's hearts would *"be enlightened."* The phrase, *"may be enlightened,"* is a perfect participle in the Greek, pointing to past action, completed action, with a resulting state of being. Wuest, therefore, interprets the verse as follows: *"the eyes of your heart having been enlightened with the present result that they are in a state of illumination."*[7] Paul desired that the eyes of his readers' hearts continually be enlightened (or illuminated). To discover what occurs when one's eyes are *"enlightened,"* read Luke 24:13-35—which explains why Paul prayed as he did for these saints.

Paul desired that these believers' eyes be opened in three specific areas, all of which are recorded in the remainder of this verse and the first phrase of verse 19.

so that you may know what is the hope of His calling, (1:18b)

God has called the New Testament believer with a *"calling"* inundated with *"hope."* We discussed this truth when we addressed *"predestined"* in Ephesians 1:5a. There we found that the saints are called in the sense of being invited to accept Christ, a calling that in no way indicates that they were selected (by God) for salvation from eternity past. It simply means that New Testament believers are invited to become children of God while in their depraved state, as are all individuals who grace the earth. We also discovered that in several instances *"calling,"* or *"called,"* references the New Testament believer's office (area of gifting—1Peter 4:10). Ephesians 1:18b seems to apply to that scenario.

Do you have *"hope,"* or is your Christian life somewhat mundane and boring? Are you as excited about pursuing Christ today as you were when you first met Him? Is His Word as interesting and refreshing as it once was? Do you have vision, or are you experiencing frustration as you pursue God's best for your life? Do you "feel" as if nothing you are doing (in Christ's strength, of course) is impacting anyone's life, including your own? The believers at Ephesus were apparently faltering. They had been exposed to the wonderful truths of verses 3-14 (and much more since Paul had taught at Ephesus for at least three years), yet Paul prayed that the eyes of their hearts might be enlightened so they might *"know what is the hope of His calling"* (Ephesians 1:18). Evidently, these believers were in a rut. They had been exposed to a wealth of truth through a man who had seen Jesus but were lacking in their ability to implement his teachings. They possessed an intellectual understanding of their future destiny (that they would one day receive a resurrected body and reign with Christ), but that event was to occur in the distant future. What they needed was a revelation of what God was doing in the midst of the mundane so hope could be experienced in the present. In much the same way, we have little difficulty appropriating hope for that day when we will receive our glorified bodies and return with Christ. Appropriating hope in the present, in the middle of clogged drains, stopped up commodes, and flat tires, is the greater challenge. For this we have Jesus, Who saves us daily *"by His life"*:

> For if while we were enemies, we were reconciled to God through
> the death of His Son, much more, having been reconciled, we shall
> be saved by His life. (Romans 5:10)

"Hope" never disappoints (Romans 5:5), allowing believers to rejoice in all circumstances (Romans 12:12) and exude boldness of speech (2Corinthians 3:12). That hope is usually attained through trial (Romans 5:1-5) should not deter us, for hope is found in *"Christ Jesus, who is our hope"* (1Timothy 1:1), *"the Lamb that was slain"* (Revelation 5:6, 8, 12, 13). As we enter into His sufferings, we know Him more deeply and, in turn, live more consistently from His perspective— viewing difficulties as opportunities to display the principle of the cross (selfless living) in all situations of life. Once we experience selfless living, hope inundates our souls to the glory of the Father. Self-centeredness, on the other hand, extinguishes hope.

These believers had reason to possess hope in the present as well as in the future, as validated by verses 3-14. *"Hope,"* according to Hebrews 6:19, is the *"anchor"* of the believer's *"soul."* Without hope, the redeemed sail aimlessly in defeat and despair. In fact, they *"grieve"* (1Thessalonians 4:13). Paul encouraged his readers to focus on the hope made available through Christ—to live by His life in the present, remembering that they would later receive glorified bodies and return with

Christ (as God's *"inheritance"*—Ephesians 1:11) to the *"glory"* of God the Father (Ephesians 1:14). Knowing (really knowing and believing) what lies ahead supplies hope for the future as well as the present. But, as was pointed out earlier, Christ's work on the cross can be viewed from two perspectives (one proper, the other improper): (1) self-centeredness, where you are concerned with how it benefits you (2) God-centeredness, where you are concerned with how it benefits God and others. Hence, Paul prayed that the eyes of their hearts would be enlightened (Ephesians 1:18) so they might bask in the hope experienced in the present and the future through selfless living.

what are the riches of the glory of His inheritance in the saints, (1:18c)

Paul also prayed that his readers would know *"what are the riches of the glory of His inheritance in the saints."* He had taught earlier, in verse 11, that these saints had been made God's inheritance. But now he prayed that their eyes would be opened to that truth—that it would become revealed truth rather than remain information. The gospel, from their vantage point, needed to become God-centered rather than remain self-centered (man-centered). They needed to begin to understand what God received through the cross and grow past the shallowness of viewing Calvary selfishly.

All New Testament saints are God's inheritance. God is glorified in them, and this glory is valuable to the Father. But just as pain (the death of God's Son) was required prior to our becoming His inheritance, pain (personal suffering) reveals to the believer the value of God's inheritance in the saints. In fact, only through living by the principle of the cross (selfless living—dying to self when the going gets tough) do we appreciate what God receives through Christ's offering and bride. Only then is our perspective of the body of Christ (the universal church) drastically revolutionized. Instead of viewing her as random individuals, some lovable and some not so lovable, we view her as precious to the Father—something worth cherishing, something worth our concern due to her great value. Can you see why a deficiency of this perspective could nurture disunity within Christ's body? May each of us love God by encouraging His inheritance in truth and loving her unconditionally!

Before we can comprehend the positive ramifications of being a part of God's inheritance, we must realize the type of work that God is doing today, even this very moment, in those who make up His inheritance. This work is an awesome work, one that can be understood through a proper knowledge of a previous topic—"the principle of the cross."

The church, made up of *"glorified"* saints (Romans 8:30) *"conformed to the image of"* Christ (Romans 8:29), will return as the body of Christ at Jesus' Second Coming. This event will occur after each member of the church has received a resurrected body (1Thessalonians 4:13-18; Revelation 19:11-16), bringing much glory to the Father. By this time the Father's inheritance (masterpiece) will be totally conformed to the image of His Son in soul and spirit, as well as body. Consequently, we will respond to all situations exactly as Christ responds.

God is in the process, even today, of bringing us to maturity. His goal is that we begin to think and respond as Christ thinks and responds. From earlier lessons, we learned that Jesus does nothing for Himself, but only for others—including the other two Persons of the Trinity. He lives, in other words, by the principle of the cross. We, therefore, must move from a self-centered gospel to a God-centered gospel. We must move past the place of serving God for our own glory (2Corinthians 4:17) and serve Him for the glory that He is to receive through His inheritance, the church (Ephesians 1:18), when she returns in glory. Only through God opening the eyes of our hearts (Ephesians 1:18), as we passionately pursue His heart, will we grow past our selfishness to comprehend *"what are the riches of the glory of His inheritance in the saints."* Thus, Paul prayed for the church at Ephesus.

Ephesians 1:19-20 —and what is the surpassing greatness of His power toward us who believe (19a). These are in accordance with the working of the strength of His might (19b) which He brought about in Christ, when He raised Him from the dead (20a), and seated Him at His right hand in the heavenly places (20b),

and what is the surpassing greatness of His power toward us who believe. (1:19a)

"Power" is from the Greek *dunamis* and points to God's power supplied to the New Testament believer, not only in the future, but also in the present. *"Surpassing"* is from the Greek *huperbaloon* meaning "to throw over or beyond," confirming that God's power exceeds any power that has or will exist. Hence, God's power fulfills the New Testament believer's *"hope"* (Ephesians 1:18b) today, tomorrow, and throughout eternity. Therefore, His power sustains the church, His *"inheritance"* (Ephesians 1:18c), both today and forever.

Because we receive this type of power (*"toward us who believe"*—Ephesians 1:19a), we have been called to live by this power as we function in the spiritual gift (1Peter 4:10) we received the moment we repented and believed, were placed in Christ and made new, and predestined to receive a glorified body. Read Psalm 18:1-19 for additional insight into the magnitude of the power made available to

God's children.

These are in accordance with the working of the strength of His might (1:19b) which He brought about in Christ, when He raised Him from the dead (1:20a),

The power described in Ephesians 1:19a is *"in accordance with the working of the strength of His might"* (Ephesians 1:19b). *"Working,"* from the Greek *energeia,* can be viewed as God's "operative power" or "energizing" (refer to notes on Ephesians 1:11). *"Strength"* is from the Greek *kratos,* meaning "strength, power, might, or force." *"Might"* is from the Greek *ischus,* meaning "strength, might, or power." Clearly, Paul is referencing power of infinite magnitude, the same power that brought Jesus out of the grave (Ephesians 1:20a) and allows New Testament believers to *"walk in newness of life"* (Romans 6:4)—walk with boldness and authority as redeemed saints of God. For this reason, Jesus stated to the disciples:

> *but you shall receive power when the Holy Spirit has come upon you;...* (Acts 1:8)

This same Spirit and power came upon us when we received Christ, for Paul writes:

> *Now we have received, not the spirit of the world, but the Spirit who is from God,...* (1Corinthians 2:12)

Paul also states:

> *But if the Spirit of Him who raised Jesus from the dead dwells in you, He who raised Christ Jesus from the dead will also give life to your mortal bodies through His Spirit who indwells you.* (Romans 8:11)

Paul is not pointing solely to that day when we will receive our resurrected bodies, but is also reminding us of the power available today through the indwelling Spirit. Paul, having as his ultimate goal to know Christ and the power of His resurrection (Philippians 3:10), teaches us a critical principle: We will never experience the power of His resurrection in the daily affairs of life until we know Him intimately. Authority and power for victorious living come only through knowing Him and living by His very life (Romans 5:10; Colossians 3:4).

and seated Him at His right hand in the heavenly places (1:20b),

The fact that Jesus is seated in heaven means that His work as our high priest, in the heavenly tabernacle, is completed (Hebrews 8:1-2). Since the earthly priests' work was never done, they were in constant motion. Not so with Christ. He could sit down because His blood (and death) produced a finished work. Consequently, future sacrifices are unnecessary.

Not only did the Father's power raise Jesus from the dead (Galatians 1:1), but this same power also seated Jesus at the Father's *"right hand"* in heaven (Ephesians 1:20b). The *"right hand"* of God has always been considered His hand of power. Moses stated:

> *"Thy right hand, O Lord, is majestic in power, Thy right hand, O Lord, shatters the enemy.* (Exodus 15:6)

(For more insight into this topic, read the following passages: Psalm 18:35; 98:1; 108:6; 118:15; 138:7; Isaiah 41:10; Matthew 26:64; Mark 12:36; 14:62; Luke 22:69; Acts 5:31; Colossians 3:1; Hebrews 8:1; 10:12—only a partial listing of the verses that address this subject are recorded here.)

Jesus holds tremendous authority at the Father's right hand. Just think of the power made available to every church saint through Christ's indwelling presence (Galatians 2:20; Philippians 4:13; Colossians 1:29). Also, Ephesians 2:6 reveals that the Father raises up New Testament believers and seats them with Him in heaven, in Christ, the moment they repent and believe while depraved. Thus, if you have accepted Christ, you too are at the Father's right hand of power—you are in heaven in Christ (Ephesians 2:6) and Christ is in you on earth (Galatians 2:20; Colossians 1:27). Note: *"The heavenly places"* (Ephesians 1:20b) is heaven itself.

Ephesians 1:21—far above all rule and authority and power and dominion, and every name that is named, not only in this age, but also in the one to come.

far above all rule and authority and power and dominion, and every name that is named, (1:21a)

Jesus, as a result of His resurrection, was given authority *"far above all rule and authority and power and dominion."* Because *"rule,"* *"authority,"* *"power,"* and *"dominion"* can be used to describe angelic beings of great rank or power, anything in the created realm, even angelic beings (both holy and unholy), must submit to Christ. In fact, any *"name that is named"* must bow before Him. Because Jesus (being God, Hebrews 1:8, and one with the Father and Spirit) outranks any power or authority that can be *"named,"* no created thing supersedes Christ in rank—not even Satan and his demons. Remember this truth when we study Ephesians 6:12:

For our struggle is not against flesh and blood, but against the rulers, against the powers, against the world forces of this darkness, against the spiritual forces of wickedness in the heavenly places. (Ephesians 6:12)

Because our Leader possesses such *"authority and power"* (Ephesians 1:21), we can take on the forces of darkness (in His strength and authority) and know the battle is won.

not only in this age, but also in the one to come. (1:21b)

Our discoveries concerning Christ's authority apply to both the present and the future. His authority will exceed anything in the created realm from now throughout the Millennium. After the Millennium, and after all things *"in the heavens"* and *"the earth"* are summed up *"in Christ"* (Ephesians 1:10), He will present what He possesses to the Father for all eternity (1Corinthians 15:28). He will, of course, retain His authority over all created things.

Ephesians 1:22—And He put all things in subjection under His feet, and gave Him as head over all things to the church,

And He put all things in subjection under His feet, (1:22a)

1Peter 3:22 states:

who is at the right hand of God, having gone into heaven, after angels and authorities and powers had been subjected to Him. (1Peter 3:22)

Jesus was taken to heaven after *"all things"* (Ephesians 1:22) in the created realm were *"subjected to Him"* (1Peter 3:22). Once in heaven, and *"seated"* at the *"right hand"* of God (Ephesians 1:20), *"above all rule and authority and power and dominion"* (Ephesians 1:21), many people accepted Him as Savior and were made part of His body. Hence, God the Father placed all things *"under His feet"* (Ephesians 1:22a). Paul uses *"feet"* because Jesus, since Acts 2 (the birth of the church), has possessed a *"body"* made up of New Testament believers (Ephesians 1:22-23). Oh, the consistency of the detail implemented within the Scriptures!

and gave Him as head over all things to the church, (1:22b)

Jesus is the *"head"* of the universal church, not just in the sense of being her

Supreme Authority, but also serving as her very *"life"* (Colossians 3:4—*"When Christ, who is our life,... "*). Thus, we live by His *"life"* (John 1:4; John 14:6) and are *"saved"* on a daily basis *"by His life"* (Romans 5:10). Note: By no means am I communicating that a church saint is a little Jesus. God's Spirit and our spirit, though in union, are two separate entities (Romans 8:16; 2Timothy 4:22).

Ephesians 1:23 which is His body, the fullness of Him who fills all in all.

which is His body, (1:23a)

Considering what we discussed earlier, we can conclude the following: Christ is the *"head"* of the church (Ephesians 1:22b), *"which is His body"* (Ephesians 1:23a). Consequently, Ephesians 1:22a does not say, "And He put all things in subjection under His head." The passage states *"And He put all things in subjection under His feet."* Who happens to make up Christ's body (His very feet and the remainder of His body)? The universal church fulfills that role, made up of all believers who have accepted Christ since Acts 2. Paul desired that the church at Ephesus understand her authority: That all things had been placed in subjection under her—she being part of Christ's body. Hence, she could stand in Christ's strength against any *"rule and authority and power and dominion, and every name that is named"* (Ephesians 1:21). We, being part of the universal body of Christ, can do the same.

the fullness of Him who fills all in all. (1:23b)

Christ's body is His *"fullness"* or His full development (Ephesians 1:23b), which means that Jesus' body (which is in the process of being developed) is incomplete (so to speak) until the church has been completed—especially since the head (Jesus) manifests Himself through the body (Philippians 2:20). All believers from Acts 2 to the Rapture make up Christ's body. Because the Rapture has not yet occurred, the body receives new members each day. Christ's body, therefore, will be made complete when the final member is added and all members receive their glorified bodies at the Rapture. Jesus will then be capable of fully expressing Himself through His holy, glorified body, the church, which returns with Him as His bride at the Second Coming (Revelation 19:11-16).

In Jesus, *"all the fullness of Deity dwells in bodily form"* (Colossians 2:9). In fact, *"it was the Father's good pleasure for all the fullness to dwell in Him"* (Colossians 1:19). Because the fullness of Deity dwells in Jesus, He is God (John 10:30; Hebrews 1:8). To see Him is to see the Father (John 14:9), for He *"is the image of the invisible God"* (Colossians 1:15). Thus, the Godhead's riches, power, and presence reside within each member of the universal body of Christ through the Person of the Son of God.

The *"fullness of Deity"* (Colossians 2:9) resides within us when Christ enters our lives (Galatians 2:20; John 1:16). Yet, we must be careful with *"fills"* in Ephesians 1:23b. Jesus *"fills"* New Testament believers who allow Him to bring them to maturity. When we live in this manner, we are *"filled up to all the fullness of God"* (Ephesians 3:19)—a subject addressed in more detail in Ephesians 3:19, 4:10, and 4:13.

Ephesians 2

Ephesians 2:1—And you were dead in your trespasses and sins,

The believers at Ephesus were spiritually *"dead"* (separated from God) before they met Christ because they were born depraved. So were we. Our bodies functioned. We could even think with our minds, feel with our emotions, and choose with our wills, but we were *"dead"* in that we were separated from God. All of Adam's descendants begin in this state, for when Adam sinned he became spiritually *"dead"*—separated from God Who *"is spirit"* (John 4:24). God had told Adam that the day he ate of the forbidden fruit he would *"die"* (Genesis 2:17)— experience instantaneous spiritual death. Thus, Adam ate and died spiritually but continued to live physically. In fact, sometime after sinning in Genesis 3:6, he had relations with Eve, who bore Cain (Genesis 4:1). Adam was very much alive physically, but for the first time in his existence possessed a nature that enjoyed sin. Suddenly, it was natural for Adam to sin due to his sinful nature. In fact, the most natural thing Adam did after willfully sinning against God was disobey God. We, being descendants of Adam, were born with a *"dead"* spirit (Ephesians 2:1); the condition that existed within Adam after he sinned. Because *"God is spirit"* (John 4:24), and we possessed no spirit life when we were born, we were dead upon arrival. We were born depraved.

Reformed Theology (extreme and hyper-Calvinism) adheres to the idea that man is born a spiritual corpse, totally incapable of believing while depraved. Is this mindset in agreement with the full counsel of God's Word? Let's answer that question using Scripture alone.

Romans 1:8-32 portrays the lifestyle of the heathen—those who, through their own choosing, reject the truth that God so graciously supplies.

> *For the wrath of God is revealed from heaven against all*
> *ungodliness and unrighteousness of men, who suppress the truth in*
> *unrighteousness,* (Romans 1:18)

The spiritually depraved can *"suppress the truth,"* proving that they are conscious (aware) of the truth. You can't *"suppress"* what has not been made accessible.

> *because that which is known about God is evident within them; for*
> *God made it evident to them.* (Romans 1:19)

Here we observe that God makes what can be *"known"* about Himself *"evident"* to the depraved (lost).

> *For since the creation of the world His invisible attributes, His eternal power and divine nature, have been clearly seen, being understood through what has been made, so that they are without excuse.* (Romans 1:20)

Creation reveals God's *"attributes,"* *"power,"* and *"divine nature."* Hence, no man can accuse God of withholding from mankind the certainty of His existence—not even the heathen.

> *For even though they knew God, they did not honor Him as God, or give thanks; but they became futile in their speculations, and their foolish heart was darkened.* (Romans 1:21)

Paul teaches that all persons know about God—know of His existence and specifics regarding His Person. The depraved who choose to dishonor Him, however, possess hearts that have been progressively *"darkened."* The fact that the choice to dishonor God results in an enhanced darkening of the heart proves that man is not at his worst at physical birth. He can (in the midst of his depravity) become increasingly *"darkened"* through intensified rebellion.

> *Professing to be wise, they became fools,* (Romans 1:22)

The depraved who profess *"to be wise"* become *"fools"* due to their own choices.

> *and exchanged the glory of the incorruptible God for an image in the form of corruptible man and of birds and four-footed animals and crawling creatures.* (Romans 1:23)

As a result of the depraved rejecting God's truth (which can be accepted if they so desire), they worship what has been created. In making that choice, they exchange *"the glory of...God"* (Who He is in His essence) for what will perish.

> *Therefore God gave them over in the lusts of their hearts to impurity, that their bodies might be dishonored among them.* (Romans 1:24)

As a result of the majority of the depraved rejecting His truth, *"God"* gives *"them over"* to *"impurity"*—but only <u>after</u> they choose to disobey.

> *For they exchanged the truth of God for a lie, and worshiped and*
> *served the creature rather than the Creator, who is blessed forever.*
> *Amen.* (Romans 1:25)

The depraved (as they progress in sin) are given *"over...to impurity"* (Romans 1:24) because they exchange *"the truth of God for a lie"* (Romans 1:25), which results in their worshipping *"the creature rather than the Creator"* (Romans 1:25). To exchange *"truth,"* you must have access to *"the truth."* You can't exchange something for an alternative if you don't first possess what you are exchanging.

> *For this reason God gave them over to degrading passions; for*
> *their women exchanged the natural function for that which is*
> *unnatural,* (Romans 1:26)

After the depraved reject the truth, God gives *"them over to degrading passions"* (Romans 1:26), which are defined in both Romans 1:26 and Romans 1:27:

> *and in the same way also the men abandoned the natural function*
> *of the woman and burned in their desire toward one another, men*
> *with men committing indecent acts and receiving in their own*
> *persons the due penalty of their error.* (Romans 1:27)

The *"degrading passions"* of verse 26 are passions that cause women to desire *"unnatural"* physical relationships with women (Romans 1:26) and men to desire unnatural and *"indecent"* physical relationships with men (Romans 1:27)— homosexual and lesbian relationships that God classifies as *"error"* (Romans 1:27).

> *And even as they did not like to retain God in their knowledge, God*
> *gave them over to a reprobate mind, to do those things which are*
> *not convenient;* (Romans 1:28 KJV)

Clearly, the depraved possess a *"knowledge"* of God, although they many times refuse to *"retain"* it (Romans 1:28). Therefore, their rejection of the truth results in their minds becoming *"reprobate"* (Romans 1:28), causing them to involve themselves in *"things which are not convenient"* (Romans 1:28)—behavior defined in Romans 1:29-31.

> *being filled with all unrighteousness, wickedness, greed, evil; full*
> *of envy, murder, strife, deceit, malice; they are gossips, slanderers,*
> *haters of God, insolent, arrogant, boastful, inventors of evil,*
> *disobedient to parents, without understanding, untrustworthy,*
> *unloving, unmerciful;* (Romans 1:29-31)

The fruit of rebellion in the depraved is an appalling state indeed!

> *and, although they know the ordinance of God, that those who*
> *practice such things are worthy of death, they not only do the*
> *same, but also give hearty approval to those who practice them.*
> (Romans 1:32)

The depraved *"know the ordinance of God"* (Romans 1:32—also read verses 25 and 28) prior to their extreme rebelliousness. Thus, a huge difference exists between knowing God's truth and yearning to apply it. Once a depraved individual repents and believes, however, he is made new—resulting in a passionate desire to know and exercise God's absolutes to the greatest degree possible.

Romans 1:18-32 validates (beyond doubt) that man, even in his depraved state, has a conscience awareness of God's existence—proving that man's depravity does not make him totally unaware of spiritual matters, and thus, a spiritual corpse. No wonder the Psalmist penned:

> *The heavens are telling of the glory of God; and their expanse is*
> *declaring the work of His hands. Day to day pours forth speech,*
> *and night to night reveals knowledge. There is no speech, nor are*
> *there words; their voice is not heard.* (Psalm 19:1-3)

Depravity does not mean that unregenerate man is "incapable" of knowing about God and His truth. Neither does depravity endorse the idea that unregenerate man possesses an "inability" to exercise personal repentance and faith—as verified by passages such as Galatians 3:24:

> *Therefore the Law has become our tutor to lead us to Christ, that*
> *we may be justified by faith.* (Galatians 3:24)

Romans 1:18-32 ties in perfectly with Galatians 3:24. The Law, given to Moses in the Old Testament, serves a very special purpose. Paul describes it as a *"tutor,"* for through the Law a spiritually unregenerated (depraved) man can recognize his need for a Savior. However, if total depravity should mean "total inability" (the Reformed view), what need would there be for the Law? If man, in his lost (depraved) state, cannot recognize sin and exercise personal repentance and faith, why would God give a Law whose purpose is to convict the depraved of their lostness?

Paul, in (1Timothy 1:8-10), confirms that the Law is for *"the ungodly"*—not the *"righteous"*:

> *But we know that the Law is good, if one uses it lawfully, realizing*
> *the fact that law is not made for a righteous man, but for those who*
> *are lawless and rebellious, for the ungodly and sinners, for the*
> *unholy and profane, for those who kill their fathers or mothers, for*
> *murderers and immoral men and homosexuals and kidnappers and*
> *liars and perjurers, and whatever else is contrary to sound*
> *teaching,* (1Timothy 1:8-10)

These verses prove, unequivocally, that the Law was given to convict the hearts of the ungodly (depraved) only. Paul confirms this same truth in Romans 3:19:

> *Now we know that whatever the Law says, it speaks to those who*
> *are under the Law, that every mouth may be closed, and all the*
> *world may become accountable to God;* (Romans 3:19)

The Law speaks to one class of people, *"to those who are under the Law."* Once again, we observe that the Law convicts the depraved of their sin so they might recognize their need for a Savior. Adding even more strength to the argument, Paul states in Romans 6:14 that the New Testament believer is *"not under law, but under grace"*:

> *For sin shall not be master over you, for you are not under law, but*
> *under grace.* (Romans 6:14)

This verse reinforces the fact that only the ungodly (the depraved) are under the Law. Paul also states (in Romans 7:4-6) that New Testament believers died to the Law through the body of Christ, freeing them to *"serve in the newness of the Spirit and not in the oldness of the letter"*:

> *Therefore, my brethren, you also were made to die to the Law*
> *through the body of Christ, that you might be joined to another, to*
> *Him who was raised from the dead, that we might bear fruit for*
> *God. For while we were in the flesh, the sinful passions, which*
> *were aroused by the Law, were at work in the members of our body*
> *to bear fruit for death. But now we have been released from the*
> *Law, having died to that by which we were bound, so that we serve*
> *in newness of the Spirit and not in oldness of the letter.* (Romans
> 7:4-6)

The Law serves to convict only the ungodly (the depraved). It was given, in other words, to lead the ungodly (the depraved) to Christ (Galatians 3:24). Hence, the depraved are capable of having the Law convict them of their ungodliness so they might repent and believe—disproving that depravity means "total inability."

To perceive the depraved as spiritual corpses, totally incapable of repenting and believing, is in violation of the full counsel of God's Word. Again we observe the consistency of the Scriptures regardless of the subject under examination.

Note how John 16:8 ties in with our present study:

> *"And He, when He comes, will convict the world concerning sin,*
> *and righteousness, and judgment;* (John 16:8)

The Scriptures teach that the Holy Spirit convicts every person on God's earth, although many of these individuals disregard His conviction. Should depravity indicate that man (while depraved) is incapable of responding to God, would God not be unwise if, through the power of the Holy Spirit, He convicted individuals who are unable to respond? Titus 2:11-12 ties in well with our discussion:

> *For the grace of God has appeared, bringing salvation to all men,*
> *instructing us to deny ungodliness and worldly desires and to live*
> *sensibly, righteously and godly in the present age,* (Titus 2:11-12)

If depravity makes man a spiritually lifeless corpse, why would Paul record that God's *"grace"* makes *"salvation"* available *"to all men"*? Why would God offer the non-elect of Calvinism what they are incapable of receiving? He would be irrational in doing so! Thus, some Reformed theologians view the *"all men"* of Titus 2:11 as pointing solely to the "elect." Such a conclusion is contextually impossible.

Titus 2:11-12 is also misused by the Universalists in an attempt to prove that all mankind will be saved. When taken through the full counsel of the Scriptures, proper context indicates that God offers *"salvation to all men,"* many of whom reject it to their own demise. 2Thessalonians 1:6-10 refutes the error that all mankind will be saved:

> *For after all it is only just for God to repay with affliction those*
> *who afflict you, and to give relief to you who are afflicted and to us*
> *as well when the Lord Jesus shall be revealed from heaven with*
> *His mighty angels in flaming fire, dealing out retribution to those*
> *who do not know God and to those who do not obey the gospel of*
> *our Lord Jesus. And these will pay the penalty of eternal*
> *destruction, away from the presence of the Lord and from the glory*

of His power, when He comes to be glorified in His saints on that
day, and to be marveled at among all who have believed — for our
testimony to you was believed. (2Thessalonians 1:6-10)

A wealth of additional passages could have been cited, but we must continue with our present topic of interest by considering Stephen's words of Acts 7:51:

"You men who are stiff-necked and uncircumcised in heart and
ears are always resisting the Holy Spirit; you are doing just as
your fathers did. (Acts 7:51)

Observe that Stephen's accusers resisted the Holy Spirit and its work of conviction. Therefore, their *"resisting"* proves that the Holy Spirit convicts the depraved. It also proves (coupled with what we will study shortly) that Stephen's accusers' choice, not God's choice, determined where they would spend eternity. Again, if God is all-knowing (omniscient), sovereign, and wise, He would be totally unwise (foolish—relinquishing His sovereignty) should He convict a person of sin whom He knew could not possibly believe. Hence, depravity and "total inability" are absolutely not synonymous. Isn't the full counsel of God's Word fascinating!

Because we were born spiritually *"dead"* (born with a nature that enjoyed sin— separated from God), we committed many *"trespasses and sins"* (Ephesians 2:1). We were not spiritually dead (separated from God) because we had committed acts of disobedience, but the habitual disobedience confirmed that we were already spiritually dead. Individuals who use Ephesians 2:1 in an attempt to prove that man is born void of a sin nature (yet receives it when old enough to sin and recognize sin) are in error, for Romans 5:12-19 (and numerous additional passages) teaches that a person possesses the sin nature at birth. Consequently, between Adam and Moses, when no Mosaic Law existed, men died without breaking the Mosaic Law (Romans 5:12-14). They died due to their sin nature inherited from Adam—due to their genes having been in Adam's gene pool when he ate of the forbidden fruit. Of course, all persons who repented and believed during this period were made part of God's family. Thus, at physical death they entered *"Abraham's bosom"* (Luke 16:22) and were later taken to heaven—a topic addressed in more detail as this study progresses.

Paul, in Romans 5:12-21, confirms that the sin nature condemns man to hell—not his acts of sin. Let's take this input and apply it to the virgin birth. Had Jesus been Joseph's son and not the Father's Son, He could not have been Savior. Why? He would have been condemned to hell because of His sin nature (inherited from Adam) even had He lived without sin. If, however, man should be born void of a sin nature, but acquire it when he sins (an error taught in some theological circles),

Jesus (based on this improper thinking) could have been Joseph's son, arrived void of a sin nature, lived a sinless life, and still (according to this erroneous view) fulfilled His mission as Savior. The full counsel of God's Word will not allowed such an interpretation. Note: I am not advocating that all who view the sin nature as acquired subsequent to physical birth reject the virgin birth. I am emphasizing, however, that individuals who strive to discredit the virgin birth could use this argument while attempting to build their case.

The words *"trespasses"* and *"sins"* (Ephesians 2:1) are somewhat synonymous. Paul possibly used both these terms to communicate the scope of disobedience experienced by the spiritually dead. *"Trespass"* is from the Greek *parapipto* and means "to fall beside, to make defection from, to deviate from uprightness and truth." *"Sin"* is from the Greek *hamartia* and means "a missing of the mark, to be in error." God's standard is absolute holiness. A person misses the mark when he fails to walk by God's standard of holiness. For this reason Paul states, *"for all have sinned* [missed the mark] *and fall short of the glory of God"* (Romans 3:23). God possesses glory due to His flawless character. He has never dropped the ball—never committed sin. Man, in his own strength, cannot live righteously because he is dead (spiritually dead–separated from God) upon arrival. Therefore, *"all have sinned and fall short of"* His *"glory"* (Romans 3:23) because man is born void of God's kind of life (spiritual life). The depraved are not spiritually dead because they committed acts of disobedience, but their habitual disobedience confirms that they were born spiritually dead. Read Matthew 12:35 and Matthew 15:18-19 for more insight into this subject matter.

Ephesians 2:2—in which you formerly walked according to the course of this world, according to the prince of the power of the air, of the spirit that is now working in the sons of disobedience.

in which you formerly walked according to the course of this world, (2:2a)

Because *"in which you formerly walked"* (Ephesians 2:2a) points back to verse one, Paul is actually saying "in which you formerly walked in trespasses and sins." The *"course"* Paul's readers chose (prior to salvation) was *"according to...this world."* The phrase, *"the course of this world,"* does not relate simply to the physical creation as we know it, but to the world's system of values and perceptions. This world system is controlled by Satan, *"the god of this world"* (note the small *"g"*—2Corinthians 4:4), who *"disguises himself as an angel of light"* (2Corinthians 11:14) but possesses no truth (John 8:44). Because we arrived with a dead spirit (a sin nature which was separated from God), and lived in rebellion toward God, we perceived Satan's lies as absolute truth. Hence, sin inundated our landscape! We not only disregarded God, but bought into a system that totally rejects God, a system where self, humanism, rebellion, worldly wisdom, power, pride, arrogance, notoriety, wealth, and immorality reign supreme—none of which bring fulfillment. Why? Truth, righteousness, humility, brokenness, and love (which bring fulfillment) always trump pride, arrogance, humanism, and power. The cross proved it to be so!

according to the prince of the power of the air, (2:2b)

Because *"prince"* means "ruler," or "chief," Satan reigns as *"the prince of the power of the air."* He gained his authority through tempting Adam and Eve—the individuals originally given dominion over the earth (Genesis 1:27-28). Once Adam and Eve declared their independence from God (through eating of the forbidden fruit), Satan usurped their authority and became *"the god of this world"* (2Corinthians 4:4). He will function in this position until the Lord's return.

Satan is the *"prince,"* or ruler, or chief, *"of the power of the air."* The phrase, *"power of the air,"* probably refers to demons—fallen angels who have aligned themselves with Satan (Matthew 25:41; Revelation 12:9). One of their main responsibilities is to war against God's holy angels (read Daniel 10:1-21). *"Air"* is used seven times in the New Testament, and in most cases references the atmosphere surrounding the earth. Satan's present abode is in the *"air,"* or atmosphere, the realm where Satan's demons and God's holy angels do battle. These demons also war against believers, for Ephesians 6:12 states:

> *For our struggle is not against flesh and blood, but against the rulers, against the powers, against the world forces of this darkness, against the spiritual forces of wickedness in the heavenly places.* (Ephesians 6:12)

This battle is real and many times extremely intense. Anyone who walks with the Lord is aware of this conflict. We will study more about spiritual warfare in Ephesians 6.

While Satan's present abode is in the *"air,"* or atmosphere, he is still permitted entrance into two additional locales. He can enter heaven (Job 1:6; 2:1) to accuse the brethren (Revelation 12:10) or, as in the case of Zechariah 3:1-2, to accuse the nation of Israel. He can also come to earth in one of two forms: (1) *"a roaring lion"* (1Peter 5:8) to destroy (2) *"an angel of light"* (2Corinthians 11:14) to deceive. His goal is to deceive, both believers (2Corinthians 11:3) and unbelievers (Revelation 20:3), by implementing a counterfeit program resembling the real thing. This program of deception is carried out by counterfeit teachers

(2Corinthians 11:13-15) who teach a counterfeit Jesus (2Corinthians 11:3-4) and perform counterfeit signs and wonders (Matthew 7:22-23).

Halfway through the Tribulation, Satan and his angels will be cast to the earth and confined there (Revelation 12:7-9). Satan's counterfeit program will, at that time, be displayed vividly through the counterfeit Father, Son, and Holy Spirit. Let's examine this counterfeit trinity for a moment.

The *"dragon,"* Satan, will give his *"authority"* to *"the beast,"* the Antichrist (Revelation 13:1-2), as the Father gave His authority to the Son (John 17:1-2). Once this transition of power occurs, many people will *"worship"* Satan (Revelation 13:2, 4). The Antichrist will be Satan's offspring as Jesus is the Father's offspring. Thus, Satan is the counterfeit Father.

The Antichrist will die and be brought back to life, causing a large portion of mankind to follow him (Revelation 13:3). John also states that the dragon (Satan) gives *"his authority to the beast"* (Revelation 13:4). Hence, the counterfeit trinity comes to full fruition when Satan (the counterfeit Father) gives his authority to the resurrected beast (the Antichrist—the counterfeit Christ). When this transfer occurs, those who follow the beast will worship the beast, just as the followers of Christ worship Christ (Revelation 13:4).

The third member of the counterfeit trinity is described in Revelation 13:11-13 as *"another beast,"* but as *"the false prophet"* in Revelation 16:13. The false prophet will come *"up out of the earth"* (Revelation 13:11) and have *"two horns like a lamb"* (he will have the appearance of a true religious system), and will speak *"as a dragon"* (speak with the authority of the dragon—the counterfeit Father). He will encourage all men to worship the Antichrist (Revelation 13:12), as the Holy Spirit encourages believers to worship Christ (John 16:14). He will also perform great signs, even call fire down from heaven (Revelation 13:13), in an attempt to counterfeit the miracles of the Holy Spirit.

"The prince of the power of the air" (Ephesians 2:2) has one goal in mind—to deceive and destroy. Only truth empowered by the Holy Spirit can thwart such deception and destruction. Satan's goal, therefore, is to busy us so we have little or no time for God's Word.

of the spirit that is now working in the sons of disobedience. (2:2c)

"The prince of the power of the air" (Ephesians 2:2b) is Satan, who is also the prince *"of the spirit that is now working in the sons of disobedience"* (Ephesians 2:2c). Thus, *"the spirit"* (Ephesians 2:2c) is not referencing Satan himself but

Satan's disposition, his perspective of life—what makes him tick. For instance, 1John 4:3 states:

> *and every spirit that does not confess Jesus is not from God; and this is the spirit of the antichrist, of which you have heard that it is coming, and now it is already in the world.* (1John 4:3)

Ephesians 2:2c shows that Satan's *"spirit"* (his way of thinking) hampers unregenerate man, which explains why unbelievers so enjoy sin and walk as *"sons of disobedience."* Their spiritual father, Satan, who is void of *"truth"* (John 8:38-44), does everything possible to prevent them from exercising personal repentance and faith while depraved. Even believers are to *"test the spirits to see whether they are from God"* (1John 4:1).

Ephesians 2:3—Among them we too all formerly lived in the lusts of our flesh, indulging the desires of the flesh and of the mind, and were by nature children of wrath, even as the rest.

Among them we too all formerly lived in the lusts of our flesh, (2:3a)

"Among them" (Ephesians 2:3a) refers to *"the sons of disobedience"* of Ephesians 2:2c. Paul's main point is not that the redeemed once lived among the sons of disobedience, but that they were once sons of disobedience. In fact, all saints (before they accept Christ) live *"in the lusts of"* their *"flesh."*

"Lusts" refers to *"evil desires or cravings."* *"Flesh,"* as it applies to this verse, can be perceived as the sinful habit patterns formed in the brain of an unbeliever (the brain being a piece of flesh) as he walks *"according to the course of this world"* (Ephesians 2:2a). Consequently, these sinful habit patterns are etched in the brains of the unredeemed. (Our *Romans 1-8* course addresses this topic in great depth.)

Conclusion: Prior to exercising personal repentance and faith while depraved and receiving God's gift of salvation, the saints at Ephesus responded naturally to the sinful habit patterns created (generated) by sin's influence. These habit patterns were lodged in their brains, a piece of flesh. These sinful patterns were based on evil desires and cravings, the very definition of lust. Therefore, Paul uses the phrase, *"the lusts of our flesh"* (Ephesians 2:3a), when describing their lost condition. Some of these sinful patterns were removed the moment they were saved/justified, while others remained until months or years later. Some even continued until physical death. This same truth applies to believers today. Again, our *Romans 1-8* course deals extensively with this subject matter.

indulging the desires of the flesh and of the mind, (2:3b)

"Indulging" can also be interpreted "fulfilling," "performing," or "accomplishing." I think *"indulging"* translates best, for the sin nature in unregenerate man results in more than a passive involvement with sin. He desires to "indulge" in sin because of the sin nature's addiction to sin. Fear of getting caught is the only factor that keeps him from sinning without restraint. That sin hurts God's heart is a nonissue.

Note: Should you possess a copy of the *Romans 1-8* course distributed by this ministry, the circle diagrams located in the Reference Section of that material will assist your understanding of the following input.

As the sin nature in unregenerate man builds sinful habit patterns in the brain (the brain being a piece of flesh), the unbeliever is programmed to pursue particular areas of sin. Thus, as unbelievers we were programmed for sinful behaviors and passions. We may have been programmed in one or several of the following areas: to pursue power, indulge in illicit sex or pornography, consume ourselves with amassing wealth, view ourselves as inferior, view ourselves as superior, be overly concerned with our appearance, be too little concerned with our appearance, feel insecure in our relationships, be unfaithful in our relationships, feel depressed when facing specific situations, deny reality, worry about everything (even those things about which we can do nothing), etc. We had no alternative but to commit habitual sin in some of these areas due to the sin nature's addiction to disobedience. Paul's use of *"indulging the desires of the flesh"* (Ephesians 2:3b) is more than appropriate, for we were programmed for failure through the sinful habit patterns etched in our brains (made of flesh).

The previously described condition would have been bad enough, but Paul also mentions the *"mind"* (Ephesians 2:3b). *"Mind"* in the Greek means "mode of thinking and feeling, disposition of mind and heart, the affections." Consequently, the sin nature, which includes the mind of an unbeliever, gave us a natural resolve to sin in our lost state (although we were capable of exercising personal repentance and faith while depraved). Hence, Paul uses the phrase, *"the desires of the flesh and of the mind"* (Ephesians 2:3b). No wonder we indulged ourselves in sin! Note: The sin nature includes the soul and spirit of unregenerate man, the soul being the mind, will, and emotions. Remember, our *Romans 1-8* course addresses this subject matter in great detail.

and were by nature children of wrath, even as the rest. (2:3c)

The sin nature inherited from Adam condemns unregenerate man to hell, not the sins he commits during his stay on earth. Stated differently, the lost are condemned by God, not because of their misdeeds, but because of who they are. Man in his lost condition is the sin nature (or Adamic nature, old man, old self, dead spirit—all synonymous terms), which was inherited from Adam due to his genes having been in Adam's gene pool when Adam sinned. Thus, Paul states, *"and were by nature children of wrath, even as the rest"* (Ephesians 2:3b). (A baby is not condemned by God should he experience physical death, for David realized that he would again see his son who died as an infant—2Samuel 12:23.)

Ephesians 2:4—But God, being rich in mercy, because of His great love with which He loved us,

Many things in life are certain—things you can hang your hat on. The first is that God loves His children. Why shouldn't He if His very nature is *"love"* (1John 4:8 and 16)? Not only does He display unconditional love toward his children, but the degree to which He loves them has no bounds. As a result, Paul references God's unconditional, limitless *"love"* in Ephesians 2:4. Therefore, if you have accepted Christ, you are not on a performance-based acceptance with God. You are on a Jesus-based acceptance!

Verse 4 communicates that God is *"rich in mercy"* toward us because of the unconditionality and completeness of His *"love"* directed our way. Oh, by the way, God also loves those who reject His free offer of salvation (John 3:16), never rejoicing over *"the death of the wicked"* (Ezekiel 33:11).

Ephesians 2:5—even when we were dead in our transgressions, made us alive together with Christ (by grace you have been saved),

even when we were dead in our transgressions, (2:5a)

Because of God's great *"love"* and *"mercy"* (Ephesians 2:4), He did something extremely special for us. He sent His Son to die so any depraved individual might exercise personal repentance and faith and receive God's gift of eternal life. As unbelievers *"we were dead"* (Ephesians 2:5a) because we, as Adam's descendants, lacked spirit life (*"God is spirit"*—John 4:24). Our bodies functioned, but we *"were dead"* spiritually (Ephesians 2:5a)—separated from *"God"* Who *"is spirit"* (John 4:24). (Remember that death in Scripture does not always mean extinction—it can also mean "separation.") Because of our sin nature (dead spirit), we committed numerous *"transgressions"* (Ephesians 2:5a). In fact, *"transgressions"* came as naturally and as frequently as our breathing. Remember: We were not spiritually dead because we had committed acts of disobedience, but the habitual disobedience confirmed that we were born spiritually dead. Yet, this spiritual death did not prevent us from turning to Christ in our depravity and, thus, prior to spiritual regeneration (2Corinthians 3:16):

> *but whenever a man turns to the Lord, the veil is taken away.*
> (2Corinthians 3:16)

Note that "man turns to the Lord" prior to the "veil" being *"taken away,"* disproving Reformed Theology (make use of the diagrams in the Reference Section if necessary, especially Diagram 11).

made us alive together with Christ (by grace you have been saved), (2:5b)

We can be certain that we have been *"made...alive...with Christ,"* for Paul is addressing New Testament believers here. When we (while depraved) repented of our sin and accepted Christ as Savior, God placed us in (baptized us into) Christ through the avenue of the Holy Spirit (1Corinthians 12:13; 2Corinthians 5:17). We received His kind of life—eternal life, life with no beginning or ending. This means that from God's vantage point, which is reality, we have always been in Christ. Therefore, when Christ was crucified, our sin nature (Adamic nature, old man, old self, dead spirit—all synonymous terms) *"was crucified with Him"* (Romans 6:6; Galatians 2:20). We were also *"buried with Him"* (Romans 6:4; Colossians 2:12) and *"raised"* to new life when He came out of the grave (Romans 6:4; Colossians 2:12-13). Hence, Paul says, *"made us alive together with Christ"* (Ephesians 2:5b). Note: *"Baptism,"* in Romans 6:4 and Colossians 2:12, does not point to water baptism, but to our Spirit baptism which placed us in Christ (1Corinthians 12:13). *"Baptism"* can also make reference to our identification with the death, burial, and resurrection of Christ, much the same as Israel was identified with Moses, their leader, through baptism (through identification) according to 1Corinthians 10:1-2.

All of these magnificent "events" occurred because of God's *"grace"* (Ephesians 2:5b). We have not only been saved by grace (Ephesians 2:5b) but are in the process of being kept by grace (1Corinthians 15:10; 2Corinthians 12:9; Hebrews 4:16; 1Peter 5:10; 1Peter 5:12). Paul, in dealing with the fact that we have been saved by grace, uses the perfect tense in the Greek—pointing to a salvation in past time that will continue throughout eternity (Ephesians 2:5b). Thus, Paul taught that the New Testament believer is *"sealed"* in Christ (Ephesians 1:13).

Ephesians 2:6—and raised us up with Him, and seated us with Him in the heavenly places, in Christ Jesus,

God actually *"raised us up with"* Jesus and *"seated us...in the heavenly places, in Christ...."* Because we are in Jesus (*"sealed"* in Jesus—Ephesians 1:13) and He is at the *"right hand"* of the Father (Ephesians 1:20), we are also at the Father's right hand. Consequently, unlimited power is available to take authority (in Christ's strength, of course) over anything Satan sends our way. We do battle in God's armor (Ephesians 6:11-12), which is actually Christ's armor (Isaiah 59:16-20), in the heavenly places. For this reason we must learn to love war!

Ephesians 2:7—in order that in the ages to come He might show the surpassing riches of His grace in kindness toward us in Christ Jesus.

God raised us up with Christ and seated us in the heavenlies (Ephesians 2:6) to show (*"in the ages to come"*) *"the surpassing riches of His grace in kindness toward us in Christ Jesus"* (Ephesians 2:7). *"Ages to come"* (Ephesians 2:7) actually means "the ages that are coming one upon another." God saved us so we might, throughout eternity future, be objects of His *"kindness"* through which He shows *"the surpassing riches of His grace"* (Ephesians 2:7). This *"grace"* is given to us *"in Christ Jesus."* Who is watching as this *"grace"* is dispensed? The angelic hosts in heaven are watching (Ephesians 3:10), who while observing bow and worship the Creator.   *"Thanks be to God for His indescribable gift"* (2Corinthians 9:15)!

Ephesians 2:8—For by grace you have been saved through faith; and that not of yourselves, it is the gift of God;

Paul emphasizes that salvation is most definitely by God's *"grace"* (also read Romans 3:24 and Titus 3:7)—reiterating what he recorded earlier in Ephesians 2:5 (*"by grace you have been saved"*). He also affirms that God's salvation is *"through faith"* (also confirmed by passages such as Habakkuk 2:4, Romans 1:17, Galatians 3:11, Philippians 3:9, Hebrews 10:38, Hebrews 11:1-2, and Hebrews 11:6).

"That," in the phrase, *"and that not of yourselves"* (Ephesian 2:8), is the source of much debate. Both sides of the argument will be addressed to present the facts regarding what is at stake. A proper view of Who God is supersedes all matters of life, so to approach this subject passively or haphazardly is grossly inadequate. For this reason, we will dig deeply in our pursuit of the truth regarding this critical

theological issue.

Reformed Theology, due to viewing the depraved as incapable of believing, normally perceives *"that"* (Ephesians 2:8) as referring to *"faith"* (Ephesians 2:8). Why? They picture God as spiritually regenerating the depraved and giving them repentance and faith before they can repent, believe, and be saved. (Observe Diagram 11 in the Reference Section.)

Other theologians view this passage differently due to recognizing that the terms *"faith"* and *"grace"* are both feminine in gender, and *"that"* is neuter. Therefore, they view *"that"* as referring to *"saved"* rather than to *"faith."* The following quote from Dave Hunt's, *What Love Is This?,* pages 452-453, expresses well the disparity that exists between "free-will" and the Reformed view (extreme and hyper-Calvinism):

> ... That faith is a gift is a major foundational principal of Calvinism. The favorite passage offered as proof is Ephesians 2:8–10. Mathison says, "Saving faith is a gift of God, a result of the regenerating work of the Holy Spirit." Storms claims, "Numerous texts assert that such [saving] faith is God's own gracious gift (see especially Ephesians 2:8–9...)." Clark declares:
>
>> A dead man cannot...exercise faith in Jesus Christ. Faith is an activity of spiritual life, and without the life there can be no activity. Furthermore, faith...does not come by any independent decision. The Scripture is explicit, plain, and unmistakable: "For by grace are ye saved through faith, and that not of yourselves, it is the gift of God" (Ephesians 2:8). Look at the words again, "It is the gift of God." If God does not give a man faith, no amount of will power and decision can manufacture it for him.
>
> On the contrary, the subject of the preceding seven verses is salvation, not faith. Verse 8 then declares concerning salvation, "by grace are ye saved...it [obviously salvation] is the gift of God." It is not saving faith, but being saved that is God's gift. We are repeatedly told that eternal life is "the gift of God" (Romans 6:23; see also John 4:10; Romans 5:18; Hebrews 6:4; etc.). No less definitive, as Calvin admitted and then tried to deny, is the statement that "faith comes by hearing and hearing by the Word of God." There is no biblical basis for suggesting that God gives saving faith to a select group and withholds it from others.

Furthermore, the construction of the Greek in Ephesians 2:8–10 makes it impossible for faith to be the gift. Such is the verdict of many Greek authorities, including Alford, F. F. Bruce, A. T. Robertson, W. E. Vine, Scofield, and others. Vance notes that "A witness to the truth of Scripture against the Calvinist 'faith-gift' interpretation can be found in the Greek grammarians." He lists W. Robertson Nicoll, Kenneth S. Wuest, Marvin R. Vincent, and others.

Among the reasons the experts cite is the fact that the word faith is a feminine noun, while the demonstrative pronoun that ("and that not of yourselves, it is the gift") is neuter and thus could not refer to faith. Nor will the grammar, as W. G. MacDonald says, "permit 'faith' to be the antecedent of 'it.'" Of course, "it is" is not in the Greek but was added for clarity by the KJV translators and thus is italicized. Nor does it require a knowledge of Greek, but simply paying attention to the entire context of Ephesians 2:8–10, to realize that salvation, not faith, is "the gift of God"—as all of Scripture testifies.

A number of other Greek authorities could be cited to that effect. Though a Calvinist, F. F. Bruce explains, "The fact that the demonstrative pronoun 'that' is neuter in Greek (touto), whereas 'faith' is a feminine noun (pistis), combines with other considerations to suggest that it is the whole concept of salvation by grace through faith that is described as the gift of God. This, incidentally, was Calvin's interpretation." Calvin himself acknowledged, "But they commonly misinterpret this text, and restrict the word 'gift' to faith alone. But Paul...does not mean that faith is the gift of God, but that salvation is given to us by God...." Thus White and other zealous Calvinists who today insist that faith is the gift are contradicting not only the Greek construction but John Calvin himself.[8]

Let's examine more closely Calvin's quote (mentioned above by Hunt) regarding Ephesians 2:8— taken from Calvin's *Commentary on the Epistle to the Ephesians,* in *The Comprehensive John Calvin Collection* (Ages Digital Library, 1998).

Many persons restrict the word gift to faith alone. But Paul is only repeating in other words the former sentiment. His meaning is, not that faith is the gift of God, but that salvation is given to us by God, or, that we obtain it by the gift of God.[9]

Note that Calvin's words contradict the Reformed position.

Sir Robert Anderson, in *The Gospel and its Ministry*, thirteenth edition revised, page 54 footnote, views *"that"* (Ephesians 2:8) as pointing to *"salvation"*:

> "The gift of God" here is salvation by grace through faith. Not the faith itself.... The matter is sometimes represented as though God gave faith to the sinner first, and then, on the sinner's bringing Him the faith, went on and gave him salvation! Just as though a baker, refusing to supply empty-handed applicants, should first dispense to each the price of a loaf, and then, in return for the money from his own till, serve out the bread! To answer fully such a vagary as this would be to rewrite the following chapter. Suffice it, therefore, to point out that to read the text as though faith were the gift, is to destroy not only the meaning of verse 9, but the force of the whole passage.[10]

How does this input tie in to Ephesians 2:9?

> *not as a result of works, that no one should boast.* (Ephesians 2:9)

Paul is confirming that *"salvation"* (Ephesians 2:8) is *"not...of works"* (Ephesians 2:9), as he communicates elsewhere. Read Romans 3:27-28, for example, realizing that *"justified"* points to salvation:

> *Where then is boasting? It is excluded. By what kind of law? Of works? No, but by a law of faith. For we maintain that a man is justified by faith apart from works of the Law.* (Romans 3:27-28)

Paul's message in Romans 3:27-28 is that salvation is not *"Of works"*—that God bestows salvation once the depraved exercise *"faith"* (along with repentance, of course). Paul also confirms that *"boasting"* is *"excluded"* among those who exercise personal *"faith"* in Christ while depraved. Thus, faith is not a work, for Paul contrasts *"faith"* with *"works"* on many occasions in the Scriptures. Consequently, choosing to exercise personal *"faith"* (in the midst of one's depravity) can never be viewed as a meritorious deed. Paul expresses this same truth in Romans 4:5, contrasting *"work"* with believing:

> *But to the one who does not work, but believes in Him who justifies the ungodly, his faith is reckoned as righteousness,* (Romans 4:5)

Paul again contrasts *"faith"* with *"works"* in Romans 9:30-33:

What shall we say then? That Gentiles, who did not pursue
righteousness, attained righteousness, even the righteousness
which is by faith; 31 but Israel, pursuing a law of righteousness,
did not arrive at that law. 32 Why? Because they did not pursue it
by faith, but as though it were by works. They stumbled over the
stumbling stone, 33 just as it is written, "Behold, I lay in Zion a
stone of stumbling and a rock of offense, and he who believes in
Him will not be disappointed." (Romans 9:30-33)

Once more we observe that salvation (*"righteousness"*) is not of *"works"* but is the
gift granted to those who exercise personal *"faith"* while depraved. The same
principle is communicated in Paul's words to the church at Galatia:

nevertheless knowing that a man is not justified by the works of the
Law but through faith in Christ Jesus, even we have believed in
Christ Jesus, that we may be justified by faith in Christ, and not by
the works of the Law; since by the works of the Law shall no flesh
be justified. (Galatians 2:16)

This is the only thing I want to find out from you: did you receive
the Spirit by the works of the Law, or by hearing with faith?
(Galatians 3:2)

The following passages also confirm that salvation (not the faith exercised prior to
salvation) is God's *"gift"* to those who become part of His family:

Jesus answered and said to her, "If you knew the gift of God, and
who it is who says to you, 'Give Me a drink,' you would have asked
Him, and He would have given you living water." (John 4:10-11)

But the free gift is not like the transgression. For if by the
transgression of the one the many died, much more did the grace of
God and the gift by the grace of the one Man, Jesus Christ, abound
to the many. 16 And the gift is not like that which came through the
one who sinned; for on the one hand the judgment arose from one
transgression resulting in condemnation, but on the other hand the
free gift arose from many transgressions resulting in justification.
17 For if by the transgression of the one, death reigned through the
one, much more those who receive the abundance of grace and of
the gift of righteousness will reign in life through the One, Jesus
Christ. (Romans 5:15-17)

*For the wages of sin is death, but the <u>free gift of God is eternal life</u>
in Christ Jesus our Lord.* (Romans 6:23)

*And the witness is this, that God has <u>given us eternal life</u>, and this
life is in His Son.* (1John 5:11)

Salvation is a free gift, given to the depraved who choose (by means of their free will) to accept Jesus as Savior. The following verses are highly problematic for those who reject the free will of man:

*"Come to Me, all who are weary and heavy-laden, and I will give
you rest.* (Matthew 11:28)

*Jesus answered and said to her, "If you knew the gift of God, and
who it is who says to you, 'Give Me a drink,' you would have asked
Him, and He would have given you living water."* (John 4:10)

*Now on the last day, the great day of the feast, Jesus stood and
cried out, saying, "If any man is thirsty, let him come to Me and
drink.* (John 7:37)

*And the Spirit and the bride say, "Come." And let the one who
hears say, "Come." And let the one who is thirsty come; let the one
who wishes take the water of life without cost.* (Revelation 22:17)

We well understand that Reformed theologians (due to their definition of depravity) view spiritual regeneration as preceding faith. However, spiritual regeneration is equivalent to salvation (read John 3:3-6). This fact refutes Reformed Theology, because no one can be saved prior to exercising personal faith. Such a scenario would cause the believer to be saved twice, forcing Christ to die a second time (an impossibility according to Hebrews 6:4-6, 9:28, and 10:10). Keep this truth in mind as we proceed.

To receive the gift of salvation (spiritual regeneration), the depraved must first believe (exercise personal faith). Therefore, faith precedes salvation (spiritual regeneration) rather than follows it, as confirmed by the following passages. (Many additional verses could have been cited.)

"He who has believed...shall be saved;... (Mark 16:16)

*"And those beside the road are those who have heard; then the
devil comes and takes away the word from their heart, so that they*

may not believe and be saved. (Luke 8:12)

"Of Him all the prophets bear witness that through His name everyone who believes in Him receives forgiveness of sins." (Acts 10:43)

And they said, "Believe in the Lord Jesus, and you shall be saved, you and your household." (Acts 16:31)

For I am not ashamed of the gospel, for it is the power of God for salvation to everyone who believes, to the Jew first and also to the Greek. (Romans 1:16)

But now apart from the Law the righteousness of God has been manifested, being witnessed by the Law and the Prophets, even the righteousness of God through faith in Jesus Christ for all those who believe;... (Romans 3:21-22)

for "Whoever will call upon the name of the Lord will be saved." (Romans 10:13)

For you are all sons of God through faith in Christ Jesus. (Galatians 3:26)

...as an example for those who would believe in Him for eternal life. (1Timothy 1:16)

And without faith it is impossible to please Him, for he who comes to God must believe that He is, and that He is a rewarder of those who seek Him. (Hebrews 11:6)

The following passages confirm that the faith exercised prior to salvation is the seeker's faith—not God's gift to the seeker. Note the words, *"your faith,"* in the verses listed below:

... "Be it done to you according to your faith." (Matthew 9:29)

And He said to the woman, "Your faith has saved you; go in peace." (Luke 7:50)

"...your faith has made you well." (Luke 17:19)

...your faith is being proclaimed throughout the whole world.
(Romans 1:8)

that your faith should not rest on the wisdom of men, but on the
power of God. (1Corinthians 2:5)

and if Christ has not been raised, then our preaching is vain, your
faith also is vain. (1Corinthians 15:14)

since we heard of your faith in Christ Jesus... (Colossians 1:4)

...but also in every place your faith toward God has gone forth...
(1Thessalonians 1:8)

Reformed theologians disagree with these findings due to viewing the faith exercised in the previous verses as originating with God—yet, becoming the possession of the elect in conjunction with their being spiritually regenerated. Reformed Theology cannot allow a person to exercise faith prior to spiritual regeneration. As a result, Reformed Theology (extreme and hyper-Calvinism) must view those who believe in free will (who believe that the depraved <u>can</u> exercise faith) as teaching a works-based salvation.

To choose Christ through personal faith (while depraved) does not mean that we approach God based on anything good we have done. All that is required is a humble heart that recognizes its need for salvation. Some would ask, "Is not humility a virtue?" God doesn't think so, or He would have omitted James 4:6:

... "God is opposed to the proud, but gives grace to the humble."
(James 4:6)

Humility and pride are opposites—never equal. You can't be prideful and humble at the same time! Hence, to see one's need for a Savior, through a broken and humble heart, would never cause one to approach God on the basis of personal merit or virtue. Yes, man is to humble himself before God (Psalm 138:6; Proverbs 3:34; Matthew 23:12; 1Peter 5:5), but never with the mindset that his humility grants him the right to boast. If so, he has never known what it means to be humble.

Because the depraved are capable of exercising personal faith (a fact proven in the Scriptures), Total Depravity (the "T" of the TULIP), as defined by Reformed Theology, cannot stand. However, let's assume for a moment that the Reformed view is correct—that man in his depravity cannot humble himself and exercise faith. Irresistible Grace (the "I" of the TULIP) would then be necessary to bring the elect to Christ. But forced grace (grace is "Irresistible" in Reformed Theology) is no longer grace, for free will belonging to the depraved (who can exercise personal repentance and faith should they see their need for salvation) is required for grace to remain grace.

Let's review for a moment why Paul's words in Ephesians 2:9 forever settle how Ephesians 2:8 is to be perceived. Paul is confirming that *"salvation"* (Ephesians 2:8) is *"not...of works"* (Ephesians 2:9), as he teaches elsewhere. Consequently, *"that not of yourselves"* (Ephesians 2:8) must point to *"saved"* (Ephesians 2:8) rather than *"faith"* (Ephesians 2:8). (*God's Heart as it Relates to Depravity*, a work generated and distributed by this ministry, communicates a great deal more regarding this subject matter.)

Ephesians 2:9—not as a result of works, that no one should boast.

Salvation is not a result of man's effort (Ephesians 2:9; Romans 3:20; 4:4-5; 5:20; Galatians 2:16; Titus 3:5); it is by God's *"grace"* (Ephesians 2:8). Were man capable of keeping the whole Law, his effort would count for something. In fact, he could *"boast"* before God (Ephesians 2:9). But Romans 3:23 confirms that *"all have sinned,"* and James 2:10 verifies that one broken commandment is equivalent to breaking them all. Only Jesus lived the Law perfectly (Matthew 5:17; 2Corinthians 5:21; 1Peter 2:21-22). Thus, righteousness comes through Him alone, the One who lived righteously (2Corinthians 5:21), the Righteous Son who now lives in every church saint (Galatians 2:20; Colossians 1:27).

Should I choose to accept a free gift, no work would be performed. In the same way, to make a choice (while depraved) to accept Christ as Savior must not be equated with performing a meritorious deed.

Ephesians 2:10—For we are His workmanship, created in Christ Jesus for good works, which God prepared beforehand, that we should walk in them.

For we are His workmanship, (2:10a)

We lacked the ability to work our way into a righteous standing with God, so we became God's *"workmanship."* In other words, God's work saves us, not our own (Ephesians 2:8-9). *"Workmanship"* can also be interpreted "a work," "creation"— even "masterpiece." This masterpiece consists of all individuals who accept Christ between Acts 2 and the Rapture of the church. As a result, the church, the body of

Christ, is God's masterpiece. We can be certain of this truth due to the next phrase in Ephesians 2:10, *"created in Christ Jesus."* Only church saints are placed *"in Christ"* (*"created in Christ Jesus"*—2:10) and <u>made</u> righteous (2Corinthians 5:21) the moment they repent and believe while depraved (1Corinthians 1:30; 2Corinthians 5:17). Old Testament believers were only <u>declared</u> righteous (*"reckoned"* as righteous—Genesis 15:6) when they repented and believed. They were not made righteous until Jesus' death. Neither were their sins forgiven until the cross (Hebrews 10:12)—their sins were only covered until Jesus died (Romans 3:25; Hebrews 9:15; 10:4, 11). Hence, the Old Testament believers are *"the spirits of righteous men made perfect"* of Hebrews 12:23.

What an awesome thought! God, at this very moment, is preparing His masterpiece (the church) to be revealed at Christ's Second Coming. Since Acts 2, each time someone accepts Christ and is placed into Christ (2Corinthians 5:17), God the Father makes an addition to His masterpiece by strategically placing that individual in the most beneficial location within Christ's body. Some New Testament believers become part of the hand, and others part of the foot, etc. (1Corinthians 12:12-27). As the church grows numerically, the Father, as the great Sculptor, fashions His work for its day of unveiling. God's masterpiece will be unveiled as Christ's body, made up of mature church saints *"conformed to the image of"* God's *"Son"* (Romans 8:29), having immortal bodies that radiate the Father's glory. Jesus' Second Coming will be incredible!

The Father is experiencing great joy while fashioning this work. He has the awesome privilege of taking new family members, who are *"holy"* (Ephesians 1:4), righteous (2Corinthians 5:21), and even *"glorified"* (Romans 8:30) in their souls and spirits, and bringing them to a place of maturity (to the place where their behavior begins to line up with who He made them into at the point of justification/salvation). The Father is assisted in this training exercise by the Son (Romans 5:10) and the Holy Spirit (Romans 8:4, 14) until New Testament believers experience physical death and the Father takes them home (2Corinthians 5:1-8). Only then will their behavior be perfected (nothing will tempt us in heaven, so sin will cease). Later, at the Rapture, all who make up the body of Christ will receive their glorified bodies (1Thessalonians 4:13-18) and be presented to Christ *"as a pure virgin"* (2Corinthians 11:2). The marriage between Christ and His bride, the church, is then consummated (Ephesians 5:27), a ceremony that takes place in heaven sometime before the Second Coming. But, at some point after the wedding, the church, who is also the Father's masterpiece, is unveiled as Christ returns to earth. She will be unveiled as Christ's body!

Can you even begin to envision the glory the Father will receive through Jesus' return? Jesus brought the Father much glory at His First Coming but not nearly the glory the Father will receive at His Second.

God is presently at work seeing that His "masterpiece" is truly that—a "masterpiece." And why does He display such intense interest in this work? The Son expresses Himself to the universe through this "masterpiece." This same "masterpiece" also serves as a *"temple"* for the Holy Spirit (Ephesians 2:19-22; 1Peter 2:4-5) and is part of the Father's family (John 1:12). Therefore, God's masterpiece is three in one. Interestingly, God is Himself three in One—Father, Son, and Spirit.

The Father is completing this masterpiece for the benefit of others—the Son, the Spirit, and the church. But we who make up Christ's body, which is also the Spirit's temple, will be the very vehicle through which the Son and Spirit glorify the Father at the Second Coming! What an awesome privilege! Are you beginning to see the advantage of viewing the cross based on what God the Father, God the Son, God the Spirit, and others receive through that selfless act—rather than viewing it based on what you alone receive? Oh, the shallowness of a self-centered life!

created in Christ Jesus for good works, which God prepared beforehand, that we should walk in them. (2:10b)

In verses 8-9 we found that salvation is by grace through faith and that no amount of good works makes man right before God. Here, in verse 10, Paul teaches that the natural byproduct of salvation, and becoming God's *"workmanship"* (Ephesians 2:10a), is a desire to perform *"good works"* (Ephesians 2:10b). Considering what Paul states in 2Corinthians 9:8, 2Timothy 3:17, and Titus 2:14, why shouldn't the apostle make this statement in Ephesians 2:10? Thus, the new person God made (after we repented and believed while depraved) desires to carry out (by yielding to Christ's indwelling presence) the works God previously prepared.

We became a *"new"* creation when we were placed *"in Christ"* (2Corinthians 5:17; Galatians 6:15), for we (once we repented and believed) were *"created in Christ Jesus"* (Ephesians 2:10b). We were also *"created in Christ Jesus for good works."* Don't overlook the fact that God prepares and accomplishes these works—*"which God prepared beforehand, that we should walk in them"* (Ephesians 2:10b). This truth ties in well with Philippians 2:13, where Paul states:

> *for it is God who is at work in you, both to will and to work for His good pleasure.* (Philippians 2:13)

Remember: The believer lives abundantly through living by the life of Another—by Christ's life (Romans 5:10; Colossians 3:4). Because Christian service always results in deeds, these deeds must be of a creative nature rather than imitative. In other words, the New Testament believer's good deeds must be accomplished by Christ—not the New Testament believer trying to imitate Christ's actions and character in his own strength. Therefore, as church saints prepare for ministry, they must view themselves as God's instrument through which He works creatively.

Paul encouraged the church at Corinth to imitate him, since he was an imitator of Christ (1Corinthians 11:1):

> *Be imitators of me, just as I also am of Christ.* (1Corinthians 11:1)

But in imitating Christ, Paul did nothing in his own strength; for Christ did nothing in His, but the Father's (John 14:10). Paul actually viewed Christ as his very *"life"* (Philippians 1:21; Colossians 3:4; Romans 5:10)—the Source of everything accomplished through him. Keep this perspective in mind as we continue, for even in Ephesians 5:1 Paul states that believers are to *"be imitators of God."* We will discuss the context of this verse when we arrive at chapter five.

Ephesians 2:10 does not teach that believers are forced to do God's work and have no choice in the matter. Paul, writing to Timothy, said:

> *But you, be sober in all things, endure hardship, do the work of an evangelist, fulfill your ministry.* (2Timothy 4:5)

This passage proves that God's children have a choice. They can either make themselves available for service as willing vessels, or they can compromise and do their own thing. But, any lasting work (any work that results in change) is done by God—not by His people. We serve only as the vehicle through which the Father works creatively. Hence, no member of the body of Christ can boast of his good deeds.

Ephesians 2:11—Therefore remember, that formerly you, the Gentiles in the flesh, who are called "Uncircumcision" by the so-called "Circumcision," which is performed in the flesh by human hands —

Paul encouraged his readers to take the truths expressed thus far in this epistle, use them as a backdrop, and consider, at least for a short time, their state before they knew Christ—*"Therefore remember, that formerly you."* The specifics of what they were to remember regarding their past are not stated until verse 12, so keep this in mind.

The Gentile believers at Ephesus are referenced as *"Gentiles in the flesh,"* a phrase emphasizing their physical distinction. (*"Flesh"* must be interpreted in context due to its different meanings in Scripture. Verse 3 is an example. There we found that *"flesh"* refers to the sinful habit patterns stored in the brain—the brain being a piece of flesh.)

To comprehend the depths of Paul's words in Ephesians 2:11, we must realize that an unbelieving Jew perceived himself as right with God because: (1) he was a descendant of Abraham and, therefore, part of God's chosen people—the Jews (2) he was part of the nation that had received the Law (3) he had been circumcised. The average Jew perceived all or any of the above as having secured his salvation. Paul, in Romans 2:17—3:8, refutes this thinking by teaching that a Jew is lost until he repents of his sin and accepts Christ as Savior. The *"Gentiles in the flesh"* (Ephesians 2:11) were different from Jews in that they were not physical descendants of Abraham, nor were they part of the nation that had received the Law of Moses, neither were they circumcised in their flesh. To the ill-informed Jew, the Gentiles were nothing more than trash—a totally worthless people. Unsaved Jews even called the Gentiles *"Uncircumcision"*—a word of contempt in Paul's day.

Romans 4:11 communicates that physical *"circumcision"* was both a *"sign"* and a *"seal."* *"Circumcision"* was a *"sign"* in that every time a Jewish male saw someone circumcised, or was reminded of his own circumcision, he was to remember that God's righteousness is bestowed upon those who repent and believe while depraved. It was a *"seal"* in that circumcision cannot be undone. It proved that once God bestows righteousness to those desiring salvation, they cannot become unrighteous. Thus, physical circumcision was an outward sign of an inward transformation. *"Circumcision...of the heart"* is (and has always been) the issue (Romans 2:28-29; Galatians 5:6; 6:15). For this reason, Paul refers to the unbelieving Jews as *"the so-called 'Circumcision'"* (Ephesians 2:11). Their circumcision was *"performed in the flesh by human hands,"* an act incapable of giving them a right standing with God.

Ephesians 2:12—remember that you were at that time separate from Christ, excluded from the commonwealth of Israel, and strangers to the covenants of promise, having no hope and without God in the world.

remember that you were at that time separate from Christ, (2:12a)

Paul communicates in verse 12 what the believers at Ephesus were to remember concerning their "pre-Christ" days. During that time they were *"separate from Christ."* This statement goes much deeper than their having been lost and without Christ. Paul is referring to their lack of knowledge of the Messiah as Gentile unbelievers. At least the Jews looked forward to the coming of the Messiah, even though their sin and resulting blindness caused them to reject His offer of salvation. The Gentiles wandered aimlessly without purpose or hope. They worshiped a host of pagan deities in the midst of their depravity—none of which brought peace, joy, or eternal life. These Gentile believers had a wealth of reasons to be grateful for what the Father had done through Christ.

excluded from the commonwealth of Israel, (2:12b)

"Excluded from" can also be interpreted "alienated from" or "be a stranger to." The Gentiles were aliens and strangers to *"the commonwealth of Israel."* *"Commonwealth"* is taken from a Greek term which can also be interpreted "citizenship" (as in Acts 22:28). Since a commonwealth is "the people of a nation or state," the phrase, *"commonwealth of Israel,"* refers to God's special relationship with His chosen people, physical Israel—He being their Head, Ruler, and King.

To understand the significance of God's special relationship with Israel, we must go back as far as the Garden of Eden. Jehovah has always been the sovereign Ruler over the earth, but He delegated a stewardship to Adam and Eve—that of caring for His creation. A true theocracy was established, a theocratic kingdom where God ruled with man having dominion over the earth (Genesis 1:26). This arrangement flourished until Adam and Eve declared their independence through sin. They, in fact, exchanged the theocratic kingdom for a kingdom controlled by Satan himself (2Corinthians 4:4)—God's chief enemy.

God later began rebuilding His theocratic kingdom through Abraham, Isaac, and Jacob—Israel, the Jewish people. Jehovah desired to rule as head over Israel much the same as a king rules over a people. For the good of the theocracy, He appointed leaders who could accept or reject His ultimate authority (patriarchs, judges, kings, etc.). The Scriptures record Israel's rebellion against God's instruction and her eventual rejection of the Messiah (Who had been expected since Genesis 3:15). God will eventually bring His theocratic kingdom to full fruition through His Son (Genesis 49:10), for Satan will be bound (Revelation 20:2-3) when Christ rules as *"King of Kings and Lord of Lords"* (Revelation 19:11-16) during the Millennium (Revelation 20:4). Only then will the unconditional promises made to Abraham and his descendants (such as in Genesis 12:1-3 and Genesis 15:18), King David (in 2Samuel 7:10-16 and 1Chronicles 17:11-15), and the Jewish nation (in Deuteronomy 30:1-10 and Jeremiah 31:31-34) be fulfilled. Jesus will sit on the throne of David in Jerusalem, ruling as King over the whole earth, making certain that every unconditional promise made to the Jewish nation is fully realized and maintained.

God gave Israel His Law, His love, His covenants, in fact, everything she would need to live abundantly. He gave these blessings to no other nation (Deuteronomy 4:7-8, 32-34; Psalm 147:19-20; Romans 3:1-2). Thus, Gentiles are excluded (alienated) from this commonwealth so long as they reject Christ. However, when they exercise personal repentance and faith while depraved, they enter into some of the blessings associated with these Jewish covenants. Don't misunderstand. The covenants themselves remain the possession of the Jewish people. Therefore, the church, made up of Jews and Gentiles, does not fulfill the unconditional covenants promised to the physical Jewish nation. These unconditional covenants will not be fulfilled in the truest sense until the Millennium—when Christ, a Jew, will rule as King over the Jews sitting on the throne of David (2 Samuel 7:10-16; 1 Chronicles 17:11-15). In fact, the entirety of the land promised to the Jews in Genesis 15:18 will not be under their control and occupation until the Millennium. Consider as well that every Jew who enters the Millennium will be born-again/saved (as a result of exercising personal repentance and faith while depraved), fulfilling the unconditional covenant God gave Israel in Jeremiah 31:31-34 to the max:

> *"Behold, days are coming," declares the LORD, "when I will make*
> *a new covenant with the house of Israel and with the house of*
> *Judah, not like the covenant which I made with their fathers in the*
> *day I took them by the hand to bring them out of the land of Egypt,*
> *My covenant which they broke, although I was a husband to them,*
> *"declares the LORD. "But this is the covenant which I will make*
> *with the house of Israel after those days," declares the LORD, "I*
> *will put My law within them, and on their heart I will write it; and I*
> *will be their God, and they shall be My people. "And they shall*
> *not teach again, each man his neighbor and each man his brother,*
> *saying, 'Know the LORD,' for they shall all know Me, from the least*
> *of them to the greatest of them," declares the LORD, "for I will*
> *forgive their iniquity, and their sin I will remember no more."*
> (Jeremiah 31:31-34)

This fulfillment will occur at the end of the Tribulation, for every Jew who survives that traumatic season will accept Christ and be ushered into the Millennium.

Some of this subject matter cannot be absorbed without a basic knowledge of end-time events. If you had difficulty following, know that understanding will come later as you dig deeper into God's Word.

God revealed Himself to the Jewish nation and chose her as His people for the specific purpose of bringing the Messiah into the world and taking the news of His coming to the Gentiles. She was not chosen in the sense that God elected every Jew to be saved, for many Jews have died who rejected God's offer of salvation. Salvation for a Jew is the same as for anyone else—through the depraved repenting and exercising faith in Christ, the *"seed"* of Genesis 3:15 (Galatians 3:16). Only then does God grant new life (2Corinthians 5:17).

and strangers to the covenants of promise, (2:12c)

Gentiles were *"strangers"* to what God had revealed to the Jews (mainly because the Jews had failed to take the good news of the Messiah to the Gentiles—Israel's original calling). God had first made an unconditional covenant with Abraham, the Father of the Jewish nation, promising to bless him and multiply his offspring (Genesis 12:1-3). God would, in fact, bless *"all the families of the earth"* through Abraham (Genesis 12:1-3). This unconditional covenant held God responsible for fulfilling its conditions regardless of Abraham's response. The Messiah, Jesus, Who is a Jew, brings this covenant to fruition. Additional unconditional covenants came later, such as the Palestinian covenant (Deuteronomy 30:1-10), the Davidic covenant (2 Samuel 7:11-16; 1 Chronicles 17:10-14), and the New Covenant (Jeremiah 31:31-34)—each of which were based on the Abrahamic covenant. The covenant of Law (God's covenant with Israel established at Mt. Sinai in Exodus 20) came <u>after</u> God's promise to Abraham (Galatians 3:17-19), but was conditional (obedience brought blessings, disobedience brought curses). Paul doesn't seem to reference this covenant in Ephesians 2:12, when he says, *"the covenants of promise."* He, more than likely, is referencing the Abrahamic covenant along with the three additional unconditional covenants—each of which had as their foundation the Abrahamic covenant.

having no hope and without God in the world. (2:12d)

Before hearing the good news of Christ, the Ephesian believers (in comparison to Israel) had *"no hope and"* were *"without God in the world."* Remember, the Jews had received God's covenants, circumcision, and were descendants of Abraham— the father of the Jewish nation. They had a definite advantage over the Gentiles. Yet, Christ is the only *"hope"* for anyone, regardless of nationality (1Timothy 1:1). Thus, some Gentiles (such as Rahab and Ruth) placed faith in Israel's Messiah (the *"seed"* of Genesis 3:15) prior to His First Coming.

Because Jesus is God (Hebrews 1:8), and the only *"way"* to the Father (John 14:6), as long as these Gentile readers were without Christ they were *"without God"* (Ephesians 2:12d). Sadly, they were *"without God in the world"*—*"without God"* in a world controlled by Satan (2Corinthians 4:4) who possesses no truth (John 8:44), whose ideas, plans, and schemes bring certain destruction.

Ephesians 2:13—But now in Christ Jesus you who formerly were far off have been brought near by the blood of Christ.

The Gentile believers at Ephesus, in fact all Gentiles who make up the body of Christ, were *"formerly...far off"* (Ephesians 2:13)—as confirmed later in Ephesians 2:17, a quote from Isaiah 57:19. Why? They had not received what Israel had received from Jehovah—the special privileges mentioned in Romans 9:4-5:

> *who are Israelites, to whom belongs the adoption as sons and the*
> *glory and the covenants and the giving of the Law and the temple*
> *service and the promises, whose are the fathers, and from whom is*
> *the Christ according to the flesh, who is over all, God blessed*
> *forever. Amen.* (Romans 9:4-5)

Remember, however, that although the Jews had received these special privileges, repentance and faith in Jesus as Messiah were required before God bestowed salvation. As mentioned earlier, no Jew is right with God due to ancestry, circumcision, or being part of the nation that received the Law. This truth adds insight to Paul's teaching in Ephesians 2:13:

> *But now in Christ Jesus you who formerly were far off have been*
> *brought near by the blood of Christ.* (Ephesians 2:13)

The Gentiles, through faith in Jesus, have access to the Father anytime they like—a privilege no unbelieving Jew has possessed, even the unsaved Jews who offered sacrifices under the Law (Hebrews 9:1-10). No unsaved Jew has the same privileges as a saved Gentile until he repents of his sin and accepts Christ as Savior. An incredible transformation transpires, however, once a Jew sees his need for Jesus—a topic addressed in the next few verses.

Ephesians 2:14—For He Himself is our peace, who made both groups into one, and broke down the barrier of the dividing wall,

King Herod's temple, the second temple built in Jerusalem, existed in Paul's day. The first temple, King Solomon's temple, was destroyed by Babylon (2 Kings 25:8-9—586 BC) but rebuilt during the days of Ezra (Ezra 6:14-15). Herod refurbished this second temple magnificently, which caused the disciples to point out the temple buildings to Jesus (Matthew 24:1). Herod's temple was completed only a few years before Titus (a Roman general) destroyed it in A.D. 70.

When Paul wrote to the Ephesians, in 60-62 A.D., a wall served as a barrier between the Court of the Gentiles and the remainder of the temple. A notice was posted to insure that no Gentile ventured past this wall. The notice, which was discovered by excavators in 1871, stated:

> "No man of another nation to enter within the fence and enclosure round the temple, and whoever is caught will have himself to blame that his death ensues" (*International Standard Bible Encyclopedia,* 1994). [11]

Both Jews and Gentiles gathered in the Court of the Gentiles, which formed a square of 750 feet. The money changers of Jesus' day conducted business in this location, selling oxen, sheep, and doves for sacrifices. Jesus cleansed this area in both John 2:13-16 and Matthew 21:12-13.

The previous input allows us to properly interpret Paul's words of Ephesians 2:14. First, Jesus gave Jews and Gentiles the opportunity to enter into a peaceful relationship with the Father. Second, He provided a way for Jews and Gentiles to live peacefully among themselves. Jews and Gentiles have always been unsuccessful in maintaining a peaceful relationship, as secular history records. Israel's constant conflict with the Arab nations is just one example. The descendants of Ishmael (Abraham's son through Hagar—a Gentile) have warred against the Jews for centuries (as God promised in Genesis 16:12), and the war continues today. Only *"in Christ Jesus"* (Ephesians 2:13) can the enmity be put to rest, *"For He Himself is our peace"* (Ephesians 2:14). Therefore, once a Jew or Gentile accepts Christ as Savior, he is placed *"in Christ Jesus"* (Ephesians 2:13), where *"both groups"* are made *"into one"* (Ephesians 2:14). This truth explains why Paul wrote to the Galatians:

> *There is neither Jew nor Greek, there is neither slave nor free man, there is neither male nor female; for you are all one in Christ Jesus.* (Galatians 3:28)

Ephesians 2:15—by abolishing in His flesh the enmity, which is the Law of commandments contained in ordinances, that in Himself He might make the two into one new man, thus establishing peace,

by abolishing in His flesh the enmity, which is the Law of commandments

contained in ordinances, (2:15a)

Every barrier (*"all enmity"*) between God and man, as well as every barrier between man and his fellow man (be he Jew or Gentile), was abolished in Christ's *"flesh"* (body)—a truth that applies to every New Testament believer. Let's expand this thought.

When Jesus experienced physical death, the veil of the temple (which was His body—Hebrews 10:19-20) was torn from top to bottom (Matthew 27:50-51)—symbolizing that access into God's presence is constantly available to believing Jews and Gentiles who live during the church age. Hence, New Testament believers become *"priests"* (Revelation 5:9-10) who can approach God any time they like (Hebrews 4:16). Under the Mosaic Law, *"the Law of commandments contained in ordinances"* (Ephesians 2:15), the high priest (and only the high priest) could enter into God's presence just *"once a year"* (Hebrews 9:6-7). But these ordinances, along with everything else that separated the Jews from the Gentiles, were abolished through the cross. Jesus did away with this ceremonial Law (all aspects of the Law, in fact) to free New Testament believers to live *"under grace"* (Romans 6:14). All of this change came about through the death of Christ's *"flesh"* (Ephesians 2:15), or body.

We, as New Testament believers, are no longer *"under Law"* (Romans 6:14). This fact is settled for all eternity. But Romans 8:3-4 teaches that as we are led by God's Spirit we find that the requirement of the Law (the requirement of the moral Law) is fulfilled in our experience. Thus, what was unattainable through attaching ourselves to the Law in our lost condition is realized through being led of God's Spirit (as we live free of the Law), because the Holy Spirit will never lead us to do anything in violation of the righteousness associated with the Law!

that in Himself He might make the two into one new man, thus establishing peace, (2:15b)

Not only did Christ's physical death (coupled with His resurrection) end the enmity brought on by the ceremonial Law, but it also serves as the avenue through which believing Jews and Gentiles are made *"into one new man"* (Ephesians 2:14-15). Paul wrote in 2Corinthians 5:17:

> *Therefore if any man is in Christ, he is a new creature; the old things passed away; behold, new things have come.* (2Corinthians 5:17)

The New Testament believer becomes a totally new man because the old man

(Adamic nature, old self, sin nature, dead spirit—all synonymous terms) inherited from Adam is crucified (eradicated) the moment he repents and believes. The person he used to be is crucified (eradicated) through the avenue of Christ's *"body"* (Romans 6:6; Romans 7:4; Galatians 2:20). Consequently, when Jews and Gentiles become *"new"* creations (2Corinthians 5:17) in Christ, peace replaces enmity in previously volatile relationships and unity prevails. (Diagram 8 in the Reference Section might be profitable to review at this time.) As was stated earlier:

> *There is neither Jew nor Greek, there is neither slave nor free man, there is neither male nor female; for you are all one in Christ Jesus.* (Galatians 3:28)

Ephesians 2:16—and might reconcile them both in one body to God through the cross, by it having put to death the enmity.

and might reconcile them both in one body to God through the cross, (2:16a)

Both Jews and Gentiles are reconciled to God through Christ's *"body"* offered on *"the cross."* We determined earlier that the sin nature (Adamic nature, old man, old self, dead spirit) inherited from Adam is responsible for condemning unregenerate man to hell—not his acts of sin (Ephesians 2:3). For man to be reconciled to God, be he Jew or Gentile, the sin nature must be eradicated. Based on Romans 6:6, Romans 7:4, Ephesians 2:14-15, and Galatians 2:20, Christ's body is the avenue through which this eradication occurs—and the New Testament believer is forever reconciled to God (Ephesians 2:16). (Consult Diagram 8 in the Reference Section for additional input as to how we could have died in Christ.)

Even though the Jews originally received the Law, the Gentiles are also under the Law so long as they are unbelievers. This truth is confirmed in Romans 7:4 where Paul, while writing to Gentiles (Romans 1:13), states:

> *Therefore, my brethren, you also were made to die to the Law through the body of Christ,...* (Romans 7:4)

Paul also wrote to Gentiles in Galatians 3:24:

> *Therefore the Law has become our tutor to lead us to Christ, that we may be justified by faith.* (Galatians 3:24)

Paul, in writing to Timothy, confirms that all the lost (both Jews and Gentiles) live under the Law:

*realizing the fact that law is not made for a righteous man, but for
those who are lawless and rebellious, for the ungodly and sinners,
for the unholy and profane, for those who kill their fathers or
mothers, for murderers and immoral men and homosexuals and
kidnappers and liars and perjurers, and whatever else is contrary
to sound teaching,* (1Timothy 1:9-10)

Because the epistle to the Galatians was written to Gentiles, the unbelieving
Gentiles were under Law like the Jews. According to Romans 7:1-4, the only way
Jews or Gentiles, who being married to the Law, can be released from the Law, is
through death:

*Or do you not know, brethren (for I am speaking to those who
know the law), that the law has jurisdiction over a person as long
as he lives? For the married woman is bound by law to her
husband while he is living; but if her husband dies, she is released
from the law concerning the husband. So then if, while her
husband is living, she is joined to another man, she shall be called
an adulteress; but if her husband dies, she is free from the law, so
that she is not an adulteress, though she is joined to another man.
Therefore, my brethren, you also were made to die to the Law
through the body of Christ, that you might be joined to another, to
Him who was raised from the dead, that we might bear fruit for
God.* (Romans 7:1-4)

Thus, the death and eradication of the *"old self"* (Romans 6:6) is what frees New
Testament Jewish and Gentile believers from the Law so both can be *"joined"* to
Christ (Romans 7:4) once repentance and faith are exercised while depraved:

*knowing this, that our old self was crucified with Him, that our
body of sin might be done away with, that we should no longer be
slaves to sin;* (Romans 6:6)

by it having put to death the enmity. (2:16b)

"It" refers to the cross. *"Enmity,"* unlike its usage in verse 15, largely refers to the
"enmity" that exists between God and unregenerate man—not just the enmity that
exists between the unredeemed Jews and Gentiles. Our *"enmity"* with God was
forever eliminated (through the cross) when we accepted Christ as Savior, for only
then was the source of our *"enmity,"* the Adamic nature (old man), eradicated.
Faith in Jesus (and God's resulting gift of salvation) also allows the enmity between
the Jews and Gentiles (addressed in depth in verse 15) to be removed, for after the

cross, believing Jews and Gentiles are placed into one body—the body of Christ (Ephesians 2:16a). Once in Christ, any disunity between Jews and Gentiles is a direct result of sin, not a result of the previous barriers that existed under the Law.

Ephesians 2:17—And He came and preached peace to you who were far away, and peace to those who were near;

On the basis of faith in Jesus' perfect sacrifice, both Jews and Gentiles are reconciled to God (Ephesians 2:16). Therefore, during His First Coming, Jesus, the *"Prince of Peace"* (Isaiah 9:6), *"preached peace"* (Ephesians 2:17; John 14:27; 16:33). He came into the world as God's *"mediator"* to restore *"peace"* between God and man (Romans 5:1; 1Timothy 2:5; Hebrews 9:15). Even in announcing His birth, the angels perceived Him as providing *"peace"* (Luke 2:14). He *"preached peace to"* those *"who were far away"* (to the Gentiles) and *"peace to those who were near"* (to the Jews)—Ephesians 2:17. In other words, He desired that any man, be he Jew or Gentile, experience *"peace"* with the Father through Himself.

Ephesians 2:18—for through Him we both have our access in one Spirit to the Father.

According to *Vine's Expository Dictionary*, the Greek word from which we get *"access"* can be defined as:

> A leading or bringing into the presence of, denotes access, with which is associated the thought of freedom to enter through the assistance of favor of another. (Vine, 1996)[12]

Jesus is *"the door"* (John 10:7-9) and *"the way"* (John 14:6) through which we (once we repent and believe while deprived) partake of the Spirit and enter the Father's presence, God being *"spirit"* (John 4:24). Only through the Spirit of God can man be placed into Christ (1Corinthians 12:13), and into the Father (John 14:20), after accepting Jesus as Savior. So, Paul stated:

> *For you have not received a spirit of slavery leading to fear again, but you have received a spirit of adoption as sons by which we cry out, "Abba! Father!" The Spirit Himself bears witness with our spirit that we are children of God,* (Romans 8:15-16)

As God's children, who possess His Spirit, we can approach the Father through the Son any time we like:

Let us therefore draw near with confidence to the throne of grace, that we may receive mercy and may find grace to help in time of need. (Hebrews 4:16)

Ephesians 2:19—So then you are no longer strangers and aliens, but you are fellow citizens with the saints, and are of God's household,

Through Jesus, the believing Gentiles at Ephesus were *"no longer strangers and aliens"* (Ephesians 2:19). In fact, they were *"fellow citizens with the saints, and...of God's household"* (Ephesians 2:19). They were also citizens of *"heaven"* (Philippians 3:20; Ephesians 2:6). These same truths apply to us today. Interestingly, *"saints"* (Ephesians 2:19) in this case refers to all Old and New Testament believers, all of whom are members of God's *"household"* (Ephesians 2:19), the *"household of the faith"* (Galatians 6:10). Note: Old Testament believers were not forgiven (Romans 3:25; Hebrews 10:4, 11-12) nor made into saints (made perfect) until Jesus died (Hebrews 10:10; 12:23). Neither did they go to heaven until Jesus' ascension, but dwelt in *"Abraham's bosom"* (Luke 16:19-31) until that glorious event. All Old Testament believers were (and are) members of *"God's household"* (Ephesians 2:19), *"the household of the faith"* (Galatians 6:10). All New Testament believers are also members of *"God's household"* (Ephesians 2:19), *"the household of the faith"* (Galatians 6:10). However, only New Testament believers make up the church, the body of Christ (Ephesians 5:22-33), which began in Acts 2.

Ephesians 2:20—having been built upon the foundation of the apostles and prophets, Christ Jesus Himself being the corner stone,

As confirmed earlier, Old Testament believers are not part of the church age. The church, made up of all the redeemed since the day of Pentecost (Acts 2), is *"built upon the foundation of the apostles and prophets, Christ Jesus Himself being the corner stone"* (Ephesians 2:20). The *"apostles"* were men trained by Jesus over an extended period of time. The *"prophets"* were those equipped with the message of the apostles during the formative years of the church. These *"prophets"* are also mentioned in Ephesians 4:11 and will be covered there. *"Christ Jesus,"* as *"the corner stone"* of *"the foundation,"* is the main support of the structure that the foundation undergirds—the reference point from which every measurement is calibrated, the stabilizing factor that unifies the entire building. (For more input concerning Jesus as *"the corner stone,"* read Isaiah 28:16, Psalm 118:22, Matthew 21:42, Mark 12:10, Luke 20:17, Acts 4:11, and 1Peter 2:6-7.) Therefore, the church has a firm foundation.

Ephesians 2:21—in whom the whole building, being fitted together is growing into a holy temple in the Lord;

The *"building"* (Ephesians 2:21), the church that the *"foundation"* of Ephesians 2:20 supports, is being built at the present time. In fact, it was *"being fitted together"* (Ephesians 2:21) in Paul's day and continues *"being fitted together"* today. This *"building...is growing into a holy temple in the Lord"* (Ephesians 2:21). Thus, the foundation, which consists of the apostles, prophets, and Christ Jesus the corner stone, supports *"a holy temple."* The stones *"being fitted together"* to form this structure are believers who have accepted Christ since Acts 2. The stones, in other words, are those individuals who make up the church. This truth is confirmed in 1Peter 2:5, where we read:

> *you also, as living stones, are being built up as a spiritual house for a holy priesthood, to offer up spiritual sacrifices acceptable to God through Jesus Christ.* (1Peter 2:5)

Ephesians 2:22—in whom you also are being built together into a dwelling of God in the Spirit.

The believers at Ephesus were *"being built together into a dwelling of God in the Spirit,"* and so are we. In fact, every member of Christ's body (the church) has had the awesome privilege of being placed, as a *"living"* stone (1Peter 2:5), within the temple wall. This temple houses the Holy *"Spirit"* (Ephesians 2:22). This temple, as confirmed earlier, is also the body of Christ and part of the Father's family. In other words, God's "masterpiece" (the church) spoken of in Ephesians 2:10 is addressed here.

Ephesians 3

Ephesians 3:1—For this reason I, Paul, the prisoner of Christ Jesus for the sake of you Gentiles —

Paul was *"the prisoner of Christ Jesus"* (Ephesians 3:1). For this phrase to fully impact our lives, we must understand the backdrop associated with his imprisonment.

While Paul was imprisoned in Rome, the Roman Empire ruled the world with Caesar as its emperor. The Romans had initially imprisoned Paul in Jerusalem (for his personal safety) after hostile Jews threatened his life for associating with Gentiles and teaching "politically incorrect" views regarding the Law (Acts 21:17-36). The Romans later sent Paul to Caesarea (Acts 23:12–26:32) and then to Rome (Acts 27:1–28:31), where he lived *"in his own rented quarters"* (Acts 28:30-31). Interestingly, Paul, under the jurisdiction of the Roman Empire during this lengthy imprisonment, did <u>not</u> say, "the prisoner of Caesar." He realized that all *"authority"* is established by God (Romans 13:1), which made him ultimately *"the prisoner of Christ Jesus"* (Ephesians 3:1). Thus Caesar, possessing a free will, was God's instrument for that season of history just as Pilate, possessing a free will, was God's instrument during Jesus' First Coming (John 19:10-11). Paul viewed himself as Christ's *"prisoner...for the sake of"* the *"Gentiles"* (Ephesians 3:1). This mindset allowed him to understand how his "circumstances" were working for his *"good"* (Romans 8:28) as well as the good of his Gentile readers (Ephesians 3:1).

Paul was an apostle *"to the Gentiles"* just as Peter was an apostle to the Jews (Galatians 2:8; Romans 15:15-16). In fact, Paul's involvement with the Gentiles put him at odds with the unbelieving Jews (read Acts 21:27-31). His teaching that Jewish and Gentile believers are one in Christ irritated his Jewish critics immensely.

Paul confirms in Ephesians 3:1 that our "circumstances" are a matter of perspective. When viewed from God's vantage point, difficulties become opportunities. Freedom naturally follows, releasing the believer to truly "live."

Ephesians 3:2—if indeed you have heard of the stewardship of God's grace which was given to me for you;

Wuest's commentary states that Paul, in penning the phrase, *"if indeed you have heard,"* reminds his readers that they had been previously introduced to what was to follow.[13] Therefore, in Ephesians 3:2-12, Paul is repeating what he had taught these believers at an earlier date. Remember that Paul spent significant time at Ephesus teaching at *"the school of Tyrannus"* (Acts 19:9-10) prior to his imprisonment.

Paul viewed himself as having been entrusted with *"the stewardship of God's grace"* (Ephesians 3:2). *"Stewardship"* refers to "the management of a household, a ministerial commission in the publication and furtherance of the Gospel." Hence, Paul perceived himself as a manager of what God had entrusted to him in the gospel. He was called as a minister of *"God's grace"* (Ephesians 3:2), thus he states in 1Corinthians 9:16-17:

> *For if I preach the gospel, I have nothing to boast of, for I am under compulsion; for woe is me if I do not preach the gospel, for if I do this voluntarily, I have a reward; but if against my will, I have a stewardship entrusted to me.* (1Corinthians 9:16-17)

Again, in Colossians 1:25, Paul addresses this same subject:

> *Of this church I was made a minister according to the stewardship from God bestowed on me for your benefit, that I might fully carry out the preaching of the word of God,* (Colossians 1:25)

God not only gave Paul the revelation of His grace, but also the responsibility of preaching and teaching this revelation to the Gentiles. Paul refused to take his calling lightly; he wrote, in fact, to the Ephesians (who were Gentiles) that this stewardship *"was given to"* him for their benefit (Ephesians 3:2). Paul realized that the ministry he had received from God was for the sake of others, specifically the Gentiles.

We must be responsible stewards over what God has entrusted to our care, be it insight, knowledge, wisdom, a particular gifting, material possessions, etc. In fact, excellently handling small responsibilities today may result in increased responsibilities tomorrow. Certainly, God grants additional insight and wisdom to those who, through His strength, properly apply the insight and wisdom they already possess? Think about it!

Ephesians 3:3—that by revelation there was made known to me the mystery, as I wrote before in brief.

The *"mystery"* of God was made known to Paul through *"revelation."* *"Revelation"* means "to uncover, to be discovered in true character." *"Mystery"* is defined by some as "that which would remain undisclosed but for revelation." That Jews and Gentiles become one once they receive Christ and are placed into Christ is the *"mystery"* revealed to Paul. Can you imagine Paul's response when he received this truth? Remember, Paul's passion was persecuting Christians prior to his conversion (Acts 8:3; Galatians 1:13). However, Paul's *"gospel"* was *"not according to man,"* nor did he receive it *"from man"* (Galatians 1:11-12). He *"received it through a revelation of Jesus Christ"* (Galatians 1:12)—a disclosure that changed him forever.

After his conversion, Paul *"went away to Arabia,"* evidently spending much time alone with the Lord (Galatians 1:15-18). On his visit to Jerusalem (*"three years later"*) he did see James and Peter, but the revelation of the mystery did not occur at this time (Galatians 1:18-20). Neither did it occur *"fourteen years"* later when he visited Jerusalem; for, to quote Paul, *"those who were of reputation contributed nothing to me"* (Galatians 2:1-6).

Jesus also disclosed to Paul the details of His First Coming—information the eleven disciples already possessed. This truth is confirmed in 1Corinthians 11:23-24:

> *For I received from the Lord that which I also delivered to you,*
> *that the Lord Jesus in the night in which He was betrayed took*
> *bread; and when He had given thanks, He broke it, and said, "This*
> *is My body, which is for you; do this in remembrance of Me."*
> (1Corinthians 11:23-24)

The Lord revealed to Paul what occurred in the upper room prior to His crucifixion (Paul would have been an unbeliever when these activities took place. How Peter, John, and the other apostles responded to Paul's knowledge of these activities would have been intriguing to behold!

Paul's entire *"gospel"* was given to him *"through a revelation of Jesus Christ"* (Galatians 1:12), even the *"mystery"* addressed in Ephesians 3:3. Evidently, the *"mystery"* was not revealed to the other disciples to the degree that it was revealed to Paul (2Corinthians 12:1-7; 2Peter 3:14-16).

The phrase, *"as I wrote before in brief"* (Ephesians 3:3), refers to one of two things: (1) an earlier letter possibly written to the Ephesians by Paul (2) his words concerning *"the mystery"* in Ephesians 1:9-10 and Ephesians 2:11-22. Based on 2Corinthians 12:1-7, the *"mystery"* was one of several *"revelations"* unveiled to this amazing apostle.

Ephesians 3:4—And by referring to this, when you read you can understand my insight into the mystery of Christ,

"Insight" means "a critical understanding." Therefore, Paul's understanding of *"the mystery of Christ"* was thorough and detailed. Paul's words in Ephesians 1:9-10 and Ephesians 2:11-22 validated the depth of his *"insight into the mystery."*

The phrase, *"the mystery of Christ,"* is captivating; for New Testament believers have access to a thrilling *"mystery"* revealed only to the body of Christ. Once a depraved individual during the church age repents and believes by responding to the limited (yet adequate) truth accessible to all the depraved, God saves him and makes him new. He is then capable of progressing to the deeper things of God—such as comprehending the *"mystery"* and living life on a totally different plane. He can see that order exists in the cosmos and that life consists of more than random happenstances lacking purpose. He knows that everything is advancing toward a day when all things will be summed up in Christ (Ephesians 1:9-10). Once he is *"in Christ"* (2Corinthians 5:17), after repenting and believing while depraved, he not only possesses the capacity to comprehend the mystery, but, being part of Christ's body (1Corinthians 12:12-13), becomes part of the fulfillment of the mystery. Consequently, just as a proper perception of future events is based on the summing up of all things in Christ, the solutions to our present difficulties are also found in Christ.

Ephesians 3:5—which in other generations was not made known to the sons of men, as it has now been revealed to His holy apostles and prophets in the Spirit;

1Peter 1:10-12 shows that men like Abraham, Moses, Joshua, King David, Isaiah, and Daniel did not know what Paul knew (nor what we have the capability of comprehending) concerning the mystery. They realized from passages such as Genesis 3:15, Psalm 22, and Isaiah 53 that a suffering Savior would die for the sin of man, but they didn't understand the details of the positive ramifications of that gruesome, yet glorious event. The Old Testament prophets prophesied much about Christ's death and His future Millennial reign, but the church age remained a mystery—a time they knew little about. Thus, Paul states:

> *which in other generations was not made known to the sons of man, as it has now been revealed to His holy apostles and prophets*

in the Spirit; (Ephesians 3:5)

"Sons of men" references mankind in general; for no one, not even the spiritual giants of the Old Testament, understood the mystery that Paul addresses in the book of Ephesians. Paul speaks of the mystery in other epistles as well (Colossians 1:27 serves as an excellent example).

This mystery *"has now been revealed to His holy apostles and prophets"* (Ephesians 3:5)—the foundation of the church (Ephesians 2:20). Therefore, the mystery was not revealed to Paul alone. The *"apostles"* (such as Peter, Andrew, John, etc.) along with certain *"prophets"* (like Luke and James—who were not apostles), understood to some degree at least the mystery. In fact, all New Testament believers have the capacity to understand it. This truth is confirmed in Romans 16:25-26:

> *Now to Him who is able to establish you according to my gospel and the preaching of Jesus Christ, according to the revelation of the mystery which has been kept secret for long ages past, but now is manifested, and by the Scriptures of the prophets, according to the commandment of the eternal God, has been made known to all the nations, leading to obedience of faith*; (Romans 16:25-26)

Don't overlook the fact that Peter, one of the apostles, evidently had difficulty accepting certain aspects of this mystery—that Jewish and Gentile New Testament believers are made part of the body of Christ with no racial distinction (read Acts 10, Galatians 2:11-16, and 2Peter 3:14-16).

The phrase, *"has...been revealed"* (Ephesians 3:5), is in the aorist tense. Coupling this fact with the word *"now,"* it becomes obvious that the holy apostles and prophets, who recorded New Testament Scripture, received revelation never before exposed to man. They received this revelation through the Person of the Spirit. Note: The phrase, *"in the Spirit,"* can also be interpreted, *"by the Spirit."*

Ephesians 3:6—to be specific, that the Gentiles are fellow heirs and fellow members of the body, and fellow partakers of the promise in Christ Jesus through the gospel,

Paul, in Ephesians 2, began proving that born-again Jews and Gentiles are one in Christ. He expands this thought in Ephesians 3:6.

Unbelieving Jews had no quarrel with Gentiles being saved. God promised as early as Genesis 12:3 that all nations would be blessed through Abraham. God expanded this thought in Genesis 22:17-18, 26:4, and 28:14, which Paul references in Galatians 3:8. The Jews realized that Gentiles could be saved (Psalm 22:27; Isaiah 11:10; 42:1, 6; 49:6; 60:1-3; Jeremiah 3:17; Daniel 7:14; Hosea 2:23; Joel 2:28), and that this salvation would come through the Messiah. But the unbelieving Jews were not waiting for a crucified Messiah Who would unite believing Jews and Gentiles into one body, but for a Messiah Who would eliminate Roman oppression. Consequently, for Paul to say that believing Jews and Gentiles become one in Christ (Ephesians 2:11-22), with no racial distinction (Galatians 3:28), was infuriating to his unbelieving Jewish critics.

Paul's gospel (which taught that believing *"Gentiles are fellow heirs"* with believing Jews—Ephesians 3:6) greatly offended his unbelieving Jewish opponents who perceived the Hebrew people as far superior to Gentiles. Acts 22:1-22 verifies the unbelieving Jews' hatred of Paul's message. Note Paul's words to the believing Gentiles at Galatia:

> *And if you belong to Christ, then you are Abraham's offspring, heirs according to promise.* (Galatians 3:29)

Paul even taught in Romans 8:17 that Jewish and Gentile New Testament believers are *"fellow heirs with Christ"* (Romans 8:17). He also taught that they are made part of Christ's body (Ephesians 3:6), for through the Holy Spirit both Jews and Gentiles (during the church age) are placed into Jesus (1Corinthians 12:12-13) after repenting and believing while depraved. Once in Him, they receive His kind of life, eternal life. In fact, He becomes their *"life"* (Colossians 3:4). By receiving this life in the same body, Christ's body, no racial distinction exists between believing Jews and Gentiles.

Gentile believers are also *"fellow partakers of the promise in Christ Jesus"* (Ephesians 3:6). Paul isn't communicating that believing Gentiles are fellow partakers of promises given to the nation of Israel alone (the Old Testament is inundated with such promises). For example, God promised Israel (the nation) the territory from *"the river of Egypt"* to *"the river Euphrates"* (Genesis 15:18). This promise, to be fulfilled during the Millennium (the one-thousand-year reign of Christ on earth), was made to the Jews—not to the Gentiles. Ephesians 3:6, on the other hand, references what Gentile believers (along with Jewish believers) receive through the Person of Christ during the church age. *"The promise in Christ Jesus"* (Ephesians 3:6) was: The Father would send His Son to die for sinful mankind and raise Him from the dead (Christ's death was prophesied as early as Genesis 3:15). As a result, Jesus inhabits both Jewish and Gentile saints during the church age (Galatians 2:20). In fact: Christ is their *"life"* (Colossians 3:4), God works *"all*

Ephesians   *Chapter 3*

things" for their good (Romans 8:28), they have been blessed *"with every spiritual blessing...in Christ"* (Ephesians 1:3), and they will never be condemned by God (Romans 8:1). Paul is saying that believing Gentiles enter into promises of God not distinctly related to the physical Jewish nation.

Paul's words in Ephesians 3:6 are fulfilled *"through the gospel,"* for *"through the gospel"* believing Jews and Gentiles become *"fellow heirs and fellow members of the body, and fellow partakers of the promise in Christ Jesus."*

Conclusion: That Jesus Christ possesses a body (made up of believing Jews and Gentiles during the church age) through which to express Himself to the universe is the wonder of God's *"mystery"* (Ephesians 3:3-4), for the mystery is *"Christ Himself"* (Colossians 2:2)—in Whom both Jewish and Gentile New Testament believers gain *"every spiritual blessing"* (Colossians 2:3; Ephesians 1:3). The mystery is also Christ's dwelling in Jewish and Gentile church saints as the means by which God's *"glory"* is manifested (Colossians 1:26-27; Galatians 2:20). Therefore, the mystery is not that Gentiles can be saved, but that born again Jews and Gentiles become one in Christ with no racial distinction:

> *There is neither Jew nor Greek, there is neither slave nor free man, there is neither male nor female; for you are all one in Christ Jesus.* (Galatians 3:28).

Ephesians 3:7—of which I was made a minister, according to the gift of God's grace which was given to me according to the working of His power.

Paul was *"made a minister,"* confirming that God ordained Paul's ministry—not Paul himself (read Acts 26:16). *"Minister"* means "one who renders service to another; an attendant, servant." Paul desired to know Christ's heart above all else (Philippians 3:10), thus His passion was Christ Himself—not the ministry to which he was called. Through pursuing Christ, his Source of empowerment was revealed—God Himself. Hence the words, *"according to the gift of God's grace which was given to me according to the working of His power"* (Philippians 3:7). God's *"grace"* not only made Paul an apostle (a position he could have rejected—as did Judas), but sustained him as he carried the gospel to the Gentiles—also confirmed by 1Corinthians 15:10:

> *But by the grace of God I am what I am, and His grace toward me did not prove vain; but I labored even more than all of them, yet not I, but the grace of God with me.* (1Corinthians 15:10)

Colossians 1:29 lines up perfectly with our findings:

> *And for this purpose also I labor, striving according to His power, which mightily works within me.* (Colossians 1:29)

We learned earlier that *"works"* (Colossians 1:29) can be perceived as God's energizing, so a review of the word *"works"* in Ephesians 1:11c might be encouraging.

Paul realized that God Himself, through His grace and power (Ephesians 3:7), would supply everything needed to fulfill the ministry to which he had been called. Paul's responsibility was to yield to Jesus' indwelling presence for purity of character (1Corinthians 9:27), for God's servants must be *"above reproach"* (1Timothy 3:2; Titus 1:6-7).

We are to pray for everyone who holds a leadership position within Christ's body. To those who are called of God to a particular position, we pray they continually remember the Source of their calling and empowerment. For believers who function in positions to which they have not been called (or gifted), we pray they might yield to individuals equipped for the responsibility. Saints who sense an obligation to serve God in a specific area, yet are ungifted for the position, many times hinder God's work and God's people.

Ephesians 3:8—To me, the very least of all saints, this grace was given, to preach to the Gentiles the unfathomable riches of Christ,

Paul probably viewed himself as *"the very least of all saints"* because of his mistreatment of believers prior to his conversion (Acts 22:4; 1Corinthians 15:9; 2Corinthians 12:11; Galatians 1:23). He credits God's *"grace"* as the source of his empowerment while preaching the gospel to the Gentiles (also read Galatians 2:2, 8-9).

Paul preached *"the unfathomable riches of Christ"* (Ephesians 3:8)— *"unfathomable"* can also be interpreted "unsearchable" or "incomprehensible." Had Paul preached a thousand years describing Christ's *"riches,"* the majority would have remained untold.

As we ponder Christ's *"riches,"* Colossians 1:16 comes to mind:

> *For by Him all things were created, both in the heavens and on earth, visible and invisible, whether thrones or dominions or rulers*

or authorities—all things were created by Him and for Him. (Colossians 1:16)

Even Hebrews 1:2 states that Jesus is the *"heir of all things"*:

> *in these last days has spoken to us in His Son, whom He appointed heir of all things, through whom also He made the world.* (Hebrews 1:2)

Jesus, the *"first-born"* Son of the Father (Hebrews 1:6), will inherit everything—and we are *"fellow heirs"* with Him (Romans 8:17):

> *and if children, heirs also, heirs of God and fellow heirs with Christ, if indeed we suffer with Him in order that we may also be glorified with Him.* (Romans 8:17)

We, as part of the body of Christ, the church, have received abundant riches through being placed into Jesus (read Ephesians 1:3, 1Corinthians 1:5, 2Corinthians 5:17, 2Corinthians 5:21, and Colossians 2:10 for starters).

We are also part of Christ's inheritance, for we belong to Him (1Corinthians 3:23). Hence, we add to His wealth.

Conclusion: Our value is great in the eyes of the Creator.

Ephesians 3:9—and to bring to light what is the administration of the mystery which for ages has been hidden in God, who created all things;

and to bring to light what is the administration of the mystery (3:9a)

Paul was called *"to bring to light...the administration"* (plan or dispensation) *"of the mystery"* (Ephesians 3:9). The *Phillips Translation* renders verse 9 as:

> *and to make plain to all men the meaning of that divine secret which he who created everything has kept hidden from the creation until now.* (Ephesians 3:9 *Phillips*)[14]

Paul's goal was to *"make plain"* (*Phillips*) the mystery which, until his day, had been hidden in God. The fact that Jews and Gentiles can become new creations in Christ (2Corinthians 5:17) and, in God's economy, live with no racial distinction

(Galatians 3:28), was a truth that consumed Paul's thought processes. He desired that all Jews and Gentiles know the profoundness of this truth. Thus, he was energized (by God's grace) to share *"the glorious gospel of the blessed God"* (1Timothy 1:11), a message which attracted persecution from the unbelieving Jews. (Note: Although Paul's ministry was to the Gentiles, he first visited the Jewish synagogues when entering a new city (Acts 17:1, 10-12). Why? The gospel was to be presented *"to the Jew first and also to the Greek"* (Romans 1:16).

which for ages has been hidden in God, who created all things; (3:9b)

The mystery that Paul preached, *"which for ages had been hidden in God,"* was revealed at a strategic time in the history of mankind—*"when the fullness of the time came"*:

> *But when the fullness of time came, God sent forth His Son, born of a woman, born under the Law,* (Galatians 4:4)

The Greeks had earlier, under the leadership of Alexander the Great, united Europe, Asia, and Africa. In the process they established the Greek language as the universal language. The Romans, who ruled after the Greeks, kept the "then known world" as one empire, but created a network of roads to make the whole of the empire accessible. Considering too that the Jews had been dispersed throughout the world, the stage was set for the mystery to be revealed to the masses—Jews and Gentiles alike. Paul was to teach this mystery to anyone who would listen, regardless of the degree to which the unbelieving Jews resisted its validity.

God, in Whom the mystery had been *"hidden,"* *"created all things"* (Ephesians 3:9b). He did so through His Son (Colossians 1:15-16), Who is *"the Word"* of God (John 1:1-3). Therefore, when the Father spoke (Genesis 1:3), all things came into existence *"by"* the Son (1Corinthians 8:6).

> *yet for us there is but one God, the Father, from whom are all things, and we exist for Him; and one Lord, Jesus Christ, by whom are all things, and we exist through Him.* (1Corinthians 8:6)

Ephesians 3:10—in order that the manifold wisdom of God might now be made known through the church to the rulers and the authorities in the heavenly places.

Paul has been addressing the "mystery"—the fact that God makes unredeemed Jews and Gentiles into new creations (once they repent and believe while depraved), places them into one body (the body of Christ), and empowers them to function as a unified army for the cause of the kingdom. God exercised *"manifold wisdom"* while implementing this glorious plan, a *"wisdom"* being communicated *"through the church"* to the angels *"in the heavenly places."* What an amazing God we serve!

The church is to make known *"the manifold wisdom of God"* to *"the rulers and authorities in the heavenly places."* Coupling the phrase, *"rulers and authorities"* (Ephesians 3:12), with Ephesians 6:12, Paul is possibly referencing holy and unholy angels alike:

> *For our struggle is not against flesh and blood, but against the*
> *rulers, against the powers, against the world forces of this*
> *darkness, against the spiritual forces of wickedness in the heavenly*
> *places.* (Ephesians 6:12)

(Also read Ephesians 1:21 and Colossians 1:16). The holy angels worship God (Revelation 5:11-12) and minister to the saints (Hebrews 1:14), while the unholy angels (demons) scheme to disrupt God's work within the church, the body of Christ. Revelation 12:7-10 confirms that an army of angels (demons) fell with Satan.

Angels understand little about redemption, for once they fall they can never be redeemed (Hebrews 2:16). So, the holy angels are mesmerized with salvation and how it relates to man (1Peter 1:12):

> *It was revealed to them that they were not serving themselves, but*
> *you, in these things which now have been announced to you*
> *through those who preached the gospel to you by the Holy Spirit*
> *sent from heaven — things into which angels long to look.* (1Peter
> 1:12)

Because the ministry of the church goes far beyond what we see in the realm of the physical, each member of Christ's body ministers to the holy angels. The holy angels enjoy worshipping God (Revelation 5:11-12), but their worship is greatly enhanced as God's *"manifold wisdom"* is revealed through *"the church"* (Ephesians 3:10).

"Manifold" (Ephesians 3:10) means "exceedingly various, immense, infinite," confirming the vastness of God's *"wisdom."* As the church (functioning as teacher) explains God's wisdom to the holy angels (the students), they are brought to a deeper understanding of Calvary—resulting in enhanced praise. Just imagine

the sense of awe experienced by the angels through their heightened understanding of Jesus' sacrifice. How rebellious Jews and Gentiles can be placed into one body and made new (after repenting and believing while depraved), functioning as the vehicle through which Christ expresses Himself to the world, must be awe-inspiring to beings incapable of experiencing the same. Yes, salvation enhances the praise offered to our God, even among the holy angels.

The church reveals God's wisdom to the fallen angels as well (Ephesians 3:10). When the church wields its spiritual weaponry (*"the word of God"*—Ephesians 6:17), empowered by God's Spirit, the unholy angels (demons) witness the enormity of God's wisdom and retreat in defeat. How could they fail to observe God's wisdom after suffering humiliation at the hands of Jews and Gentiles who formerly hated each other and blatantly disobeyed God's commands? Only God could rectify such hostility between two groups of polarized individuals and mold them into a war machine capable of defeating any foe—even Satan himself. As God empowers the church to defeat Satan and his demons, the holy angels witness an additional aspect of God's infinite wisdom—resulting in enhanced praise.

Paul, in 1Corinthians 11:3-16, addresses women wearing long hair to display submission to their husbands. Note his words in 1Corinthians 11:10:

> *Therefore the woman ought to have a symbol of authority on her head, because of the angels.* (1Corinthians 11:10)

Paul is evidently referencing the holy angels' observance of the wife's submission to the husband—a picture of the church's submission to Christ. Through this observance, the holy angels' submission to God is heightened—resulting in greater praise. The unholy angels (demons) may be observing as well, hoping to somehow disrupt the husband-wife relationship and, in turn, the unity within the church.

Paul's instruction to Timothy should also be considered:

> *I solemnly charge you in the presence of God and of Christ Jesus and of His chosen angels, to maintain these principles without bias, doing nothing in a spirit of partiality.* (1Timothy 5:21)

Angels are extremely interested in the correlation between proper leadership within the church and proper behavior among the members of the church body. Why shouldn't they be if they are called to minister to and serve the members of Christ's body (Hebrews 1:14)? You and I, therefore, have *"entertained angels without knowing it"* (Hebrews 13:2). The holy angels are continually observing the saints for additional insight into God's limitless wisdom. By the way, angels always appear as men, for they are male in gender.

Ephesians 3:11—This was in accordance with the eternal purpose which He carried out in Christ Jesus our Lord,

"Eternal purpose" can actually be translated "the purpose of the ages." This *"purpose"* has existed in God's heart from eternity past and, of course, has *"eternal"* significance. God's *"eternal purpose"* is the unveiling of the mystery through the Person of His Son.

As the church's understanding of Jesus grows, and as she increasingly comprehends the privilege of living *"in Him"* (2Corinthians 5:17; Ephesians 2:6), Who is the *"mystery"* (Colossians 2:2), she cherishes more deeply His Person— which results in greater praise. The angels' adoration of God is also naturally bolstered. Yes, God desires praise from His children (Hebrews 13:15), His angels (Psalm 148:2; Hebrews 1:6), in fact, all His creation (Psalm 10:6; 69:34; 148:3-9). Before concluding, however, that God yearns to be worshiped due to an unhealthy ego, or that He can't exist without it, consider the following passage:

> *neither is He served by human hands, as though He needed anything, since He Himself gives to all life and breath and all things;* (Acts 17:25)

God suggests worship for our benefit, not His. Only through beholding God's glory and majesty do we grasp His perception of life (2Corinthians 3:18) and enter into His *"joy"* (Psalm 16:11; 147:1). God desires to be worshiped for the good of the worshiper, again proving His commitment to the principle of the cross, a selfless principle that has governed the Godhead from eternity past. What has been stated relates well to verse 12.

Ephesians 3:12—in whom we have boldness and confident access through faith in Him.

If God's desire is that the created realm worship Him, then the body of Christ must understand what grants New Testament believers access to His throne. Many saints are deficient in the area of worship because they "feel" unworthy to enter God's presence. The key words in verse 12, therefore, are *"in whom,"* especially since the last words in verse 11 are *"in Christ Jesus our Lord."* Only because we are in Jesus do *"we have boldness and confident access"* (Ephesians 3:12). In Ephesians 1:3-4 we discovered that *"in Him"* we have been made into holy and blameless saints, blessed with every spiritual blessing. We are not lowly sinners saved by grace! In fact, once we repented and believed while depraved, God made us the righteousness of Himself (2Corinthians 5:21)! Hence, Paul states, *"in whom we have boldness and confident access through faith in Him"* (Ephesians 3:12). The apostle John, realizing this truth, writes:

> *...And if anyone sins, we have an Advocate with the Father, Jesus Christ the righteous*; (1John 2:1)

Jesus, our *"great high priest"* (Hebrews 4:14), not only died for us, but also intercedes on our behalf (Romans 8:34) before the Father. Thus, when sin disrupts our fellowship with the Father (notice that I said "fellowship" and not "relationship"), confession restores our passion for worship. The enemy would have us believe that worship can coexist with unconfessed sin—a lie from the pit.

Ephesians 3:13—Therefore I ask you not to lose heart at my tribulations on your behalf, for they are your glory.

Many *"tribulations"* came Paul's way as he preached the mystery. In fact, after completing his third missionary journey, Paul's return to Jerusalem was inundated with false accusations from the unbelieving Jews (Acts 21:17-22:24) due to his involvement with the Gentiles (Acts 21:27-29; 22:21-22). The church at Ephesus was well aware of the price Paul paid. Thus, he encourages the Gentiles at Ephesus *"not to lose heart"* at his *"tribulations"* (Ephesians 3:13). Evidently, Paul's many trials were disheartening to his readers. Paul basically says, "Don't concern yourself with what I have suffered, *'for they are your glory'"* (Ephesians 3:13). Paul's sufferings actually enhanced the cause of Christ (Philippians 1:12) and were of great value to the Ephesians, for as Paul was strengthened in his sufferings the Ephesians would be strengthened in theirs—resulting in much *"glory"* (2Corinthians 4:17). Consequently, Paul states regarding his sufferings, *"for they are your glory"* (Ephesians 3:13).

Ephesians 3:14—For this reason, I bow my knees before the Father,

Paul begins verse 14 with, *"For this reason."* Because the Ephesians were discouraged and on the verge of losing heart (Ephesians 3:13), Paul prays for them—*"I bow my knees before the Father"* (Ephesians 3:14). No doubt existed as to Whom Paul was bowing when he prayed. He bowed *"before the Father,"* the God capable of answering prayer.

Intercessory prayer brings about remarkable results from the Father (read Exodus 17:8-13). Paul, a true prayer warrior, who believed so much in prayer that he encouraged the church at Thessalonica to *"pray without ceasing"* (1Thessalonians 5:17), used the most powerful resource imaginable to minister to the needs of the church at Ephesus. He prayed for them! His use of the phrase, *"I bow my knees,"* does not necessitate that this same posture be assumed by everyone who prays. Although passages such as Psalm 95:6, Ezra 9:5, and Daniel 6:10 confirm that kneeling is proper, prayer is a matter of the heart—not the position of the body.

The prayers of the saints have sustained me while pursuing God's call upon my life. I am certain that you could say the same in regard to your particular calling. Because God honors the prayers of His people, Paul prayed for the church at Ephesus.

Ephesians 3:15—from whom every family in heaven and on earth derives its name,

"Every family in heaven and on earth derives its name" from the Father (Ephesians 3:14-15), *"from whom are all things"* (1Corinthians 8:6). Scripture confirms that two orders of intelligent beings exist—angelic and human. The angelic order contains three classes: (1) cherubim (2) seraphim (3) angels. The human order consists of classes such as Jew and Gentile. But be it the angelic or human realm, every family derived its name from the Father. The Jews were named the Jews (Israel), the Gentiles the Gentiles, the cherubim the cherubim, etc., each name originating with the Father. However, the fact that everything in the human realm is the *"offspring"* of God (Acts 17:28-29) does not communicate that all mankind is saved/justified (John 3:16). To become a child of God requires repentance and faith while depraved (Romans 5:1; 2Timothy 2:25; Acts 11:18), so Paul is not (by any stretch of the imagination) teaching universal salvation. The lost have Satan as their *"father"* (John 8:44).

The heavenly Father, Who created all things through the Son, lived inside the believers at Ephesus (John 14:23; Ephesians 2:22). Thus, limitless power was accessible even in their disheartened state (Ephesians 3:13). Paul asks the omnipotent (all powerful) Father, Who lived inside them, to provide strength—as verified by verse 16.

Ephesians 3:16—that He would grant you, according to the riches of His glory, to be strengthened with power through His Spirit in the inner man;

The Father is rich in *"glory"* due to the perfection of His Being. His character, love, power, and wisdom are without flaw. Hence, when He appears, *"glory"* is manifested (Exodus 3:1-5; 19:16-18; 24:15-18; 33:17-23; 40:34-38; 2 Chronicles 5:11-14; John 1:14). Due to His impeccable nature, He possesses the resources to strengthen the disheartened. Evidently, the Ephesians were failing to appropriate faith, not due to blatant sin but because of losing heart (Ephesians 3:13). Had blatant sin been to blame, Paul would have, at some point in these passages, asked them to repent. Yet, no such plea is present. He is basically encouraging *"the fainthearted,"* as he did with the church at Thessalonica in 1Thessalonians 5:14.

Paul prays: *"that He would grant you..... to be strengthened with power through His Spirit in the inner man"* (Ephesians 3:16). The *"inner man,"* since Paul is addressing New Testament believers, is the *"new"* creation (2Corinthians 5:17), or the *"new self"* (Ephesians 4:24; Colossians 3:10), who replaces the *"old self"* (Romans 6:6; Ephesians 4:22; Colossians 3:9) at the point of salvation/justification. The child of God is *"strengthened with power...in the inner man"* (Ephesians 3:16) through the avenue of the *"Holy Spirit"* (Acts 1:8; Romans 15:13; Ephesians 3:16). Paul, realizing this truth, prays that the Ephesians might be strengthened as such. (*"The inner man,"* or new self, is the New Testament believer, *"the divine nature"* of 2Peter 1:4, who consists of soul and spirit. The physical body is not redeemed at salvation/justification, for church saints will not receive resurrected bodies until the Rapture of the church.)

Paul's prayer verifies that although we become *"saints"* when we accept Jesus as Savior (Ephesians 1:1), and are *"blessed...with every spiritual blessing...in Christ"* (Ephesians 1:3), we must be empowered by *"His Spirit"* to live a lifestyle pleasing to God (Ephesians 3:16). To glorify the Father is impossible unless we are in tune with, and enabled by, His Spirit (Romans 8:5-6, 12-13; 2Corinthians 3:18; 4:16; Galatians 5:16). Should God grant that the Spirit strengthen these believers *"according to the riches of His glory"* (Ephesians 3:16), the Ephesians would consistently reflect His glory through a holy and powerful lifestyle enabled through the Spirit's energizing. We can understand why Paul prayed so fervently on their behalf.

Ephesians 3:17—so that Christ may dwell in your hearts through faith; and that you, being rooted and grounded in love,

so that Christ may dwell in your hearts through faith; (3:17a)

Paul previously referred to his readers as *"saints"* (Ephesians 1:1) who had been *"sealed in"* Christ (Ephesians 1:13). Therefore, when he writes, *"that Christ may dwell in your hearts through faith,"* he is not questioning their salvation. *Wuest's* commentary records the following regarding *"dwell"*:

> "dwell" is *katoikesai*, made up of *oikeo*, "to live in as a home," and *kata*, "down," thus "to settle down and be at home." The tense is aorist, showing finality. The expanded translation is "that Christ might finally settle down and feel completely at home in your hearts. (Wuest, 1989, p. 132)[15]

Many New Testament believers fail to allow Jesus to "settle down and be at home" within them. He moves in (Galatians 2:20), and is their *"life"* (Colossians 3:4), but is seldom allowed opportunity to affect their daily living. Evidently, the Ephesians had begun to lose heart (Ephesians 3:13) and struggled to appropriate faith. Only an awakened faith, energized by the Holy Spirit, would result in Paul's readers making godly choices—freeing Christ to reside comfortably in His earthly dwelling (1Corinthians 3:16; 6:19).

At times, we too "feel" incapable of appropriating faith. We know that God is alive and in charge, but victorious living eludes us. The Holy Spirit can grant strength during these seasons, transforming our doldrums into triumphant praise. If you have yet to experience such seasons, just wait. They will surely come, although they seem to appear out of nowhere. These passages take on new meaning when saints trudge through one of those lonely valleys. Even Paul experienced times, earlier in his ministry, when faith seemed to flee (2Corinthians 7:6)—possibly explaining his passionate intercession for his readers.

Conclusion: We receive Jesus' presence at the point of salvation/justification, but we must practice His presence to live victoriously.

and that you, being rooted and grounded in love, (3:17b)

When faith is waning, we sometimes struggle to appropriate our true identity—that we are holy and blameless saints before the Father. But a renewed *"faith"* (Ephesians 3:17a), energized by the *"Holy Spirit"* (Ephesians 3:16), restores perspective. This foundation of *"faith"* (Ephesians 3:17a) is attained through a proper understanding of God's *"love"* (*"being rooted and grounded in love"* 3:17b). Paul, in Galatians 5:6, goes so far as to say that *"faith"* works *"through love."* A person who lacks a proper understanding of God's love will, therefore, struggle appropriating faith.

Paul understood the key to godly living:

> *For the love of Christ controls us,...* (2Corinthians 5:14)

May God grant us, through the power of the Holy Spirit, the ability to progressively comprehend His *"love"*!

As a farmer, I learned the importance of being firmly *"rooted"* (Ephesians 3:17b). I noticed time and time again that an abundance of moisture early in the crop year didn't ensure a bountiful yield. So long as plentiful moisture existed, the root systems of the young plants remained shallow. If the abundant moisture persisted and the roots failed to gain depth, the plants writhed during the hot and dry months of July and August. Also, the slightest wind late in the season could uproot the shallow root systems and, some years, destroy the entire crop. However, if dry conditions existed shortly after the planting season, the root systems would spear deeply into the soil, seeking the moisture well below the surface. The dry, hot days of July and August affected these plants to a lesser degree, as did the late season winds. Paul employs this principle in Ephesians 3:17. Our roots must be *"grounded"* deeply in God's *"love"* if faith is to withstand the storms and droughts certain to come our way. Paul confirms in Galatians 5:6 that *"faith"* naturally follows a deeply rooted and grounded *"love"* for God and His Word. Therefore, faith goes unappropriated in minds yet to understand God's affection for His people.

Fresh insight into God's *"love"* also yields an enhanced love for others. Paul addresses this truth in Ephesians 3:18.

Ephesians 3:18—may be able to comprehend with all the saints what is the breadth and length and height and depth,

After the discouraged New Testament saint is *"strengthened"* by the Holy Spirit (Ephesians 3:16), and faith is bolstered through an enhanced understanding of God's *"love"* (Ephesians 3:17), he passionately pursues intimacy with God and fellowship with His people. Paul, consequently, wrote to Philemon:

> *and I pray that the fellowship of your faith may become effective through the knowledge of every good thing which is in you for Christ's sake.* (Philemon 6)

As the disheartened saint regains perspective through focusing on *"every good thing which is in"* him *"for Christ's sake"* (Philemon 1:6), the *"fellowship"* of his *"faith"* becomes *"effective"* (Philemon 1:6). He, all of a sudden, pursues (with passion) fellowship with God and His children. This change pays huge dividends, freeing him to *"comprehend with all the saints what is the breadth and length and height and depth"* (Ephesians 3:18). Let's examine this phrase more extensively.

"Comprehend" means "to understand" or "to apprehend in the sense of laying hold of with the mind, to mentally grasp some idea or truth." What is to be comprehended (apprehended) is available to *"all the saints"* (Ephesians 3:18), not just the spiritual "elite" (should such individuals even exist). Paul also seems to be saying that this comprehension is enhanced through fellowship with the saints (*"may be able to comprehend with all the saints"*— Ephesians 3:18). Thus, certain truths remain dormant without corporate fellowship with other believers.

Fellowship among believers has played an important role since the church's inception (Acts 2:42), and rightly so. When the body of Christ comprehends the Scriptural view of God's love and operates in it (John 13:34; 1Peter 1:22), the supernatural is always manifested. The world suddenly realizes that we are Jesus' disciples (John 13:35), we experience optimum spiritual growth (Ephesians 4:11-13), we learn to live by Christ's life (Romans 5:10; Colossians 3:4), and we jettison the death associated with the letter of the Law (2Corinthians 3:6). Lone Rangers would become extinct within the Kingdom should Scriptural fellowship become the norm.

Opinions vary as to what Paul is referencing in the phrase, *"what is the breadth and length and height and depth"* (Ephesians 3:18). Because the general subject matter of verses 17-19 is Jesus' *"love,"* Paul is probably addressing this topic. To know *"the breadth and length and height and depth"* of anything is to know it fully. God's love, above all else, needs to be known in this manner since His very nature *"is love"* (1John 4:8, 16).

The *"breadth"* of Christ's love is displayed not only by means of the cross (He died for all persons, not just some), but in His acceptance of both Jews and Gentiles into His body (Ephesians 3:13-15). His love also lasts throughout eternity (Hebrews 7:25), meaning its *"length"* is limitless. The *"height"* of Christ's love is boundless due to our having been placed into Christ (2Corinthians 5:17) *"in the heavenly places"* (Ephesians 2:6; 4:10), *"far above all rule and authority and power and dominion"* (Ephesians 1:21). And finally, His love possesses the *"depth"* to reach down to man and grant him the freedom to exercise personal repentance and faith while depraved. What love!

Ephesians 3:19—and to know the love of Christ which surpasses knowledge, that you may be filled up to all the fullness of God.

and to know the love of Christ which surpasses knowledge, (3:19a)

When Paul inserts the phrase, *"to know the love of Christ"* (Ephesians 3:19), he is referencing something other than a conceptual knowledge of Christ's love. He is speaking of the knowledge of His love gained through the Holy Spirit as the saint passionately pursues His heart. In fact, *"know"* (Ephesians 3:19) is the same Greek word as is used in Philippians 3:10, where Paul states:

> that I may <u>know</u> Him, and the power of His resurrection and the
> fellowship of His sufferings, being conformed to His death;
> (Philippians 3:10)

To know Christ is to know His love, for *"God is love"* (1John 4:8, 16)—and Jesus is God (Hebrews 1:8). We can possess all the conceptual knowledge imaginable, but until the Holy Spirit opens our eyes to His Person and His love, it remains just that—conceptual knowledge. This opening of our eyes is called *"revelation."*

I view Christ's love quite differently than when I first believed on Him. I know Jesus loves me, but this understanding is not based on "knowledge" alone. It came through the Holy Spirit revealing God's Person through His Word. Oh, by the way, *"the mystery"* was revealed to Paul in this same manner (Ephesians 3:3).

that you may be filled up to all the fullness of God. (3:19b)

Paul speaks of *"the fullness of God"* in Ephesians 3:19b, *"the fullness of Christ"* in Ephesians 4:13, and the fullness of *"the Spirit"* in Ephesians 5:18. Jesus, the *"fullness of Deity"* (Colossians 1:19; 2:9), Who is God (Hebrews 1:8), takes up residence in a New Testament believer (along with the Father and the Spirit—John 14:17, 23) at the point of salvation/justification (Galatians 2:20). This means that God's *"fullness"* came to live in us when we became believers (John 1:16). But only as we allow Christ to *"dwell"* (feel at home) in our *"hearts"* (Ephesians 3:17), and *"know"* His *"love"* (Ephesians 3:19a), are we *"filled up to all the fullness of God"* (Ephesians 3:19b). In fact, we walk in God's *"fullness"* only when we are emptied of our selfish motives and desires and allow Christ to direct and empower our daily routines. Therefore, we can lose perspective and cease walking in *"the fullness of God"* (without losing our salvation), *"fullness"* being a place of blessing and empowerment available to New Testament believers throughout their earthly pilgrimage.

Ephesians 3:20—Now to Him who is able to do exceeding abundantly beyond all that we ask or think, according to the power that works within us,

We must be careful not to apply this passage to all believers, for its context pertains to believers who have an abiding passion to know God's heart. Stated differently, it applies to saints in pursuit of experiential holiness, righteousness, and godliness. Consequently, Ephesians 3:20 applies to believers who allow Jesus to *"dwell* [feel at home] *in their hearts"* (Ephesians 3:17), who are *"rooted and grounded in love"* (Ephesians 3:17), and who pursue being *"filled up to all the fullness of God"* (Ephesians 3:19). We can make this assumption because the Father *"is able to do exceeding abundantly beyond all we think or ask,"* and does so *"according to the power that works within us"* (Ephesians 3:20). God's power fills vessels who find pleasure in knowing and obeying His Word. (*"Works"* can actually be viewed as God's energizing—refer to notes on Ephesians 1:11). Paul's life was characterized by this power only because of his unwavering commitment to knowing Jesus' heart (Philippians 3:10), which resulted in a lifestyle of obedience (1Corinthians 9:27) to the indwelling Christ (Galatians 2:20). And was he ever empowered by God's Spirit (1Corinthians 2:4)! Hence, he wrote the following to Timothy, his son in the faith:

> *Therefore, if a man cleanses himself from these things, he will be a vessel for honor, sanctified, useful to the Master, prepared for every good work. Now flee from youthful lusts, and pursue righteousness, faith, love and peace, with those who call on the Lord from a pure heart.* (2Timothy 2:21-22)

The verb *"ask"* (Ephesians 3:20) is in the middle voice, meaning "to ask for one's self or in one's own interest" (*Wuest*).[16] This truth validates God's capability of doing, on behalf of those walking in submission and obedience, anything they might *"ask"* (a truth in agreement with John 14:12-14). Individuals who walk as such are applying the principle of the cross—living for the benefit of God and others, which greatly affects the content of their prayers. Believers who walk in disobedience, yet refuse to confess and repent of their wrongdoing, shouldn't expect God to respond as Paul describes in Ephesians 3:20.

God is capable of doing *"beyond all that we ask"* as well as *"beyond all that we...think"* (Ephesians 3:20). How exciting to know that Jesus' resources are limitless in that He creates the visible from the realm of the invisible:

> *By faith we understand that the worlds were prepared by the word of God, so that what is seen was not made out of things which are visible.* (Hebrews 11:3)

Thus, dream all you like, plan the most wonderful life imaginable, and God can exceed your wildest expectations. What an adventure—this life of faith! Anything else is a boring, extremely tiring existence.

Ephesians 3:21 to Him be the glory in the church and in Christ Jesus to all generations forever and ever. Amen.

"Him" refers to the Father, the recipient of all *"the glory in the church and in Christ Jesus"* (Ephesians 3:21). This passage confirms that we, the *"body"* of Christ (Romans 12:5), along with Jesus, *"the head"* (Ephesians 5:23), will bring glory to the Father *"forever and ever"* (Ephesians 3:21). The phrase, *"forever and ever,"* can also be interpreted "of the age of the ages." Hence, we will bring glory to the Father *"to all generations of the age of the ages."* What an awesome privilege!

Ephesians 4

Ephesians 4:1—I, therefore, the prisoner of the Lord, entreat you to walk in a manner worthy of the calling with which you have been called,

Chapters 4-6 of this epistle explain how the doctrines taught in chapters 1-3 are to be applied to daily living. Thus, by employing *"therefore,"* Paul is encouraging his readers to link the truths of Ephesians 1-3 to the practical applications addressed in the remaining chapters.

Paul refers to himself as *"the prisoner of the Lord"* (Ephesians 4:1) although he was at that time imprisoned by the Romans. (He referred to himself as *"the prisoner of Christ Jesus for the sake of you Gentiles"* in Ephesians 3:1, so you might want to review the commentary associated with that passage.) Paul was *"a bond-servant of Christ"* (Romans 1:1) in the truest sense of the word.

Now, Paul entreats his readers to *"walk in a manner worthy of the calling"* (Ephesians 4:1). *"Entreat"* means "to call to or for, to exhort, to encourage," while *"walk"* refers to "behavior" (the same root word used for *"walk"* in Ephesians 4:1 is interpreted *"behavior"* in Romans 13:13 and 1Thessalonians 4:12). The meaning of *"worthy"* can be depicted by a weighing device that pivots in the middle like a seesaw. The goods being purchased are placed on one side with a corresponding weight placed on the other until the scales are balanced. Paul's point here is that we must learn to walk in a manner (by yielding to Christ's indwelling presence) that corresponds with *"the calling with which we have been called"* (Ephesians 4:1). In other words, the behavior that best exemplifies our *"calling"* should be the norm for our lives. What is our *"calling"*? Follow closely.

As we discovered earlier (under Ephesians 1:4c and 1:5a), Greek words such as *kletos, kaleo, kaleomai,* and *klesis* are normally translated "called" or "calling" and point to two different truths recorded in Scripture: (1) that we have been invited to receive Christ (2) that the New Testament believer receives a specific office (gifting or purpose) once he is in Christ (saved/justified). Paul states in 1Corinthians 1:9:

> God is faithful, through whom you were called into fellowship with
> His Son, Jesus Christ our Lord. (1Corinthians 1:9)

Yes, we were *"called"* (invited) into fellowship with Christ, as is every person. Yet, not everyone accepts the invitation.

The most common use of *"called"* or *"calling"* is in relation to the believer's gifting, or purpose. Ephesians 4:1, in context with Ephesians 4:1-16, shows that Paul is addressing the different giftings, or offices, within the body of Christ. The believers at Ephesus were to *"walk in a manner worthy of"* their office, or gifting (Ephesians 4:1). We, like the believers at Ephesus, were *"called as saints"* (Romans 1:7) once we were placed in Christ (1Corinthians 1:2) subsequent to repenting and believing while depraved. What a wonderful purpose—to live, through Christ's strength, as a saint should live. Consequently, the fact that the New Testament believer is *"called"* can point to something other than being "called" or "invited" to be saved. New Testament believers, in association with being saved, are *"called"* to a particular office or purpose within Christ's body. These believers at Ephesus were to *"walk in a manner worthy of"* their *"calling."*

Ephesians 4:2—with all humility and gentleness, with patience, showing forbearance to one another in love,

Certain character traits epitomize the lifestyle of a New Testament believer who walks worthily in his calling. *"Humility...gentleness...patience,"* along with *"showing forbearance to"* fellow believers *"in love,"* should be obvious.

"Humility" can also be rendered "lowliness of mind." Don't misunderstand. The humble are not to perceive themselves as worthless and without hope. Neither are they weak with no backbone to stand in battle. Rather, they are individuals who regard others *"as more important than"* themselves (Philippians 2:3). Anyone who lives by the principle of the cross demonstrates humility as a way of life.

Moses was the most humble man on the earth (Numbers 12:3) but could never be accused of wimping out (going passive) in a bind. David (2Samuel 7:18), Josiah (2Kings 22:19), Isaiah (Isaiah 6:5), John the Baptist (John 3:30), Paul (2Corinthians 12:7-10), and, of course, Jesus (Matthew 11:29), all exemplified humility as they carried out the Father's will. But to a man, they possessed the boldness of a lion. So *"humility"* (Ephesians 4:2) is not synonymous with "weakness."

God makes the following promises to the humble: He will teach them His way (Psalm 25:9); they will prosper (Psalm 37:11) and be rewarded with riches, honor, and life (Proverbs 22:4); they will possess wisdom (Proverbs 11:2) and honor (Proverbs 29:23) and receive abundant grace (1Peter 5:5). Humility most definitely is the way to travel, especially when you consider the alternative.

The opposite of humility is pride. Pride caused Lucifer's fall (Isaiah 14:12-14), was the basis of Adam and Eve's sin (Genesis 3:5-6), and is the root of sin in mankind in general (1John 2:16). A life of pride results in forgetting God (Deuteronomy 8:14; Hosea 13:6), engaging in corrupt action (2 Chronicles 26:16), being unthankful to the Lord (2 Chronicles 32:25), opposing God and man (Psalm 10:2-4), being rebuked by the Lord (Psalm 119:21), receiving dishonor (Proverbs 11:2), bringing destruction upon one's self (Proverbs 25:15; 16:18), stirring up strife (Proverbs 28:25), stumbling and falling (Proverbs 16:18; Jeremiah 50:32), never being satisfied (Habakkuk 2:5), seeking evil gain (Habakkuk 2:9), experiencing self-deception (Galatians 6:3), opposing the Father (1John 2:16), being unfaithful to the Lord (2 Chronicles 26:16), and being humbled (Proverbs 29:23; Isaiah 2:11, 17; Daniel 4:37; 5:20; Matthew 23:12). Why Paul encouraged the believers at Ephesus to walk in *"humility"* (Ephesians 4:2) is apparent.

"Gentleness" (Ephesians 4:2) is a natural byproduct of humility. *"Gentleness,"* a fruit of the Spirit (Galatians 5:23), can also be interpreted "meekness"; but in no way means "weakness." Jesus was gentle and meek (2Corinthians 10:1), but cleansed the temple after observing its abuse (Matthew 21:12-13; John 2:13-17). Consequently, the gentle (meek) can display righteous anger without committing sin (Ephesians 4:26). In fact, controlled anger (directed toward what opposes God and is harmful to others) is permissible when coupled with wisdom and discretion. However, unrighteous anger (uncontrolled anger based on selfish motives) toward those in opposition is sin. We are to love and pray for our enemies (Matthew 5:10-12, 44; Luke 6:28)—never attempt to "whip them into line" by using weapons of the flesh.

Once humility and gentleness take root, patience follows. How so? Humility and gentleness are gained through a proper view of God's awesome character, power, and sovereignty. Once a believer perceives God as sovereignly working all things for his good (Romans 8:28), he is more apt to wait patiently on God's timing rather than attempt to resolve difficulties in the power of the flesh. Those who marginally know God possess little patience. Those who know Him intimately (know His heart) learn that everything must be done in His timing, for the right thing done at the wrong time is sin. God teaches us patience by allowing our faith to be tried (James 1:3). Once tried, we learn that God always knows best and answers prayers with: "Yes!" "No!" or "Wait!" Abraham learned this truth while waiting on God's promise regarding Isaac (Romans 4:18-21; Hebrews 6:13-15).

When a believer possesses humility, gentleness, and patience, he is equipped to *"show forbearance"* to others *"in love"* (Ephesians 4:2). *"Forbearance"* means "to hold up or to bear with." *"Love"* is *agape* love, unconditional love. Unsurprisingly, our agape love validates to the world that we are Jesus' disciples (John 13:35). Paul desired that the Ephesians display all of these qualities.

Ephesians 4:3 being diligent to preserve the unity of the Spirit in the bond of peace.

To be *"diligent"* is "to endeavor earnestly, strive, to make haste." In other words, Paul desired that his readers put forth an earnest and determined effort to *"preserve the unity of the Spirit in the bond of peace"* (Ephesians 4:3). *"Preserve"* means "to watch over or to guard." Thus, the Ephesians were to guard *"the unity of the Spirit,"* confirming that *"unity"* among believers is a work of the Holy Spirit. The church cannot generate unity. The church is to *"preserve the unity"* generated by the Spirit *"in the bond of peace"* (Ephesians 4:3). Hence *"peace,"* a *"fruit of the Spirit"* (Galatians 5:22), is the glue that preserves the unity that the Spirit provides. The foundation of this peace is *"love"* (Ephesians 4:2), *"the perfect bond of unity"* (Colossians 3:14).

As we *"walk in a manner worthy of the calling with which we have been called"* (Ephesians 4:1), respond to one another in *"love"* (Ephesians 4:2), and live in *"peace"* (Ephesians 4:3), the world will see Jesus!

Ephesians 4:4 There is one body and one Spirit, just as also you were called in one hope of your calling;

Paul, once again, stresses unity within Christ's body because all things *"in the heavens and...upon the earth"* will eventually be summed up *"in Christ"* (Ephesians 1:10), every member of the church is *"sealed"* in Christ (Ephesians 1:13), both Jewish and Gentile believers are one in Christ (Ephesians 2:11-22; 3:4-6), believers are *"to comprehend with all the saints"* (Ephesians 3:18), and believers are to be *"diligent to preserve the unity of the Spirit in the bond of peace"* (Ephesians 4:2-3). Paul continues the theme of unity in Ephesians 4:4-6 by using *"one"* on seven different occasions. Verse 4 deals with the Holy Spirit, verse 5 the Lord Jesus Christ, and verse 6 the Father. Paul realized that the unity within the Trinity (having existed since eternity past) is accessible to all who believe. (Remember what we learned in Ephesians 1 regarding this subject while studying the principle of the cross.)

"One body" (Ephesians 4:6) exists not two, three, or four *"one body"* that we were placed into through the Person of the Holy Spirit:

> *For by one Spirit we were all baptized into one body, whether Jews or Greeks, whether slaves or free, and we were all made to drink of one Spirit.* (1Corinthians 12:13)

The church is *"one body"* made up of holy and blameless saints from all cultural, social, racial, and economic backgrounds. No barriers should stand within this body (Galatians 3:28).

"One Spirit" (Ephesians 4:4) exists as well. In fact, *"we were all made to drink of one Spirit"* (1Corinthians 12:13); meaning that all members of Christ's body (the church) are being built into a holy temple—*"into a dwelling of God in the Spirit"* (Ephesians 2:18-22). No wonder Paul teaches that New Testament believers are *"a temple of the Holy Spirit"* (1Corinthians 3:16; 1Corinthians 6:19).

Without doubt, the Father desires that His people live in unity. But the foundation of meaningful relationships among fellow believers is personal intimacy with Christ. As we know Him more deeply (through the truth of His Word), we mature through the Spirit's guidance (2Corinthians 3:18); and meaningful horizontal relationships, previously impossible, are readily supplied. Only then is *"the unity of the Spirit"* (Ephesians 4:3), already resident within the church, manifested for all to see.

The phrase, *"one hope of your calling"* (Ephesians 4:4), is necessary to comprehend. The New Testament believer's *"calling"* was addressed earlier in Ephesians 1:5, so we will build on what was discovered there. We found that: (1) God called us (just as He calls everyone) to become part of His family (Matthew 22:14), but most people reject His offer (2) in conjunction with making us new, after we exercised personal repentance and faith while depraved, God gave us a particular *"calling"* or gifting (office, position) within Christ's body to nurture the body. Therefore, the *"one hope"* of our *"calling"* is that one day, as a result of the Godhead working through the gifted saints within Christ's body, we will mature in our behavior and later reign with Christ. The realization of this *"hope"* results from our having been placed into Christ's body through the avenue of the Holy Spirit—after we exercised repentance and faith while depraved in response to God having called us to be saved. God calls everyone to be saved, not desiring that any perish (1Timothy 2:4; 2Peter 3:9)—although only the depraved who choose to exercise personal repentance and faith receive eternal life.

Ephesians 4:5—one Lord, one faith, one baptism,

Verse 5 speaks of the *"one Lord,"* Jesus Christ. In fact:

> *"And there is salvation in no one else; for there is no other name under heaven that has been given among men, by which we must be saved."* (Acts 4:12)

The *"one Lord"* (Ephesians 4:5) is Jesus, Whom God made *"both Lord and Christ"* (Acts 2:36).

"One faith" (Ephesians 4:5) exists as well. Some theologians view these words as referencing the principle of faith, Jesus being the object of such faith. Other theologians consider the *"one faith"* to be the body of doctrine revealed in the Old and New Testaments (Jude 1:3)—a view I also hold. Jesus is the fulfillment of this doctrine and the focal point of all New Testament Scripture. Because only *"one faith"* (Ephesians 4:5) exists (not two, three, four, etc.), unity should characterize the body of Christ.

The *"one baptism"* is Spirit baptism, the avenue through which a New Testament believer is placed into Christ's *"body"* (1Corinthians 12:13). Thus, only *"one baptism"* is associated with spiritual regeneration/salvation. Because all New Testament believers are Spirit baptized into one body, unity should abound among the body's members. Note: Water baptism, in all its significance, is but a picture of the Spirit baptism associated with salvation. New Testament believers are Spirit baptized into the body of Christ, not two or three times (*"one baptism"*—Ephesians 4:5). Hence, your salvation is secure, never to be taken from you so as to require additional Spirit baptisms.

Ephesians 4:6—one God and Father of all who is over all and through all and in all.

As verse 4 dealt with the Spirit, and verse 5 the Lord Jesus Christ, verse 6 addresses truth concerning God the Father. He is *"one God and Father,"* a fact the nation of Israel understood long ago:

> *"Hear, O Israel! The LORD is our God, the LORD is one!*
> (Deuteronomy 6:4)

This mindset carried over into the New Testament, as evidenced by Mark 12:29, Mark 12:32, and 1Corinthians 8:4-6.

God is the *"God and Father of all"* (Ephesians 4:6) New Testament believers. He is *"over all"* (Ephesians 4:6) New Testament believers just as He is the sovereign Ruler over all creation (Psalm 103:19). He also works *"through all"* (Ephesians

4:6) New Testament believers (Philippians 2:13) and is *"in all"* (Ephesians 4:6) New Testament believers (John 14:23). Therefore, if the Father is *"in all"* church saints (along with the Son and the Spirit—John 14:23; 1Corinthians 3:16), and the three Persons of the Trinity live in flawless unity (even though they have varied roles and responsibilities), the members of Christ's body should abound in unity (John 17:11). Is it not amazing what the Father has made available to the church, by His Spirit, through Jesus His Son?

Paul, by discussing the three members of the Godhead separately (Ephesians 4:4-6), is not implying that the three Persons of the Trinity work independently of each other. The Three have functioned as One since eternity past, an arrangement that will continue throughout eternity future (John 10:30). (Only when Jesus bore the sin of man on the cross did the Father and Son break fellowship—Matthew 27:46). Isn't it wonderful that this Father is our Father (Romans 8:15; Galatians 4:6)!

Ephesians 4:7—But to each one of us grace was given according to the measure of Christ's gift.

In verses 7-16, Paul discusses the gifts given to church saints for the purpose of maintaining unity within Christ's body. These gifts are also bestowed to bring the church to spiritual maturity.

Paul begins verse 7 with, *"But to each one."* *"Each"* New Testament believer has been *"given"* *"grace"* (*charis*) *"according to the measure of Christ's gift"* (Ephesians 4:7), confirming that the *"grace"* (*charis*) that empowers the spiritual gifts within Christ's body is totally free. This *"grace"* energizes the spiritual gifts, allowing each church saint to employ his *"special gift"* (singular—1Peter 4:10) to God's glory. Consequently, the *"grace"* (*charis*) addressed in Ephesians 4:7 is *"given according to the measure of Christ's gift."*

Consider, too, that all spiritual gifts are bestowed through the working of God's *"grace"* (Romans 12:6):

> *And since we have gifts that differ according to the grace given to*
> *us, let each exercise them accordingly:....* (Romans 12:6)

Thus, the Greek word for *"gift"* in Ephesians 4:7 is *dorea*, pointing to the freeness of the gift. Consequently, through God's grace we both receive and exercise our spiritual gift to His glory. Note: The grace that Paul addresses here is different from the grace the believer must appropriate while facing difficulties (review notes on Ephesians 1:2). The grace needed in the midst of adversity is unlimited

(2Corinthians 12:9-10), while the grace associated with a spiritual gift is fixed according to the particular gift received (Romans 12:6; Ephesians 4:7).

These spiritual gifts, though diverse and unique, are necessary if the church is to function in *"the unity of the Spirit"* (Ephesians 4:3) and as *"one body"* (Ephesians 4:4). All New Testament believers receive a special spiritual gift (1Peter 4:10), one of its purposes being to assist in maintaining unity among God's people. Hence, no one is like you, for your gift cannot be duplicated. For instance, should you have the gift of teaching, no one can teach like you teach. Your gift can also be a combination of several gifts. Therefore, since your gift is distinct, be sure to use it properly. Otherwise, the body of Christ will miss a tremendous blessing.

Ephesians 4:8—Therefore it says, "When He ascended on high, He led captive a host of captives, And He gave gifts to men."

During Old Testament times, all the souls and spirits of the dead (believers as well as unbelievers) went to Sheol (Deuteronomy 32:22; 1 Kings 2:6; Job 24:19; 26:6; Psalm 9:17; 16:10; etc.), or Hades (Matthew 11:23; Luke 16:23; Acts 2:27, 31; Revelation 20:13; etc.), while their bodies returned to the earth (to dust). Sheol (Hebrew), or Hades (Greek), was divided—one side for the lost, the other side for the saved (Luke 16:19-31). The saved side was called *"Abraham's bosom"* (Luke 16:22), or *"Paradise"* (Luke 23:43), while the lost side (the side we normally call hell) is a place of torment for the unrighteous dead (Luke 16:22-24). It also houses a specific class of demons (2Peter 2:4-5; Jude 6). This input should assist our understanding as we continue.

According to Matthew 27:45-46, darkness fell upon the earth during the three hours that the Father judged sin through His Son. Jesus was separated spiritually from the Father (He died spiritually) when He took on the sin of mankind (the sin of the "elect" as well as the "non-elect"). After Jesus' spiritual death, however, and while His body remained alive on the cross, He was *"made alive in the spirit"* (1Peter 3:18). Therefore, Christ died spiritually and was raised spiritually before He died physically. Later, when Jesus died physically (John 19:28-30), His body was placed in the tomb (for three days); but His soul and spirit traveled to the saved side of Hades (or Sheol)—to *"Paradise"* (Luke 23:43; Ephesians 4:9), or *"Abraham's bosom"* (Luke 16:22). During His three-day-stay in Hades, He *"made a proclamation to the spirits now in prison"* (1Peter 3:19). In other words, He *"made a proclamation"* (an announcement) to a particular group of beings in hell—*"to the spirits now in prison,"* a topic addressed in more detail shortly. (Notice that He *"made a proclamation"* rather than preached the gospel.) But how was it possible for Christ, dwelling in Paradise (Abraham's bosom), to make an announcement to beings restrained to hell? According to Luke 16:19-31, the lost rich man (in hell) could speak with Abraham (in Abraham's bosom). Thus Jesus, by no stretch of the imagination, entered hell—as some theologians have incorrectly assumed.

When Peter speaks of Jesus' *"proclamation to the spirits...in prison"* in Hades (1Peter 3:19), he mentions a particular class of beings who were disobedient during *"the days of Noah"* (1Peter 3:20). Genesis 6:1-4 confirms that after God pronounced judgment on the serpent through the *"seed"* of the woman (Genesis 3:15), *"the sons of God"* (Genesis 6:2—fallen angels in this case) joined themselves to *"the daughters of men"* (to natural women). These fallen angels were attempting to negate, or corrupt, God's promise of Genesis 3:15—that a *"seed"* would be born through a particular *"woman,"* and that this *"seed"* would *"bruise"* Satan's *"head"* (usurp Satan's authority over earth). Had these fallen angels polluted the lineage to the seed, the seed could not have been born. Peter mentions these particular beings for this reason. Jesus' *"proclamation"* (1Peter 3:19) proved to the lost side of Hades that He had overcome. Peter addresses these same disobedient angels in 2Peter 2:4.

Jesus departed from Sheol (Hades), for according to Psalm 16:10 (and Acts 2:27) the Father didn't allow Him to linger there. He was brought up from Sheol to be joined with His resurrected body. Jesus' subsequent ascension to heaven (Acts 1:1-11) allowed the souls and spirits of the inhabitants of Abraham's bosom (Paradise) to be taken to heaven, while the souls and spirits of the lost remained in the same place of torment—as they do today. Thus, Abraham's bosom no longer exists.

Therefore it says, "When He ascended on high, (4:8a)

Paul refers to Psalm 68:18 by saying, *"When He ascended on high, He led captive a host of captives, And He gave gifts to men"* (Ephesians 4:8a). Paul's words are not a direct quote of the Psalm, which has led some theologians to conclude that Paul makes a general reference for the sake of analogy. *The New Bible Commentary Revised* also states:

> The quotation from Psalm 68:18 is adapted to produce a reading which closely follows the Syriac version known as the Peshitta: "Thou didst ascend on high, and take captivity captive; and Thou gavest gifts to men"; and a similar version in the Aramaic Targum (i.e. paraphrase of the Old Testament text) shows that the sense of "He gave unto men" was an old Jewish interpretation on which Paul is evidently drawing in this citation. (*The New Bible Commentary Revised*, 1984)[17]

Whatever the case, Christ's ascension allowed Him to give gifts to men. When He exited the grave (Matthew 28:1-10) and forty days later was taken to heaven (Acts 1:1-11), everything was set for the Holy Spirit to descend on the day of Pentecost (Acts 2:1-13), establish the church, and give *"gifts to men"* (Ephesians 4:8c).

We can't begin to imagine the warfare accompanying Jesus' trek through the atmospheric heavens (Acts 1:9-11; Hebrews 4:14) on His way to the Father. Satan had done everything possible to thwart Christ's birth and had (of late) unsuccessfully prevented His resurrection, so his onslaught against Jesus' ascension must have been incredible. Evidently, every demon in the enemy's camp was assigned to the task (Colossians 2:15). But Jesus was taken up in *"a cloud"* (Acts 1:9), *"a cloud"* of glory—glory that stems from God's holiness, purity, righteousness, omniscience, love, and power. Because righteousness consistently overpowers evil, Jesus' ascension was completed as planned.

He led captive a host of captives (4:8b)

Jesus *"led captive a host of captives"* (Ephesians 4:8b). The King James renders the phrase, *"He led captivity captive."* For proper interpretation we need only consider Paul's words to the church at Colosse:

> *When He had disarmed the rulers and authorities, He made a public display of them, having triumphed over them through Him.* (Colossians 2:15)

"Disarmed" can also be rendered "renounced," or "stripped off," or "put off." Thus, during Jesus' ascension, He "put off" every demon that came His way. In fact, *"He made a public display of them"* (Colossians 2:15), or "made a public show or spectacle of them." In other words, He showed *"the rulers and authorities"* (Colossians 2:15)—all forces of evil listed in Ephesians 6:12—Who is Boss. He *"triumphed over them"* (Colossians 2:15), meaning that He, like the Roman generals who led their captives triumphantly through the streets of Rome, led the demons in triumphal procession through the atmospheric heavens. What a sight this must have been! The demons' goal was to prevent Jesus from serving as our Great High Priest. How disappointed they must have been!

Jesus' ascension allowed Old Testament believers' souls and spirits to move from Abraham's bosom to heaven. It also paved the way for the soul and spirit of a New Testament believer to be ushered into heaven at the point of physical death (2Corinthians 5:8; Philippians 1:23).

and He gave gifts to men." (4:8c)

After Jesus *"led captive a host of captives"* (Ephesians 4:8b), *"He gave gifts to men"* (Ephesians 4:8c). Paul uses the Greek *doma* for *"gifts"* in this instance but *charisma* for *"gifts"* in Romans 12:6-8 and 1Corinthians 12:4-30. This fact may indicate that Paul is referencing the spiritually gifted men of Ephesians 4:11 who serve in designated positions within Christ's body to help mature the Son's bride (read Ephesians 4:11 with 4:12-13). After all, the *"gifts"* alluded to in verse 8 are listed specifically in verse 11, with verses 9-10 serving as a parenthetical expression. Don't misunderstand. The spiritual gifts listed in Romans 12:6-8 and 1Corinthians 12:4-30 are given to individuals (1Corinthians 12:11) for the benefit of the entire body of Christ. But in Ephesians 4:8 and Ephesians 4:11, Paul seems to reference gifted men rather than the individual gifts themselves. We will discuss this matter in more depth when we arrive at verse 11.

Ephesians 4:9—(Now this expression, "He ascended," what does it mean except that He also had descended into the lower parts of the earth?

We know from previous observations that Jesus *"descended into"* Hades (Sheol) before He ascended into heaven. He did not enter hell, but Abraham's bosom, the saved side of Hades (Sheol).

Ephesians 4:10—He who descended is Himself also He who ascended far above all the heavens, that He might fill all things.)

This passage provides the chronological order of events associated with Christ's ascension. Before He *"ascended,"* He first *"descended"* (Ephesians 4:10). However, after descending, He *"ascended far above all the heavens"* (Ephesians 4:10) *"to appear in the presence of God for us"* (Hebrews 9:24).

Jesus *"ascended"* for a very special purpose—*"that He might fill all things"* (Ephesians 4:10). The words, *"might fill,"* are in the subjunctive mood in the Greek, confirming the impossibility of determining the time of the action from this verse alone. The full counsel of God's Word provides the needed input:

> *The last enemy that will be abolished is death. For HE HAS PUT ALL THINGS IN SUBJECTION UNDER HIS FEET. But when He says, "All things are put in subjection," it is evident that He is excepted who put all things in subjection to Him. And when all things are subjected to Him, then the Son Himself also will be subjected to the One who subjected all things to Him, so that God may be all in all.* (1Corinthians 15:26-28)

Jesus (Who is *"God"*—Hebrews 1:8) will *"fill all things"* (Ephesians 4:10) when *"the last enemy," "death,"* is *"abolished"* (1Corinthians 15:26). His resurrection and ascension paved the way for this order of events to transpire.

We also learned from Ephesians 1:23b and Ephesians 3:19b (you may need to review those notes) that Jesus fills every New Testament believer. Because He lives in church saints (Galatians 2:20), however, doesn't mean that they are perfected in their behavior prior to physical death. Many of our behavioral imperfections won't be eliminated until our bodies cease functioning, after which we will receive our glorified bodies at the Rapture of the church (1Thessalonians 4:13-18)—an event that occurs at some undisclosed time in the future. Thus, when we return with Christ at His Second Coming (Revelation 19:11-16), inhabiting immortal bodies, we will live in sinless perfection while reigning with Him (Revelation 20:4). But in the meantime, He has endowed certain believers with specific spiritual gifts to help bring us to maturity. Some of these gifted men are listed in Ephesians 4:11.

Ephesians 4:11—And He gave some as apostles, and some as prophets, and some as evangelists, and some as pastors and teachers,

Before examining verse 11, consider that Luke, in Acts 1:1, relates that he recorded in the Gospel of Luke (which deals with Jesus' birth, life, death, and resurrection) what *"Jesus began to do and teach"*:

> *The first account I composed, Theophilus, about all that Jesus*
> <u>*began*</u> *to do and teach,* (Acts 1:1)

"Began" is underlined for emphasis, because Jesus continues His work on earth through His body, the church, who is being equipped for her work through the gifted men of Ephesians 4:11. The gifted men given to the church are *"apostles," "prophets," "evangelists,"* and *"pastors and teachers."* Let's discuss the apostles first.

And He gave some as apostles, 4:11a

Of all the positions of leadership within the body of Christ in Paul's day, no position held more authority than that of *"apostle."* Notice the emphasis on chronology in 1Corinthians 12:28:

> *And God has appointed in the church, first apostles, second*
> *prophets,...* (1Corinthians 12:28)

The Gospel of Mark has this to say regarding the twelve:

> *And He appointed twelve, that they might be with Him, and that He might send them out to preach,* (Mark 3:14)

An apostle was a messenger of God—one sent by *"Jesus Christ, and God the Father"* (Galatians 1:1). The twelve apostles (Paul replacing Judas) laid the doctrinal foundation of the church (Acts 2:42; Ephesians 2:20; 3:5; 2Peter 3:2), having been given the responsibility of imparting the truth taught by Christ. They were the final authority in the early church (1Corinthians 14:37), their ministry confirmed *"by signs and wonders and miracles"* (2Corinthians 12:12). After all, they had *"seen Jesus"* (1Corinthians 9:1).

Do apostles exist today? Those who believe they do cite verses such as Acts 14:14, 1Thessalonians 2:6, and Romans 16:7 to confirm that certain men outside of "the twelve" were referred to as apostles. Even Paul, in 1Thessalonians 2:6 (when linked with 1Thessalonians 1:1), refers to Silas and Timothy as fellow apostles— Paul being one of the original twelve, having replaced Judas.

Individuals who perceive the apostolic office as extinct cite 2Corinthians 8:23 (*"messengers"* can be interpreted *"apostles"*) to support their argument:

> *As for Titus, he is my partner and fellow worker among you; as for our brethren, they are messengers of the churches, a glory to Christ.* (2Corinthians 8:23)

They conclude that the apostles outside of the twelve were *"messengers"* (apostles) *"of the churches"* (2Corinthians 8:23), while the original twelve were *"apostles of Jesus Christ"* (Galatians 1:1; 1Peter 1:1; etc.). Also, no record exists of any apostle being replaced at death outside of Judas (Acts 1:15-26). Neither is the term "apostle" found in the book of Acts after Acts 16:4. Ephesians 2:20 is also cited, where Paul confirms that the *"apostles and prophets"* form the *"foundation"* of the church—a *"foundation"* on which the whole building is *"being built"* (Ephesians 2:21; 1Peter 2:5), believers today *"being"* added to the building, not the foundation. They perceive the foundation as consisting of the twelve apostles, along with the *"prophets"* (Ephesians 2:20), who were instrumental in forming and proclaiming the doctrine of the church—which had begun a short time earlier in Acts 2. Of course, *"the corner stone"* of this foundation is Jesus (Ephesians 2:20).
I personally view the office of "apostle" as primarily pointing to the original twelve. No doubt, other persons throughout the church age have taken the body of truth contained in God's Word to geographical locations that have never heard the gospel. In a secondary sense, these individuals are apostles. Their teaching, of

course, must agree with the doctrine of the original twelve.

and some as prophets, (4:11b)

In the New Testament, the term *"prophets"* (Ephesians 4:11) has two applications: (1) individuals who foretold the future (Acts 11:27-28) (2) individuals who taught God's Word for the purpose of encouraging and strengthening the church (Acts 15:32; 1Corinthians 14:3). A prophet's message was to be disregarded should it contradict the apostles' doctrine (1Corinthians 14:37), for the apostles carried more authority than the prophets (1Corinthians 12:28).

The *"prophets"* addressed in Ephesians 4:11 were spiritually gifted men responsible for equipping and maturing the saints (Ephesians 4:12-13). God used these men to simplify what the apostles expounded doctrinally (Acts 13:1; 15:30-35, 1Corinthians 14:3). They seemed to differ somewhat from men with the gift of prophecy (1Corinthians 12:10). They were designated leaders who were recognized as men of authority, men, who outside of the apostles, had the final say in regard to doctrinal matters within the church.

Does the office of *"prophet"* exist today? Individuals who think not use Ephesians 2:20 to support their position, arguing that the apostles' and prophets' responsibility of establishing the church in truth (along with writing the New Testament canon) fulfilled these offices. Also, in 2Peter 2:1, Peter seems to indicate that the teacher replaced the prophet—the prophet's message coming by direct revelation from God, the teacher's message consistently based on truth gathered from the Scriptures. Unquestionably, the office of "prophet" was mightily used in the formative years of the church.

Individuals who view the office of "prophet" as functioning today normally cite 1Corinthians 12:10 for support:

> *and to another the effecting of miracles, and to another prophecy,*
> *and to another the distinguishing of spirits, to another various*
> *kinds of tongues, and to another the interpretation of tongues.*
> (1Corinthians 12:10)

These persons usually perceive the gifts recorded in Romans 12, 1Corinthians 12, and Ephesians 4 as functioning today. If, indeed, the office of "prophet" remains today, those who serve in this capacity must make certain that their words (and lives) agree with the doctrine recorded in the full counsel of the Scriptures. Many "self-proclaimed" prophets have done significant harm to Christ's body by leading the immature down a path of error and deceit.

and some as evangelists, (4:11c)

"Evangelists" are gifted men who express the plan of salvation with clarity and conviction to the lost. These men function in large group settings as well as one-on-one (as was the case with Philip the evangelist—Acts 8:26-40; 21:8). *"Evangelists"* are not solely responsible for encouraging the lost to accept Christ, for Peter exhorts all church saints to *"make a defense to everyone"* who asks why they believe (1Peter 3:15). Yes, all New Testament believers are called to evangelize, but not all New Testament believers are *"evangelists."*

The church has failed to honor this office as it should, for many "so called" evangelists have forgotten (or never learned) that God's *"kindness"* (not His wrath) *"leads"* the unredeemed *"to repentance"* (Romans 2:4). Don't misunderstand. Hell is a real place, a place of torment for those who die without Christ. But a steady diet of God's wrath is not the remedy for convicting the lost of their need for a Savior. His *"kindness,"* and only His *"kindness,"* will motivate the depraved to repent and believe (Romans 2:4):

> *Or do you think lightly of the riches of His kindness and*
> *forbearance and patience, not knowing that the kindness of God*
> *leads you to repentance?* (Romans 2:4)

and some as pastors and teachers, (4:11d)

The Greek word for *"Pastors"* is *poimenas,* normally translated *"shepherd"* (Matthew 9:36; 25:32; 26:31; John 10:11, etc.). According to 1Peter 5:1-2, pastors (shepherds) are also *"elders"* (*presbuteros*) as well as overseers (*episkopos*) or bishops. This truth is confirmed in Acts 20:17, where Paul sent for *"the elders"* (*presbuteros*) who lived at Ephesus and in verse 28 said to them:

> *"Be on guard for yourselves and for all the flock, among which the*
> *Holy Spirit has made you overseers (episkopos), to shepherd*
> *(poimaino) the church of God which He purchased with His own*
> *blood.* (Acts 20:28)

During the early days of Christendom, such men served one church and were limited to one locale.

As a new believer, I viewed the phrase, *"pastors and teachers"* (Ephesians 4:11), as referencing two separate groups of individuals. I considered *"pastors"* to be one group and *"teachers"* the other. But the Greek combines them into "pastor-teacher." Thus, a pastor-teacher is both pastor and teacher:

> *Let the elders who rule well be considered worthy of double honor,*
> *especially those who work hard at preaching and teaching.*
> (1Timothy 5:17)

Consider as well that the qualifications of an *"overseer"* (bishop) are listed in 1Timothy 3:1-7. Each *"overseer,"* as a teacher (1Timothy 3:2), is to *"take care of the church of God"* (1Timothy 3:5). Also note that *"elders"* (*presbuteros*) and *"overseers"* (*episkopos*) are viewed as one in Titus 1:5-7—with the responsibility of feeding God's Word to the church (Titus 1:9). No church will be properly nurtured unless it is taught the full counsel of the Scriptures by the pastor-teacher.

1Peter 5:1-3 reveals that the pastor-teacher is a servant rather than a dictator:

> *Therefore, I exhort the elders among you, as your fellow elder and*
> *witness of the sufferings of Christ, and a partaker also of the glory*
> *that is to be revealed, shepherd the flock of God among you,*
> *exercising oversight not under compulsion, but voluntarily,*
> *according to the will of God; and not for sordid gain, but with*
> *eagerness; nor yet as lording it over those allotted to your charge,*
> *but proving to be examples to the flock.* (1Peter 5:1-3)

Every pastor-teacher must realize that the flock belongs to God—never himself. Nothing, absolutely nothing, must be tolerated that would prevent Jesus Christ from serving as the ultimate Authority in the church. This truth is confirmed in Acts 15:28, where the elders' decree was validated by the Holy Spirit:

> *"For it seemed good to the Holy Spirit and to us to lay upon you no*
> *greater burden than these essentials*: (Acts 15:28)

Ephesians 4:12—for the equipping of the saints for the work of service, to the building up of the body of Christ;

The Lord gave the gifted men of verse 11 to the church for the *"equipping (katartismos) of the saints for the work of service."* The phrase, *"for the equipping of the saints,"* is interpreted *"for the perfecting of the saints"* in the King James Version. The KJV rendering is somewhat misleading since a saint (his person—his soul and spirit) is made *"perfect"* at the point of salvation/justification (Hebrews 10:14). The gifted men of verse 11 were given to the church, not to make the saint more perfect in his person, but to encourage the saint to pursue holiness in his behavior.

Interestingly, the Greek *katartismos* is from the root word *katartizo,* which is rendered *"mending"* in Matthew 4:21. The disciples were *"mending"* (equipping) *"their nets"* for service—for the purpose of catching fish. This same Greek word is employed in Hebrews 13:21, which addresses the believer's need to be equipped for service:

> *Now the God of peace, who brought up from the dead the great*
> *Shepherd of the sheep through the blood of the eternal covenant,*
> *even Jesus our Lord, equip you in every good thing to do His will,*
> *working in us that which is pleasing in His sight, through Jesus*
> *Christ, to whom be the glory forever and ever. Amen.* (Hebrews
> 13:20-21)

Also consider Paul's statement in 2Corinthians 13:9, *"this we also pray for, that you be made complete"*—the root for *"complete"* (2Corinthians 13:9), *"equipping"* (Ephesians 4:12), and *"mending"* (Matthew 4:21) being the same Greek word.

Equipped *"saints"* are to involve themselves in *"the work of service"* (Ephesians 4:12)—not the gifted men who equip them. This truth is critical, yet a foreign concept to many of God's people. Hoards of believers perceive the evangelist and pastor-teacher as responsible for performing *"the work of service"* (Ephesians 4:12). They view the evangelist as obligated to evangelize the lost, and the pastor-teacher as responsible for meeting the new convert's need—along with a <u>majority</u> of the needs within the church. In fact, the pastor-teacher's job description (in their minds) is similar to: (1) visit the sick (all the sick) of the church (2) answer the phone each time it rings (3) be actively involved with every committee within the church (4) be present at all church functions—all socials included (5) be available every time someone has the slightest need (6) and on top of all of the above, preach two to three times each week. This job description is equivalent to James and John (Matthew 4:21) attempting to catch fish, not with their nets, but with their bare hands. Had this scenario occurred, James and John would have been perceived as less than sane! No wonder a high percentage of pastors live on the brink of exhaustion, burnout, and mental breakdown.

I will never forget a conversation I heard one Sunday morning at church. Those participating were discussing the pastor's responsibilities. One man said, "His most important priority should be to visit the sick." I didn't say a word, but waited to hear additional responses. As I listened, I was almost overwhelmed by the number of people who agreed with the first man's statement. No wonder a crisis exists within the church in America! No wonder she is anemic and forlorn and without proper leadership. A pastor-teacher's main responsibility is to feed the flock of

God (1Timothy 4:6, 11, and 13; 2Timothy 4:2), not hold everyone's hand when the slightest need arises. The members of the church, equipped with the truth of God's Word, are to visit the sick and minister to the needs of the flock. The pastor-teacher is to equip himself with truth and preach (teach) it with conviction—a taxing endeavor indeed (1Timothy 5:17). This order of responsibility doesn't mean that the pastor-teacher never visits the sick or invests time in the lives of the people. It does mean, however, that his main responsibility is to feed God's Word to God's people for the purpose of building them up (Acts 20:32).

The pastor-teacher can't take a congregation to a spiritual depth that he doesn't experience himself. Thus, before God can widen the pastor's ministry, He must first deepen the pastor's message. A pastor's message (in fact, any person's message) is deepened only through a constant intake of truth coupled with prayer:

> *"But we will devote ourselves to prayer, and to the ministry of the word."* (Acts 6:4)

As Oswald Sanders pens it:

> the highest positions are for those who have qualified in secret.[18]

We must be people who protect the pastor-teacher from the encumbrances that prevent him from prayerfully studying and teaching God's Word. Only then will the church function according to design.

Two things happen when the pastor-teacher is allowed to equip God's people. First, the members of the church are pleased to share Christ with the lost. Second, each member builds up Christ's body through his *"special"* spiritual *"gift"* (1Peter 4:10). Paul had these facts in mind when he stated, *"to the building up of the body of Christ"* (Ephesians 4:12).

Ephesians 4:13—until we all attain to the unity of the faith, and of the knowledge of the Son of God, to a mature man, to the measure of the stature which belongs to the fullness of Christ.

until we all attain to the unity of the faith, (4:13a)

As the gifted men of verse 11 function according to design, believers learn to exercise their individual gifts, resulting in *"the building up of the body of Christ"* (Ephesians 4:12). As a church grows spiritually, each believer within that church body can *"attain to the unity of the faith"* (Ephesians 4:13a). *"The faith"* points to the body of truth, or doctrine, outlined in the Word of God. Therefore the phrase, *"unity of the faith,"* refers to the *"unity"* experienced by Christ's bride as she learns (and walks in) the truth of the Scriptures. We can only speculate how the body of Christ would be perceived by the world should such unity exist. My guess is that a majority of lost mankind would stampede the doors of the churches to discover what was inside.

and of the knowledge of the Son of God, (4:13b)

"Knowledge" is from the Greek *epignosis*, pointing to "a full, accurate, precise, and correct knowledge." Paul isn't referencing salvation here, but the knowledge he addresses in Philippians 3:10—a deep, intimate knowledge of the Person of Jesus:

> *that I may know Him, and the power of His resurrection and the*
> *fellowship of His sufferings, being conformed to His death;*
> (Philippians 3:10)

As we learned earlier, Jesus, the Father, and the Spirit have lived in unity from eternity past. This unity exists because the principle of the cross has been applied to all facets of their relationships. Every individual decision has benefited the other two parties. As we know Jesus more intimately and begin to respond as He responds, we too make decisions that benefit others rather than ourselves. Such behavior results in unity, true unity, the unity of the faith which maintains the unity of the Spirit discussed in Ephesians 4:3.

We should never expect to know the Son on an intimate level (Philippians 3:10) until we know the body of doctrine that makes up *"the faith"* (Ephesians 4:13a). In other words, God's Word, illuminated by the Holy Spirit, reveals His Person. To approach God's Word for the purpose of intimately knowing the Son, and in turn the Godhead, is the greatest privilege made available to believers.

to a mature man, to the measure of the stature which belongs to the fullness of Christ. (4:13c)

This passage describes the behavior exemplified by a *"mature man"* of God: He walks in *"the fullness of Christ"* (Ephesians 4:13c). Discovering the meaning of the phrase, *"the fullness of Christ,"* is a joyful journey.

In our study of Ephesians 3:19b, we found that Jesus is *"the fullness of Deity"* (Colossians 1:19; 2:9). We learned as well that He (Jesus) takes up residence in a New Testament believer at the point of salvation/justification (Galatians 2:20; John

1:16). However, only when the New Testament believer allows Him to dwell (feel at home) in his heart (Ephesians 3:17) and knows His love (Ephesians 3:19a) is he *"filled up to all the fullness of God"* (Ephesians 3:19b)—Jesus being *"God"* (Hebrews 1:8). Consequently, a New Testament believer walks in *"the fullness of Christ"* (Ephesians 4:13) when he is emptied of his selfish motives and lives by the life of Another—by Christ's very life. (A person walking in *"fullness"* knows well the principle of the cross.) We can lose perspective and cease walking in "the *fullness of Christ,"* but even in the midst of such times *"the fullness"* can be restored through repentance and confession.

Ephesians 4:14—As a result, we are no longer to be children, tossed here and there by waves, and carried about by every wind of doctrine, by the trickery of men, by craftiness in deceitful scheming;

"As a result" (Ephesians 4:14) of the instruction from the gifted men of Ephesians 4:11-13, the saints *"are no longer to be children"* (Ephesians 4:14). *"Children"* is from the Greek *nepios*, meaning "not speaking, infants." The saints who *"mature"* (Ephesians 4:13) are no longer infants (Ephesians 4:14) incapable of verbalizing and applying the truth. Neither are they *"tossed here and there by waves"* (they are not wishy-washy in their beliefs and are not easily agitated), nor are they *"carried about by every wind of doctrine"* (their minds do not go into a mental whirlwind when confronted with error). They know God's Word well enough to instantaneously detect false doctrine. Neither are they deceived *"by the trickery of men"* (Ephesians 4:14). *"Trickery"* (*kubia*) can also be translated "cube"— pointing to throwing (or playing with) dice. As professional gamblers often load the dice for personal gain, *"trickery"* points to any sort of dishonesty. Hence, just as an infant is easily led astray, our enemy effortlessly tricks immature believers. The enemy must employ a more sophisticated strategy when attacking the mature in Christ.

"Craftiness" (Ephesians 4:14), from the Greek *panourgia,* can be defined as "doing everything, hence, unscrupulous conduct" (also study Luke 20:23, 2Corinthians 11:3, and 2Corinthians 12:16). *"Scheming"* (Ephesians 4:14), from the Greek *methodia*, is rendered *"schemes"* in Ephesians 6:11 and means "to lie in wait, a deliberate planning or system." Thus, the King James Version translates this last phrase of Ephesians 4:14 as: *"whereby they lie in wait to deceive."* Rest assured that Satan delights in an immature believer mistaking error for truth. The Scriptures are filled with warnings against being led astray—the following verses only a partial listing: Acts 20:30-31; Romans 16:17-18; 2Corinthians 11:3-4, 14; Galatians 1:6-7; Colossians 2:8; 1Timothy 1:3; 2Timothy 3:6-9; Hebrews 13:9; 2Peter 2:1-3; 3:17; 1John 2:26.

Ephesians 4:15—but speaking the truth in love, we are to grow up in all aspects into Him, who is the head, even Christ,

The opposite of remaining immature and walking in error (Ephesians 4:14) is to *"grow up"* through listening to *"truth"* spoken *"in love"* (Ephesians 4:15). *"Speaking"* (*aletheuo*) can be defined as: "to speak or maintain the truth, to act truly or sincerely." Regardless of how a New Testament saint is gifted (pastor-teacher, service, exhortation, mercy—Ephesians 4:11; Romans 12:7-8), he should function in his gifting by speaking (or maintaining) *"the truth in love"* (Ephesians 4:15)—a response requiring considerable maturity. No environment is more conducive to spiritual growth than one inundated with truth spoken with compassion and sensitivity. The quote, "Truth without love is brutality," is absolutely correct. Speak truth without love and the listener fails to *"grow up in all aspects unto Him"* (Ephesians 4:15)—even had he previously desired to mature in the faith. Ill-advised instruction of this sort also disillusions the lost who might otherwise consider Christ. We must not forget that *"the kindness of God leads...to repentance"* (Romans 2:4)—never His wrath.

"Speaking the truth in love" (Ephesians 4:15) doesn't mean that we refrain from correcting or rebuking the disobedient. Scripture (truth) was given *"for teaching, for reproof, for correction, for training in righteousness"* (2Timothy 3:16). Because truth brings conviction, it pricks the listener's heart regardless of how lovingly it is expressed. Hence, to speak the truth in love is not to be equated with speaking only what pacifies the listener's ear. A loving rebuke is many times used to great advantage.

When the corporate body of Christ has the maturity to speak (and maintain) the *"truth in love,"* the individual members of the body *"grow up in all aspects into Him, who is the head, even Christ"* (Ephesians 4:15). *"Into Him"* can also be translated *"unto Him."* Because Jesus causes spiritual growth in all church saints (Ephesians 4:15-16), along with the Father and Spirit (Colossians 2:18-19; 2Corinthians 3:18), we must look to Him for grace and power as we choose His approach to life. How did He live while on earth? He lived by His Father's life (John 6:57; 14:10). We must grow past attempting to imitate Jesus and begin to live by His indwelling presence. Only then will we *"grow up in all aspects into Him, who is head, even Christ"* (Ephesians 4:15). The byproduct is a life bearing the unmistakable *"fragrance of Christ"* (2Corinthians 2:14-16), a life of maturity.

Ephesians 4:16—from whom the whole body, being fitted and held together by that which every joint supplies, according to the proper working of each individual part, causes the growth of the body for the building up of itself in

love.

Ephesians 4:16 also deals with spiritual growth and the Lord's use of New Testament believers to bring about this growth. My prayer is that we might understand the depths of this passage!

from whom the whole body, (4:16a)

Because Christ is the subject matter of the latter portion of verse 15, *"from whom"* (Ephesians 4:16) refers to Christ. As was determined earlier, Jesus generates spiritual growth within New Testament believers—as do the Father and Spirit. As each member of Christ's body (the church) begins to live by the life of *"the head"* (Ephesians 4:15), the supernatural becomes the norm. In fact, *"the whole body"* (Ephesians 4:16a) matures due to Christ's transforming power dwelling in each believer!

being fitted and held together by that which every joint supplies, (4:16b)

We have already seen that the spiritual growth within New Testament believers has its origin in the Godhead (Father, Son, and Spirit), Jesus being the head of the body. But Jesus uses His body as a means to bring about this growth, the joints playing a vital role in the process (*"being fitted and held together by that which every joint supplies"*—Ephesians 4:16b). As is the case with our physical bodies, the hand and the lower arm are connected by a joint. The hand is unlike the lower arm but needs a properly functioning lower arm to reach its potential. Similarly, the lower arm needs a properly functioning hand to reach its potential. But neither the hand nor the lower arm could reach its full potential if not for the joint that connects the hand and the arm—the joint being a point of contrast. Consequently, the body of Christ, just as the human body, consists of many body parts (1Corinthians 12:12-27) connected by *"joints"* (Ephesians 4:16; Colossians 2:19) and *"ligaments"* (Colossians 2:19). For the entire body to function according to design, each individual body part must reach its full potential.

"Being fitted" and *"held together"* are present passive participles, the present tense confirming that this process is occurring even now. The passive voice verifies that the spiritual growth within Christ's body, both in its individual members as well as the body as a whole, results from Christ's power (the passive voice indicating that the subject is being acted upon by an outside source). Jesus holds His body together *"by that which every joint supplies"* (Ephesians 4:16b). As with our physical bodies, the joints are points of contrast. Thus, in the body of Christ, the joint allows two believers, each possessing a unique spiritual gift, to connect. Therefore, the joint serves as a conduit through which the benefits of the individual

spiritual gifts within Christ's body pass from one believer to the other for the purpose of bringing the entire body to maturity.

according to the proper working of each individual part (4:16c)

Optimal spiritual growth occurs within the church when each member is properly exercising his unique spiritual gift. Consequently, we must press on to maturity so the Lord might use us to bring about optimal spiritual growth within other believers. Such growth can only transpire by our applying "the principle of the cross"—positively responding to others for their benefit rather than our own.

causes the growth of the body for the building up of itself in love. (4:16d)

"Love" (Ephesians 4:16d), the first *"fruit of the Spirit"* mentioned in Galatians 5:22, makes faith work in the life of a believer (Galatians 5:6). If Christ's body is to grow and be built up, *"love"* will play a major role in the process.

For the spiritual gifts to properly function within Christ's body, meaningful and intimate relationships must be developed among its members. But gifted individuals possess dissimilar personalities, sometimes generating conflict. So in walks *"love"*! *"Love"* allows the believer to enter into positive relationships for what others receive. Wasn't this the principle demonstrated at Calvary? Should the body of Christ adopt this mindset as a lifestyle, believers would be strong, mature, grown up, and built up in love. All the big smiles and unhappy eyes would be transformed into big smiles and happy eyes—and maybe someone would want what we have in Christ. What motivation to press on to maturity, waving good-by once and for all to self-centeredness, mediocrity, and compromise!

Ephesians 4:17—So this I say therefore, and affirm together with the Lord, that you walk no longer just as the Gentiles also walk, in the futility of their mind,

So this I say therefore, and affirm together with the Lord, (4:17a)

"So this I say" refers to statements which follow. *"Therefore"* points back to Paul's encouragement to *"walk in a manner worthy of the calling"* (Ephesians 4:1). Clearly, the Lord was in agreement with Paul's teaching—*"and affirm together with the Lord"* (Ephesians 4:17)—because *"all Scripture is inspired by God"* (2Timothy 3:16).

that you walk no longer just as the Gentiles also walk, (4:17b)

Paul, having begun the practical section of this epistle with Ephesians 4:1, again encourages his readers to *"walk"* in a certain manner. He exhorts them to *"walk no longer just as the Gentiles also walk"* (Ephesians 4:17b). *"Walk"* means "to maintain a certain walk of life and conduct." Scripture uses *"Gentiles"* in two different ways: (1) nations or peoples as distinguished from the Jews (Romans 9:24) (2) heathen, ungodly, unregenerate, pagan persons (1Thessalonians 4:5). Paul seems to employ the second application in Ephesians 4:17b.

To comprehend the significance of Paul's words (*"that you walk no longer just as the Gentiles also walk"*—Ephesians 4:17b), we must understand the spiritual climate inside the city of Ephesus. Ephesus was one of the leading Gentile cities within the Roman Empire and the commercial center of Asia Minor. It housed the famous temple of Diana (Roman name) or Artemis (Greek name), one of the seven wonders of the ancient world (Acts 19:35). Because Diana was a sex goddess, this temple was the scene of unbridled wickedness, with sexual perversion leading the way. Idols of Diana, made of silver and other costly materials, were commonplace in Ephesus and a tremendous boost to the city's economy (Acts 19:23-27).

Due to the wickedness that encircled the church at Ephesus, Paul wrote, *"that you walk no longer just as the Gentiles also walk"* (Ephesians 4:17b). The believers at Ephesus were to separate themselves from the sin that permeated their surroundings and *"walk in a manner worthy of the calling"* (Ephesians 4:1). So should we! Peter's words in 1Peter 4:1-5 serve as a wonderful reminder when tempted to adopt the passions of the unredeemed.

in the futility of their mind, (4:17c)

"Futility" is from a Greek word which can also be interpreted "vanity, folly, or emptiness." *"Mind"* can mean "frame of mind." *"Futility,"* vanity, folly, and emptiness characterize the unredeemed. Their self-centered and self-absorbing lifestyles generate an environment that breeds discontentment, disappointment, resentment, and despair. Jesus, the Source of *"truth"* (John 14:6; Ephesians 4:21), taught that life is found when lived for the good of others (Matthew 10:39). No wonder the unredeemed world searches passionately, yet unsuccessfully, for a reason to live. Even the great King Solomon, after gaining the world's wealth, notoriety, wisdom, and power, classified the entirety of it all as *"futility and striving after wind"* (Ecclesiastes 1:12-2:26).

Ephesians 4:18—being darkened in their understanding, excluded from the life of God, because of the ignorance that is in them, because of the hardness of their heart;

being darkened in their understanding, (4:18a)

"Darkened" is a perfect passive participle that can be rendered *"having been darkened"*—the passive participle confirming that a source (the powers of darkness controlled by Satan himself) acted upon these individuals, causing them to become more severely *"darkened."* This intensified darkness increases, proving that the depraved are not born as bad as they can be—not born spiritual corpses. Corpses don't respond to anything, even error. That darkness can intensify in the depraved heart proves that at least a smidgen of light exists as they progress in sin. This small amount of light is sufficient for them to recognize their need for a Savior, repent, exercise faith, and be saved.

"Understanding" points to "the mind, intellect, feelings, and affections." Thus, sin darkens the *"understanding"* of the lost—again proving that the depraved need not be classified as spiritual corpses. So long as the depraved choose blatant rebellion over truth, God gives them up to their destructive desires (Romans 1:21-32)—all the while desiring that none perish (2Peter 3:9), but that all mankind be saved (1Timothy 2:4).

excluded from the life of God, because of the ignorance that is in them, because of the hardness of their heart (4:18b)

"Excluded," a perfect passive participle, can also be interpreted "to be alienated from, to be a stranger to." As the depraved (lost) walk *"in the futility of their mind"* (Ephesians 4:17c) and are progressively *"darkened in"* their *"understanding"* (Ephesians 4:18a), they become alienated from, and a total stranger to, *"the life of God"* (Ephesians 4:18b). This condition exists *"because of the ignorance that is in them"* (Ephesians 4:18b), an *"ignorance,"* not of worldly matters, but of the things of God (Acts 3:17; 17:30; 1Peter 1:14; 2:15)—an *"ignorance"* that remains due to their rejection of *"the truth"* (Romans 1:25) which they are capable of believing, even though depraved. The reason unbelievers walk *"in the futility of their mind"* (Ephesians 4:17c), are *"darkened in"* their *"understanding"* (Ephesians 4:18a), are *"excluded from the life of God"* (Ephesians 4:18b), and possess *"the ignorance that is in them"* (Ephesians 4:18b) is *"the hardness of their heart"* (Ephesians 4:18b). The root cause of this *"hardness of...heart"* (Ephesians 4:18b) is the sin nature (Adamic nature) they inherited from Adam (Ephesians 2:3). Due to this rebellious nature, the unbeliever basks in sin—yet can accept Christ in his depraved state whenever he chooses. If he continues in blatant disobedience and refuses to repent, sin progressively blinds him to desire the most repugnant immoralities imaginable. God gives him over to such sins (Romans 1:18-32), all along desiring that none perish (2Peter 3:9)—validating that He loves man enough to allow man to live void of His presence

should man desire. This enhanced blindness within the depraved confirms that they are not born spiritual corpses, for a progressive blindness validates a previous presence of sight—some sight, at least, and enough to repent and believe.

The sin nature (Adamic nature) is eradicated (during the church age) when a person receives Jesus (Romans 6:6; Galatians 2:20; 2Corinthians 5:17) after exercising repentance and faith while depraved. You may want to refer to the notes associated with Ephesians 2:3 for more input concerning the origin of this nature.

Ephesians 4:19—and they, having become callous, have given themselves over to sensuality for the practice of every kind of impurity with greediness.

Unbelievers (the depraved) pay an exorbitant price for their disobedience. They are blinded by Satan (2Corinthians 4:4) and eventually *"become callous"* (Ephesians 4:19) to the things of God. (Why would Satan be required to blind the depraved to the truth should they be born spiritual corpses? He wouldn't, negating the Reformed view of depravity—that the depraved cannot repent and believe due to an inability to understand truth. Our *God's Heart* series addresses this subject in great depth.)

"Callous" (Ephesians 4:19) can be interpreted "to become insensible" or "to cease to care." When a person ceases caring about God and others, he eventually stops caring about himself and how he is perceived by mankind in general. In this state, he openly commits sins that he once tried to conceal.

Desensitized individuals wallow in *"sensuality"* (Ephesians 4:19), a life surrendered to an unrestrained self. They *"practice...every kind of impurity with greediness"* (Ephesians 4:19) because habitual sin yields a greedy lifestyle. They elevate self for the sake of personal gain, a problem birthed in the Garden (Genesis 3).

Ephesians 4:20—But you did not learn Christ in this way,

Because the New Testament believer becomes a new creation at the point of salvation/justification (2Corinthians 5:17), his "want to" undergoes a radical transformation. In other words, if you took a hog (pig), removed its nature and replaced it with the nature of a cat, the resulting animal would use a litter pan. In fact, should it fall in a mud hole it would lick itself clean! Why? A cat now lives in the body that once housed a hog, even though the body's appearance remains that of a hog. (This same illustration is covered in greater depth in our *Romans 1-8* study.) Considering that Paul has just addressed the sinful routine of unbelievers (Ephesians 4:17-19), he reminds his readers of the behavioral transformation that accompanies new birth (Ephesians 4:20). Christ's followers exchange their old way of living for a lifestyle that detests sin (Romans 6:1-2). Hence, individuals who profess to know Jesus, yet enjoy basking in blatant, habitual sin, need to get on their knees, repent, and submit to Christ (James 4:4; 1John 2:15).

Due to *"learn"* being in the aorist tense, most scholars view Paul as referencing salvation while writing, *"But you did not learn Christ in this way"* (Ephesians 4:20). Whatever the case, what we *"learn"* regarding Jesus, either at salvation or subsequently, will confirm that believers are to be separate from the world (Luke 6:26; 2Corinthians 2:14-15; 1John 2:15-16)—Paul's point in Ephesians 4:20.

Ephesians 4:21—if indeed you have heard Him and have been taught in Him, just as truth is in Jesus,

New Testament believers are taught *"in Jesus"* because they live in Jesus (1Corinthians 12:13; 2Corinthians 5:17; Ephesians 2:6). No wonder Paul wrote, *"if indeed you have heard Him and have been taught in Him"* (Ephesians 4:21). What Paul's readers had *"heard"* from Jesus and had been *"taught in Him"* was correct because *"truth is in Jesus"* (Ephesians 4:21; John 14:6) alone. Believers today are *"taught"* in Jesus as well.

Ephesians 4:22—that, in reference to your former manner of life, you lay aside the old self, which is being corrupted in accordance with the lusts of deceit,

that, in reference to your former manner of life, (4:22a)

When a person is taught truth in Jesus (Ephesians 4:21) relating to a lifestyle of righteousness and holiness, he normally views his *"former manner of life"* (Ephesians 4:22) as *"futile"* (1Peter 1:18)—something of which to be *"ashamed"* (Romans 6:21). Yet, our mistakes as unbelievers can be included in our testimonies for the good of others, for even Paul mentioned his *"former manner of life"* in Galatians 1:13-14. He also spoke of his pre-Christ days in Acts 22:3-5 and Acts 26:4-14 to better relate to his audience. We must never use our past mistakes, however, as an opportunity to glorify the flesh.

you lay aside the old self, which is being corrupted in accordance with the lusts of deceit, (4:22b)

For proper understanding of this passage, we must realize that the *"old self"* is synonymous with the sin nature, Adamic nature, old man, or dead spirit. The *"old self"* was inherited from Adam due to our genes having been in his gene pool when he sinned.

If we fail to exercise caution we might perceive Ephesians 4:22b as teaching that the old self is still alive in the New Testament believer—that the saint is to *"lay aside the old self"* on a daily basis. This error stems from a misunderstanding of the aorist infinitive *"lay aside"* (Greek infinitives are sometimes difficult to translate). However, should Ephesians 4:22b teach that the *"old self"* remains alive (but wounded) after spiritual regeneration/salvation (as is communicated in many Christian circles), it contradicts Romans 6:6 and Colossians 3:9:

> *knowing this, that our old self was crucified with Him, that our*
> *body of sin might be done away with, that we should no longer be*
> *slaves to sin;* (Romans 6:6)

> *Do not lie to one another, since you laid aside the old self with its*
> *evil practices,* (Colossians 3:9)

These passages clearly teach that the *"old self"* has been crucified and eradicated in all church saints. As I sought to reconcile this truth with Paul's words of Ephesians 4:22b, I discovered that John Murray believed that both the grammar allowed and the exegesis demanded that the infinitive *"lay aside"* is an infinitive of result. He went on to say that the "past tense" is indicated here. Combining verses 21 and 22, his final translation read:

> You were taught in Christ with regard to the fact that your old man
> was laid aside. (Ephesians 4:21-22)[19]

Thus, Ephesians 4:22, Romans 6:6, and Colossians 3:9 are in agreement, confirming that our old self was eradicated at the point of salvation/justification. This means that our enemy is not the old self (sin nature), but something else. We will next address the "something else."

One fact is clear: A battle rages inside every New Testament saint. But who are the participants in the battle? It can't be the old self warring against the new self (2Corinthians 5:17), because the *"old self"* has been eradicated (Ephesians 4:22; Romans 6:6; Colossians 3:9). Romans 7:23 provides the answer, placing the battle between the new self and the power of sin—the power that lives in the <u>body</u> of every believer:

> *but I see a different law in the members of my body, waging war*
> *against the law of my mind, and making me a prisoner of the law of*
> *sin which is in my members.* (Romans 7:23)

Paul, describing the battle that raged within him as a believer, reveals that the new man (new self) sins when the New Testament believer sins—the New Testament believer being the new man. This new man is *"holy"* (Ephesians 1:4) and *"perfect"* (Hebrews 10:14) in his person (soul and spirit) but needs his behavior to increasingly agree with who God made him into at the point of salvation/justification. Our *Romans 1-8* course provides a more detailed explanation of this subject matter.

Paul makes an intriguing statement regarding the old self in the last phrase of verse 22. He writes, *"which is being corrupted in accordance with the lusts of deceit"* (Ephesians 4:22). Because *"being corrupted"* is a present passive participle, Paul proves that the old self is progressively *"corrupted"* as it controls the unbeliever. No wonder we witness an exacerbated depravity within the society of our day. Yet, the depraved aren't void of all moral restraint, for the number of ethical, upstanding humanitarians proves otherwise. Nevertheless Paul, in Romans 2:1-16, confirms their condemned state.

The *"old self"* becomes increasingly corrupt through *"the lusts of deceit"* (Ephesians 4:22). *"Lusts"* points to "a craving, a passionate desire, good or evil, depending upon the context." The context here is evil. Therefore, the old self becomes progressively corrupt due to the evil cravings of *"deceit,"* *"deceit"* meaning "deception." Satan, the master of deception who possesses no truth (2John 1:7; John 8:44), is the source behind this progressive corruption.

Paul proves once again that the depraved are not born spiritual corpses. How could they be when they are progressively corrupted through an increased involvement with sin?

Ephesians 4:23—and that you be renewed in the spirit of your mind,

Paul employs *"be renewed"*—a present passive infinitive that can be interpreted *"and being renewed."* Thus, *"the spirit of your mind"* is being *"renewed"* by God if you are pursuing Christ. Romans 12:2, Colossians 3:10, and Titus 3:5 also relate to this teaching.

The *"spirit of"* the *"mind"* (Ephesians 4:23) encourages believers to think along lines compatible with truth. It gives them a God-centered purpose, which results from being a new creation. Unbelievers (the depraved) cannot be renewed in this fashion until they repent and believe on Jesus. Note: Just as the *"old self"* (Ephesians 4:22; Romans 6:6) includes the mind of an unbeliever, *"the new self"* (Ephesians 4:24), which is the *"new"* creation (2Corinthians 5:17), includes the mind of the New Testament believer.

Ephesians 4:24—and put on the new self, which in the likeness of God has been created in righteousness and holiness of the truth.

"Put on" (Ephesians 4:24) is an aorist infinitive in the Greek. As we discovered in Ephesians 4:22 (where *"lay aside"* is also an aorist infinitive), the past tense is indicated. Thus, Paul isn't exhorting his readers to put on the *"new self."* He is encouraging them to realize that they are already the *"new self"* (new man)— 2Corinthians 5:17; Colossians 3:10. Because the New Testament believer is the *"new self"* (new man, new creation), he is *"holy"* (Ephesians 1:4), *"justified"* (Romans 5:1), *"forgiven"* (Ephesians 4:32; Colossians 2:13), *"complete"* (Colossians 2:10), *"the righteousness of God"* (2Corinthians 5:21), *"sanctified"* (Hebrews 10:10; 10:14), *"glorified"* (Romans 8:30), and a saint (1Corinthians 1:2) the moment he is made new—after repenting and exercising faith while depraved. Peter even proclaims that church saints are *"partakers of the divine nature"* (2Peter 1:4). Hence, Paul writes regarding the *"new self"* (new man): *"which in the likeness of God has been created in righteousness and holiness of truth"* (Ephesians 4:25). God makes no mistakes nor cuts corners when creating the new self (new man). Consequently, we are not lowly sinners saved by grace. We are saints who sometimes sin. We are indeed special due to God having eradicated the old man (Adamic nature, sinful nature, old self, dead spirit) at the point of salvation/justification. Should the old man remain alive, we would walk in spiritual adultery based on Romans 7:1-4:

> *Or do you not know, brethren (for I am speaking to those who know the law), that the law has jurisdiction over a person as long as he lives? For the married woman is bound by law to her husband while he is living; but if her husband dies, she is released from the law concerning the husband. So then if, while her husband is living, she is joined to another man, she shall be called an adulteress; but if her husband dies, she is free from the law, so that she is not an adulteress, though she is joined to another man. Therefore, my brethren, you also were made to die to the Law through the body of Christ, that you might be joined to another, to Him who was raised from the dead, that we might bear fruit for God.* (Romans 7:1-4)

For additional input relating to the eradication of the old man, review the notes associated with Ephesians 2:16a.

Ephesians 4:25—Therefore, laying aside falsehood, speak truth, each one of you, with his neighbor, for we are members of one another.

Paul begins this verse with *"Therefore"* to connect his prior teachings to the subject matter of verses 25-32. He has previously taught that God makes every New Testament believer into a holy and blameless saint (Ephesians 1-3); that He has gifted the members of the body of Christ so the body might grow in unity and maturity (Ephesians 4:1-16); that every member of Christ's body is no longer the old self, nor a combination of the old self and new self, but the new self only (Ephesians 4:17-24). Because of what God has done for the members of Christ's body, they, by His grace, can live in a manner that begins to match who God made them into at the point of salvation/justification. Therefore, Paul addresses the saints' behavior in Ephesians 4:25-32.

The words *"laying aside"* (Ephesians 4:25) are an aorist participle, meaning that Paul is actually communicating, "having laid aside once and for all." Hence, *"falsehood"* (Ephesians 4:25), or as some versions render it, *"lying,"* has been laid aside as a lifestyle for the saint of God. Because the old self naturally committed sin, the old self (who we were before we met Jesus) lived a lifestyle of habitual *"falsehood"* (Ephesians 4:25). But our old self has been eradicated (Ephesians 4:22; Romans 6:6; 7:4; Colossians 3:9) and replaced with the new self (Ephesians 4:24; Colossians 3:10; 2Corinthians 5:17; Galatians 2:20), freeing us to live a lifestyle of righteousness and holiness. We sin at times, but sin is an unnatural act. In fact, for a child of God to continue a lifestyle of habitual sin is impossible (1John 3:6-8). Thus, when Paul writes, *"laying aside falsehood,"* which can be interpreted *"having put off once and for all falsehood"* (*Wuest Commentary*),[20] he is communicating that a lifestyle of falsehood (habitual falsehood) is no longer part of the believer's experience.

"Falsehood" can go undetected if we fail to remain alert; for blatant lying and slightly exaggerating the truth are included in this same category. The believer is no longer bound to such behavior:

> *Do not lie to one another, since you laid aside the old self with its*
> *evil practices, and have put on the new self who is being renewed*
> *to a true knowledge according to the image of the One who created*
> *him* (Colossians 3:9-10)

Instead of speaking falsehood, we are to *"speak truth, each one of you, with his neighbor, for we are members of one another"* (Ephesians 4:25). Christ's body, the church, functions most efficiently when each member communicates *"truth"* with its adjacent members according to God's blueprint. As a matter of illustration, just imagine the resulting chaos should the brain generate a constant stream of lies (the brain being the computer that takes messages from our physical senses and transmits them to the mind). The eye could be focusing on a butterfly yet the mind think "viper" as a result of the brain's miscommunication. This scenario would generate bedlam within the entire body! Consequently, only when believers *"speak truth"* to their *"neighbor"* (Ephesians 4:25—to fellow believers) does the body function according to design. Truth is properly communicated through allowing *"the Spirit of truth"* (John 14:17; 15:26; 16:13) to teach each member of Christ's body the Word of *"truth"* (John 17:17) which, in turn, reveals the Source of *"truth,"* Jesus Christ (John 14:6). Hence, the supernatural seeks environments where truth is exchanged among saints. Spiritual growth transpires, resulting in the corporate body epitomizing the truth through daily living. Lying stymies this growth and destroys the common life in the body (Romans 12:5; 1Corinthians 12:14-27).

To communicate publicly what has been entrusted to us in private conversation is betrayal. However, to purposely withhold information in an attempt to mislead or deceive is falsehood (lying). Also, to *"speak truth"* in the form of a loving rebuke (when needed) is healthy for everyone involved.

Ephesians 4:26—Be angry, and yet do not sin; do not let the sun go down on your anger,

Be angry, and yet do not sin; (4:26a)

"Angry" is from the Greek *orge.* The anger that Paul addresses here is evidently anger directed toward what opposes God. Jesus displayed such anger while cleansing the temple (John 2:13-17), yet remained sinless.

do not let the sun go down on your anger, (4:26b)

"Anger" in this case is *parorgismos* and differs from *orge* in Ephesians 4:26a. Debate exists as to the righteousness or unrighteousness of this response. One thing is certain. Once displayed it must be laid aside (*"do not let the sun go down on your anger"*—Ephesians 4:26).

Ephesians 4:27—and do not give the devil an opportunity.

When *"anger"* (Ephesians 4:26b) of this sort remains overnight, bitterness results—giving *"the devil an opportunity"* (Ephesians 4:27). We understand well that Satan needs no *"advantage"* (2Corinthians 2:10-11). When he tempts us to pay back evil for evil, passages such as Proverbs 20:22, 24:29, and Romans 12:17-21 must come to mind.

Ephesians 4:28—Let him who steals steal no longer; but rather let him labor, performing with his own hands what is good, in order that he may have something to share with him who has need.

"Steal" is from the Greek *klepto*, from which we get "kleptomaniac." Yes, a holy and blameless saint can be deceived into taking what is not rightfully his—but it does not make him a thief. A saint who has sinned, yes—never a thief! He will be chastened of God (Hebrews 12:5-10), unlike unbelievers who go their merry way indulging in a lifestyle of thievery (1Corinthians 6:9-12). Some of the saints at Ephesus were evidently stealing from others (Ephesians 4:28), behavior unacceptable before God. (We must take nothing that is not rightfully ours—even when filing our income tax, when we are undercharged for purchased items, when punching a time clock, etc.)

Believers are to give up stealing (a sin which many times indicates laziness and lack of initiative) and go to work. We must understand what it means to *"labor"* (Ephesians 4:28). (Read Proverbs 6:9, 13:4, 15:19, 20:4, 21:25, and 24:30-34 to discover the consequences reaped by those lacking initiative.) Paul taught that if you don't work you don't eat (2Thessalonians 3:10), for such lackluster behavior results from a lack of discipline (2Thessalonians 3:11). In fact, he considered those who failed to provide for their families as having *"denied the faith, and...worse than an unbeliever"* (1Timothy 5:8). Paul could teach in this manner because he lived what he taught (Acts 20:34).

Paul, in using the phrase, *"performing with his own hands"* (Ephesians 4:28), emphasizes the importance of working for our possessions. Individuals who are given everything normally fail to appreciate the benefit of labor, many times leading an undisciplined and fruitless existence. The believer is to labor in *"what is good"* (Ephesians 4:28). Consequently, employment that requires us to compromise God's Word must be jettisoned if possible.

We are to *"labor"* for two reasons: (1) to provide for our families; (2) to have something *"to share with him who has need"* (Ephesians 4:28). We should, therefore, be *"cheerful"* givers (2Corinthians 9:7), knowing that *"it is more blessed to give than to receive"* (Acts 20:35). In fact, we need to follow the pattern of those saints described in 2Corinthians 8:1-5. Only through yielding to Christ can a lifetime of stealing be exchanged for a lifestyle of sharing with those in need (Proverbs 29:7).

Ephesians 4:29—Let no unwholesome word proceed from your mouth, but only such a word as is good for edification according to the need of the moment, that it may give grace to those who hear.

"Unwholesome" means "corrupt, depraved, vicious, foul, rotten, or impure." Words that fit these categories are not to *"proceed from your mouth"* (Ephesians 4:29), for they are normally spoken to harm others. We are to refrain from gossip and all forms of evil speaking, for David writes:

> *Who is the man who desires life, and loves length of days that he may see good? Keep your tongue from evil, and your lips from speaking deceit.* (Psalm 34:12-13)

What, then, is to come forth from the believer's mouth? *"Only such a word as is good for edification according to the need of the moment"* (Ephesians 4:29). *"Edification"* means "to build up, improve, or encourage." Consequently, if what we say doesn't build up, improve, or encourage, it should be left unsaid (1Thessalonians 5:11). The wise speak proper words at proper times, meaning that their words meet *"the need of the moment"* (Ephesians 4:29)—bringing delight and *"healing"* to the listener (Proverbs 12:18; 15:23; 25:11). Therefore, to *"associate with a gossip"* is unwise (Proverbs 20:19). Because the tongue can be *"a restless evil and full of deadly poison"* (James 3:6-8), Paul wrote:

> *But now you also, put them all aside: anger, wrath, malice, slander, and abusive speech from your mouth.* (Colossians 3:8)

Our words of edification can *"give grace to those who hear"* (Ephesians 4:29), but raw truth, spoken void of love and compassion, can destroy. Hence, Paul wrote:

> *Let your speech always be with grace, seasoned, as it were, with salt, so that you may know how you should respond to each person.* (Colossians 4:6)

Salt preserves in that it extends the shelf life of certain foods. In the same way, our words can help retard the growth rate of the moral decay around us. They can also *"give grace to those who hear"* (Ephesians 4:29). Jesus' words were *"gracious"* (Luke 4:22; Isaiah 50:4), so why should our words be anything less (Ephesians 4:29)?

Ephesians 4:30—And do not grieve the Holy Spirit of God, by whom you were sealed for the day of redemption.

The Holy Spirit is not an "it" but a *"He"* (John 14:16-17; 16:13)—a real Person. In fact, He is so much a Person that He can be blasphemed (Matthew 12:32; Mark 3:29), lied to (Acts 5:3), tested (Acts 5:9), resisted (Acts 7:51), grieved (Ephesians 4:30), quenched (1Thessalonians 5:19), and insulted (Hebrews 10:29). Scripture also communicates that the Holy Spirit has many responsibilities. He baptizes (Acts 1:5; 1Corinthians 12:13), speaks (Mark 13:11; Acts 10:19; 11:12; 13:2; 21:11; 1Timothy 4:1; Hebrews 3:7; Revelation 2:7, 11, 17, 29; 3:6, 13, 22; 14:13; 22:17), fills (Luke 1:15, 41, 67; Acts 2:4; Ephesians 5:18), teaches (Luke 12:12; 1Corinthians 2:13; Hebrews 9:8; 1John 5:7), gives life (John 6:63; 2Corinthians 3:6), guides (John 16:13), commissions (Acts 13:4; 20:28), reasons (Acts 15:28), restricts (Acts 16:6), testifies (Acts 20:23), circumcises (Romans 2:29), leads (Romans 8:14; Galatians 5:18), intercedes (Romans 8:26), possesses intellect (Romans 8:27), searches (1Corinthians 2:10), justifies (1Corinthians 6:11), distributes spiritual gifts (1Corinthians 12:11), seals (Ephesians 1:13), reveals (Ephesians 3:5), strengthens (Ephesians 3:16), vindicates (1Timothy 3:16), empowers (1Peter 1:12; 2Peter 1:21), and still finds time to be our wonderful *"Helper"* (John 14:26). He is also the *"Holy Spirit of God"* (Ephesians 4:30), confirming His status as one of the three Persons of the Trinity (the Trinity consisting of God the Father, God the Son, and God the Holy Spirit).

We learned earlier, while studying the principle of the cross, that each of the three Persons of the Trinity never makes a decision to benefit Himself. Each always chooses what will benefit the other two Persons, as well as what will benefit others. The Scriptures just studied bear this out, for the Holy Spirit never serves Himself. No wonder *"love, joy, peace, patience, kindness, goodness, faithfulness, gentleness,"* and *"self-control"* are evident in those He leads (Galatians 5:22-23).

We *"were sealed for the day of redemption"* (Ephesians 4:30)—the day when our bodies will be glorified (resurrected). This truth agrees with Ephesians 1:13-14, where we discovered that the Holy Spirit sealed us in Christ and serves as God's irrevocable pledge (down payment and guarantee) that more is to come—the resurrection of the body (1Corinthians 15:42-55). This seal confirms that the transaction has been completed, that God owns us, that we have received His stamp of approval, and that we are secure in Him. What Paul is saying in Ephesians 4:30

is: "If the Holy Spirit did this much for you, how can you possibly act in such a way as to grieve Him?"

Ephesians 4:31—Let all bitterness and wrath and anger and clamor and slander be put away from you, along with all malice.

"Bitterness," from the Greek *pikria*, is used in Acts 8:23, Romans 3:14, and Hebrews 12:15. It can be defined as "bitterness of spirit or language, harshness." Paul desired that his readers rid themselves of this sin because of its devastating impact. No one enjoys being around those who are "down in the mouth" and "sour on the world."

"Wrath" (*thumos*) means "indignation, rage, anger, or passion." *"Anger"* (*orge*), according to *Vine's Expository Dictionary*, "is less sudden in its rise than *thumos*, but more lasting in nature. *Thumos* indicates a more agitated condition of the feelings, an outburst of wrath from inward indignation, while *orge* suggests a more settled or abiding condition of mind, frequently with a view of taking revenge."[21]

"Clamor" (*krauge*) "denotes an outcry, and signifies the tumult of controversy" (*Vine's Expository Dictionary*).[22] It points to public outbursts of strife that are characterized by loss of control. *"Slander"* (*blasphemia*) is interpreted "abusive language" in 1Timothy 6:4 and *"railing"* in Jude 1:9, pointing to speech that brings injury to others by speaking evil of others. *"Malice"* (*kakia*) is "wickedness," or as it is interpreted in Romans 1:29, 1Corinthians 14:20, and 1Peter 2:16, *"evil."* For the church to function according to design, the believer must *"put away"* (Ephesians 4:31) these behaviors.

Ephesians 4:32—And be kind to one another, tender-hearted, forgiving each other, just as God in Christ also has forgiven you.

We, as believers, instead of exhibiting the negative behavior described in Ephesians 4:31, are to be *"kind"* (gentle, good, gracious), *"tender-hearted"* (compassionate), and *"forgiving"* toward *"each other"* (Ephesians 4:32). Why? Jesus *"has forgiven"* (Ephesians 4:32) us.

"Has forgiven" (Ephesians 4:32) is in the aorist tense and points to past action. Thus, we were forgiven all past, present, and future sins the moment we repented and believed while depraved—meaning we received all the forgiveness we will ever need at the point of salvation/justification. (We must never lose sight of the fact that all sin for all time was placed on Christ according to passages such as

Hebrews 10:12, yet sin is not forgiven unless a person repents, believes, and is saved.) When we (as believers) commit sin, we confess and repent—not for the purpose of receiving forgiveness, but to have fellowship restored with the Father. We were forgiven once—when we repented and believed while depraved. No need exists to seek forgiveness for sins already forgiven.

We as church saints should never be heard praying the prayer: "Father, if I have done anything wrong today, forgive me." Jesus would need to be crucified each time we sin should such a prayer be proper, yet Jesus was crucified *"once"* (Hebrews 10:10, 14)—an act that can never be repeated. (For more input regarding this subject, review the notes associated with Ephesians 1:7b. Also, our *Romans 1-8* study has much to say concerning this wonderful truth.) If unity is to inhabit the church, we must learn to forgive each other as God has forgiven us (Ephesians 4:32). No other remedy exists!

Ephesians 5

Ephesians 5:1—Therefore be imitators of God, as beloved children;

Paul begins with *"Therefore,"* directing his readers to apply his previous statements regarding God's forgiveness (Ephesians 4:32) to this chapter. The saints at Ephesus were to *"be imitators of God"* (Ephesians 5:1), forgiving one another as God had forgiven them (Ephesians 4:32). *"Imitators"* (Ephesians 5:1), from the Greek *mimetes* (from which we get the English "mimic"), can also be interpreted *"followers"* as in the King James. We must be careful here. Paul is not teaching that God's people are to "imitate" or "mimic" Him by attempting to copy His behavior. Had this been Paul's intent, New Testament believers would be required to submit to the Law (which reveals His awesome character). Hence Paul, in Galatians 3:3, confirms that self-effort (legalism) can never produce righteous behavior:

> *Are you so foolish? Having begun by the Spirit, are you now being perfected by the flesh?* (Galatians 3:3)

Galatians 3:1-14 verifies that the Galatian saints had been misled to believe that they were saved by faith but kept by the deeds of the Law. *"Flesh"* (Galatians 3:3) in this case points to the believer attempting to live, in his own strength, according to God's righteous standard prescribed by the Ten Commandments. Many saints endeavor to mimic Christ, or even worse, attempt to abide by the standards prescribed in the Sermon on the Mount (Matthew 5-7)—standards even more impossible to attain through the power of the flesh (a topic covered in depth in our study, *The Gospels from a Jewish Perspective*). Believers can never experience victory through hooking the flesh to rules and regulations (Romans 8:4-6; Colossians 2:20-23). At some point in the maturing process, church saints must realize that the power required to change lives is not imitative in nature, but creative in nature.

For years, I strived to imitate God, only to experience frustration and despair. I discovered the solution to my dilemma only through realizing that God's *"Beloved"* Son (Ephesians 1:6) demonstrated how God's *"beloved children"* (Ephesians 5:1) are to live. He lived by the life of Another (by the life of His Father), trusting Him to perform every deed (John 14:10). Instead of imitating the Father, Jesus lived by the Father's very life. For this reason the events surrounding His earthly ministry were creative in nature rather than imitative in nature. Thus, deeds resulting from attempting to imitate God are of no benefit (John 15:1-5;

Colossians 2:20-23). (For more input, review the notes associated with Ephesians 2:10b).

Scripture teaches that God's *"life is in His Son"*:

> *And the witness is this, that God has given us eternal life, and this life is in His Son.* (1John 5:11)

> *"I and the Father are one."* (John 10:30)

Therefore, to live by the life of Another (to live by the Father's life) is to live by Christ's life. Paul says it well in Romans 5:10 and Romans 5:17:

> *For if while we were enemies, we were reconciled to God through the death of His Son, much more, having been reconciled, we shall be saved by His life.* (Romans 5:10)

> *For if by the transgression of the one, death reigned through the one, much more those who receive the abundance of grace and of the gift of righteousness will reign in life through the One, Jesus Christ.* (Romans 5:17)

The phrase, *"reign in life through the One, Jesus Christ"* (Romans 5:17), can also be interpreted, *"reign in life by the One, Jesus Christ"* (emphasis added). Hence, to live according to God's blueprint is to live by the Son's life. Wasn't this God's original plan in the Garden? Adam and Eve were to partake of the tree of life, not for the purpose of imitating God's life, but to share His life—live by His life. Had they obeyed, all their offspring would have lived in like manner, and the first Adam would have fulfilled God's ultimate plan for man. This scenario would have resulted in God's family living, on a moment-by-moment basis, by His very life. However, because *"the first Adam"* sinned, God sent *"the last Adam"* (Jesus—1Corinthians 15:45) not only to die for sin but to demonstrate what it means to live by the life of Another—by the Father's very life.

We are now equipped to properly interpret the phrase, *"be imitators of God, as beloved children"* (Ephesians 5:1). The Father's child (Jesus), as *"the Beloved"* Son (Ephesians 1:6), lived by the Father's life (John 14:10). Not once did He imitate the Father. We, as the Father's children, must also live by the Father's life if we desire to live supernaturally. The Father's life is in His Son (1John 5:11; John 10:30). Thus, by living by Jesus' life we live by the Father's life flowing through the Son.

No doubt, Scripture teaches that we are to be imitators of believers who walk righteously (1Corinthians 4:16-17; 11:1; 1Thessalonians 1:6; 2:14; Hebrews 6:12; Hebrews 13:7) and imitators of *"what is good"* (3John 1:11). This arrangement is fine so long as we imitate those who have learned to live by the life of "Another" for the purpose of learning to live in the same manner. Imitating legalists, bound by the letter of the Law, brings nothing but despair.

Because Christ *"is our life"* (Colossians 3:4), we have one basic goal as a believer: to know Him as intimately as possible (Philippians 3:10). As we pursue Him, His divine power works creatively in and through us! As we know Him more intimately, our behavior is changed (2Corinthians 3:18), He ministers to others through us (1Corinthians 15:10; Philippians 2:13), and He sustains us (Philippians 4:13)—while we remain in a state of *"rest"* (Hebrews 4:9-11): No more struggling to change our behavior through rules and regulations, and no more striving to accomplish what only God can bring about. Why would we choose to live in such drudgery when enjoying Him and living by His life (Galatians 2:20) is all He desires? (DeVern Fromke's, *The Ultimate Intention,* is a wonderful read on this subject.)

Paul states that we are to *"be imitators of God, as <u>beloved</u> children"* (Ephesians 5:1). Believers are *"beloved"* of the Father (Ephesians 5:1) because they are special to the Father. This special status grants us the privilege of living *"in the Beloved"* Son (Ephesians 1:6) throughout eternity. Amazing!

Ephesians 5:2—and walk in love, just as Christ also loved you, and gave Himself up for us, an offering and a sacrifice to God as a fragrant aroma.

If Christ *"is our life"* (Colossians 3:4), if we are saved on a moment-by-moment basis *"by His life"* (Romans 5:10), if we *"reign in life"* through Him (Romans 5:17), then we should *"walk in love, just as Jesus also loved"* (Ephesians 5:2). The Greek word for *"love"* in this instance is *agape*, pointing to selfless, unconditional love. Consequently, only when we live by the life of Another (live by Christ's life) do we *"walk in love, just as Christ also loved"* (Ephesians 5:2). Should the body of Christ comprehend this truth, unconditional love would run rampant, relationships once considered irreconcilable would be reconciled, healthy relationships would be deepened, and the unredeemed world would witness Jesus' character through His beautiful masterpiece—the church (John 13:34-35; Ephesians 2:10).

Agape love, God's kind of love, loves unconditionally. The recipient of *agape* is not required to earn it, deserve it, or even understand it—for its Source is God

Himself. Without God's *agape* love, none of us would have had the opportunity to become part of His family. Therefore, since God's love allowed Him to sacrifice His Son on our behalf, our lifestyles should be motivated by love and characterized by selfless living.

None of what has been discussed regarding Ephesians 5:1-2 can occur unless we are empowered by God's Spirit. In fact, to live by the life of Another is to walk by God's Spirit. The first *"fruit of the Spirit"* listed in Galatians 5:22 is *agape "love."* No saint can *"walk in love"* (Ephesians 5:2), nor can he live by the life of Another, void of the empowerment of the Holy Spirit. For this reason Paul encouraged his readers to refrain from grieving the Holy Spirit (Ephesians 4:30).

Only through walking to the cross by the life of Another (by His Father's life) could Jesus give *"Himself up for us"* (Ephesians 5:2). He also, through living by the life of the Father, gave Himself as *"an offering and a sacrifice to God"* (Ephesians 5:2). This response makes perfect sense considering the interaction between the three members of the Godhead since eternity past. They have done nothing based on selfish motives. Consequently, each individual member of the Godhead viewed the cross based on what the other two Persons of the Trinity, along with all the redeemed, would receive through that selfless act. Thus, Jesus offered Himself for the benefit of the Father (as *"an offering and a sacrifice to God as a fragrant aroma"*), for the benefit of the Spirit, and to provide an opportunity for all mankind to believe—although only the depraved who choose to exercise personal repentance and faith will be saved.

Christ's *"offering and...sacrifice"* was a *"fragrant aroma"* (Ephesians 5:2) to the Father, confirming that it pleased the Father. Philippians 4:18 speaks of how acceptable sacrifices please God:

> *But I have received everything in full, and have an abundance; I am amply supplied, having received from Epaphroditus what you have sent, a fragrant aroma, an acceptable sacrifice, well-pleasing to God.* (Philippians 4:18)

The Old Testament sacrifices mentioned in Leviticus 1:9, 13, 17; 2:2, 9, 12; 3:5, and 16 were a soothing aroma to the Father because they were a picture of what Christ would later accomplish on the cross.

Because *"God is love"* (1John 4:8, 16), every decision, response, motive, in fact, everything He is and does is based on *"love."* *"Love"* must motivate us as well (2Corinthians 5:14-15; Galatians 5:6; Jude 21) or we will soon lose heart. Interestingly, those who perceive God as having forgiven them little find themselves loving Him little (Luke 7:47). Only through a proper view of our total inability to save ourselves, the limitlessness of His forgiveness, and the awesomeness of everything that occurred at Calvary, do we begin to comprehend His love. Hence, the deeper we know Him through prayerfully reading His Word, the more we appreciate the uniqueness of His affection for the entirety of mankind:

> *"For God so loved the world, that He gave His only begotten Son,*
> *that whoever believes in Him should not perish, but have eternal*
> *life.* (John 3:16)

Obviously, Ephesians 5:1-2 is sandwiched between Ephesians 4:1 and Ephesians 6:24. Because Ephesians 4:1—6:24 is the practical section of this epistle, dealing with the believer's behavior, could Paul be confirming that to live by the life of Another is the key to seeing these practical truths fulfilled in one's experience? This conclusion seems to agree with Romans 8:4, where Paul validates that the believer's behavior parallels the righteous requirement of the Law only as he is controlled by God's Spirit:

> *in order that the requirement of the Law might be fulfilled in us,*
> *who do not walk according to the flesh, but according to the Spirit.*
> (Romans 8:4)

Ephesians 5:3—But do not let immorality or any impurity or greed even be named among you, as is proper among saints;

The first subject addressed after Ephesians 5:1-2 is *"immorality"* (Ephesians 5:3). *"Immorality"* (*porneia*), the total antithesis of love, can be defined as "illicit sexual intercourse in general." Individuals involved in immoral relationships fail to display God's love toward the person with whom they are immorally involved. Let me explain.

Much of our society (including the body of Christ) has bought the lie that relationships are established for personal gain. Thus, relationships are entered into, not to give, but to get—the perfect formula for disaster. This arrangement endures only so long as the "partner" is pleasant, attractive, healthy, meets all needs, and surpasses expectations. The moment the feelings flee, however (and they will flee), the unfulfilled partner is free to pursue whomever he/she pleases. Satan dangles this lifestyle before the unwise to their ruin, for death is partner with *"the course of this world"* (Ephesians 2:2). Only Jesus can save us from such nonsense.

God despises sexual sin for an abundance of reasons, for sex was originally intended for marriage—for blessing (pleasing) the person with whom you enter into covenant (1Corinthians 7:2-5) and for bearing children (Genesis 1:27-28). Hence, Jehovah entered into relationship with Israel (Exodus 24:1-8; Deuteronomy 5:1-3) not only to bless her (Deuteronomy 7:6-11), but to bear His Son, Jesus Christ, the *"seed"* of Genesis 3:15 (Galatians 3:16), through a *"virgin"* (Isaiah 7:14) of Jewish descent. Yet, Israel committed adultery and played the harlot through worshipping foreign gods (Hosea 4:11-14). Besides breaking God's heart, Israel's disobedience communicated the lie that He alone was insufficient to meet her needs. It also revealed that Israel desired relationship without commitment. No wonder the Creator so despises adultery! Homosexuality (1Corinthians 6:9; 1Timothy 1:8-10) is even worse, making the bold statement that God is not needed at all. No wonder a homosexual-laced society teeters on the brink of destruction (Romans 1:18-32). God loves the adulterer and homosexual, but abhors their sin. So should we.

Unconditional *"love"* (Ephesians 5:1-2), *agape* love, God's kind of love, chooses to respond favorably with no strings attached. Worth, performance, and attractiveness are never required. Neither is *agape "love"* based on emotion (although the "feelings" or emotions are positively affected when *agape* enters the scene). *Agape* love is based on choice and commitment, the only love capable of generating the fruitful and lasting relationships the soul desires.

"Impurity" (Ephesians 5:3) is from the Greek *akatharsia* and points to both physical (Matthew 23:27) and moral uncleanness (Romans 1:24; 6:19; 2Corinthians 12:21; Galatians 5:19; Ephesians 4:19; 5:3; Colossians 3:5; 1Thessalonians 2:3). We can be safe in saying that *"impurity"* (Ephesians 5:3) points to sexual sin in general, such as impure thoughts, fantasies, lust, and a variety of sexual perversions within the mind.

"Greed" (*pleonexia*), which accompanies immorality and impurity (Ephesians 5:3), is an unrestrained desire to possess more. Thus, the passions and cravings accompanying sexual sin are never satisfied. No wonder *"immorality"* and *"impurity"* breed unfaithful relationships, either due to: (1) infidelity or (2) indecent sex acts, of barbaric proportions, performed between the partners.

The number of men, women, and children carrying emotional (and physical) scars due to these uncontrolled passions is appalling. Therefore, when tempted to compromise in these areas, Proverbs 7 and Romans 1:18-32 are necessary reading.

Because *"be named"* (Ephesians 5:3) can also be interpreted "be mentioned," for saints to so much as "mention" what can be categorized as *"immorality," "impurity,"* or *"greed"* is not *"proper."* A *"saint"* is a "holy one," and his behavior should be progressing in holiness due to the holy, perfect, and blameless soul and spirit he has already become.

Ephesians 5:4—and there must be no filthiness and silly talk, or coarse jesting, which are not fitting, but rather giving of thanks.

Other patterns of behavior *"are not fitting"* for the saint to entertain. *"Filthiness"* (Ephesians 5:4) is "obscenity" or "all that is contrary to purity" (*Vine's*)—such as indecent, disgraceful, or filthy speech. *"Silly talk"* is sinful dialogue void of forethought and wisdom, while *"coarse jesting"* occurs when, for the sake of attention and wit, a person turns an innocent statement into the suggestive, obscene, or indecent.

Paul exhorts his readers to be consumed with the *"giving of thanks,"* and in 1Thessalonians 5:18, even encourages believers to thank God for everything. Thanking God results in humility, unselfishness, and love—which helps guard against the sins previously described, sins resulting from pride, selfishness, and a deficiency of love.

Ephesians 5:5—For this you know with certainty, that no immoral or impure person or covetous man, who is an idolater, has an inheritance in the kingdom of Christ and God.

Paul's readers knew *"with certainty"* that not everyone will repent and believe, forever eliminating the gross error of universalism. How did they come to understand this truth? Paul had taught the Ephesians that *"no immoral or impure person or covetous man, who is an idolater, has an inheritance in the kingdom of Christ and God"* (Ephesians 5:5). These persons' habitual sin reveals their corrupted hearts (1John 3:4-10). Similar terminology is used in verses 5 and 3— terms such as *"immoral,"* *"impure,"* and *"covetous"* in Ephesians 5:5, *"immorality,"* *"impurity,"* and *"greed"* in Ephesians 5:3. The believer is not to even *"mention"* such sin (Ephesians 5:3), much less wallow in it—as do the unredeemed (Ephesians 5:5).

Because *"immoral,"* *"impure,"* and *"covetous"* (Ephesians 5:5) are derived from the same root words as *"immorality,"* *"impurity,"* and *"greed"* (Ephesians 5:3), the notes from Ephesians 5:3 can be referenced for additional input. *"Covetous"* is linked with *"idolater"* in Ephesians 5:5, meaning that a *"covetous"* individual is an *"idolater"*—a person who worships idols (things) rather than God. This lifestyle results from a lack of gratitude for Jehovah—a lack of *"giving of thanks"* (Ephesians 5:4). Unsurprisingly, *"idolatry"* is linked with *"greed"* and *"immorality"* in Colossians 3:5:

> *Therefore consider the members of your earthly body as dead to*
> *immorality, impurity, passion, evil desire, and greed, which*
> *amounts to idolatry.* (Colossians 3:5)

A nation can't survive the consequence of this type of evil.

During the Millennium, the church will reign *"with Christ"* (Revelation 20:4) over *"The kingdom of Christ and God"* (Ephesians 5:5). An amazing adventure awaits New Testament saints!

Ephesians 5:6—Let no one deceive you with empty words, for because of these things the wrath of God comes upon the sons of disobedience.

"Empty" (*kenos*) is rendered "vain" on most occasions in New Testament Scripture but can also be interpreted "foolish" or "futile." Hence, *"empty words" "deceive"* the listener (Ephesians 5:6). The believer should disregard words of this type, for they are void of truth—their source being Satan who possesses no truth (John 8:44). *"Sons of disobedience"* (Ephesians 5:6), individuals void of the Holy Spirit (Romans 8:9, 14, 16) who receive God's *"wrath"* (Ephesians 5:6), readily accept these lies due to their folly. The Spirit of truth allows the believer to steer clear of this emptiness so long as the believer remains alert.

Those who advocate that God's love prevents Him from condemning the lost (the unwise and foolish) are communicating *"empty words"* (Ephesians 5:6). Individuals who listen and believe accordingly are *"sons of disobedience."* They are Satan's offspring possessing natures that enjoy sin (John 8:44).

Ephesians 5:7—Therefore do not be partakers with them;

Believers, under no circumstance, should *"be partakers"* (joint-partakers) *"with"* those who disregard truth and wallow in the world's vices.

Ephesians 5:8—for you were formerly darkness, but now you are light in the Lord; walk as children of light

for you were formerly darkness, (5:8a)

As was verified in Ephesians 2:1-3, Adam's sin resulted in spiritual death for himself and his offspring. Consequently, we were born children of *"darkness"* (Ephesians 5:8a). We *"were formerly darkness"* (Ephesians 5:8a) because we were sons of Satan (John 8:44), *"the power of darkness"* (Luke 22:53), whose dominion is *"darkness"* (Ephesians 6:12; Colossians 1:13). Therefore, we possessed both moral and intellectual darkness due to the sin nature inherited from Adam, a nature that made sin natural behavior. Yet, we possessed enough light in our depravity to repent and believe, for the darkness experienced by the depraved can be enhanced through exacerbated sin (review notes associated with Ephesians 2:1). A darkness that can be enhanced is never void of light, or else its enhancement would be impossible. The removal of light generates darkness—proving that the depraved, whose darkness intensifies with increased sin, possess at least a measure of light.

A totally darkened environment is thoroughly void of truth. Hence, the lost will live in eternal *"darkness"* (Matthew 8:12; 2Peter 2:17). As a good friend once said, "God's love frees man to not only choose darkness over light, but to live in darkness for all eternity due to that choice." Man basically rejects light because of its ability to expose sin:

> *"And this is the judgment, that the light is come into the world, and men loved the darkness rather than the light; for their deeds were evil. "For everyone who does evil hates the light, and does not come to the light, lest his deeds should be exposed.* (John 3:19-20)

but now you are light in the Lord; walk as children of light (5:8b)

Because *"God is light, and in Him is no darkness at all"* (1John 1:5), Jesus, being *"God"* (Hebrews 1:8), was *"the light of the world"* during His First Coming (John 8:12; 9:5). Therefore, all who are *"in Christ"* (2Corinthians 5:17), and thus, in God the Father (John 14:20), *"are light in the Lord"* (Ephesians 5:8b). They come to the light because they desire to practice the truth (John 3:21)—unlike those who choose to reside in darkness (John 3:19-20). Isn't it wonderful to know that when God *"called"* (invited) us *"into His marvelous light"* (Colossians 1:13; 1Peter 2:9) and we chose to accept that invitation, He delivered us *"from...darkness"*? Hence, Jesus said of believers, *"You are the light of the world"* (Matthew 5:14).

We (as believers) are to *"walk as children of light"* (Ephesians 5:8b) because God, Who *"is light"* (1John 1:5), granted us His kind of life, *"eternal life"* (John 3:15-16; 5:24; 6:40, 47; 10:28; etc.), when we became His (1John 3:1-2). Because *"walk"* (Ephesians 5:8) is a present imperative in the Greek, we are to walk consistently as children of light rather than irregularly. We *"walk"* in this manner by yielding to the indwelling Christ (Romans 5:10)—not by submitting to valueless rules and regulations (Colossians 2:20-23).

Ephesians 5:9—(for the fruit of the light consists in all goodness and righteousness and truth),

This verse (a parenthetical expression) is inserted between verses 8 and 10 to provide clarity. *"Fruit"* (*karpos*) is the same Greek word used in Galatians 5:22 for *"fruit"* of the spirit. Just as spirit-led believers exhibit *"the fruit of the Spirit"* (*"love, joy, peace,"* etc.), *"children of light"* (Ephesians 5:8) exhibit *"the fruit of the light"* (Ephesians 5:9). *"The fruit of the light"* is *"goodness and righteousness and truth"* (Ephesians 5:9).

"Goodness" (Ephesians 5:9) can also be interpreted, "profitable, generous, beneficial, upright, or virtuous." Thus, those who exhibit *"the fruit of the light"* live in such a way as to "profit" and "benefit" others. They are "generous" toward others. No wonder Paul wrote:

> *See that no one repays another with evil for evil, but always seek after that which is good for one another and for all men.* (1Thessalonians 5:15)

Don't overlook the fact that *"goodness"* is also a *"fruit of the Spirit"* (Galatians 5:22).

A saint of God desires to walk in *"righteousness"* (Ephesians 5:9). Romans 1:17, 4:5-6, Galatians 3:11, and 2Corinthians 5:21 confirm that God grants righteousness, not through *"works"* (Titus 3:5), but *"through faith in Christ"* (Romans 1:17; Philippians 3:9). One who is born-again will demonstrate a lifestyle of righteousness (Romans 6:18; 1John 3:7), but will sin at times (1John 1:8). However, his overall lifestyle will be characterized by godliness and holiness.

Because God's Word is both light and truth (Psalm 119:105), *"children of light"* (Ephesians 5:8) walk in (know, understand, and apply) *"truth"* (Ephesians 5:9). A combination of *"truth"* (Ephesians 5:9) and *"light"* (Ephesians 5:9) are required for a believer to practice God's nearness (Psalm 43:3)—to walk in intimacy and fellowship with Jehovah. Therefore, passionless saints live fruitless lifestyles. *"Truth"* (Ephesians 5:9) sets the believer *"free"* (John 8:32) to exhibit the *"fruit of the light"* (Ephesians 5:9), a thrilling adventure indeed:

so that you may walk in a manner worthy of the Lord, to please
Him in all respects, bearing fruit in every good work and
increasing in the knowledge of God; (Colossians 1:10)

Ephesians 5:10—trying to learn what is pleasing to the Lord.

The phrase, *"trying to learn,"* can also be interpreted "proving," while *"pleasing"* can be rendered "acceptable." Thus, saints who *"walk as children of light"* (Ephesians 5:8) prove *"what is pleasing"* (Ephesians 5:10), or "acceptable," *"to the Lord."* They have the delightful privilege of "proving" to believers as well as unbelievers what satisfies God. In the process, they also prove (to the world) that they are *"children of light"* (Ephesians 5:8) through their living by the life of Another.

Ephesians 5:11—And do not participate in the unfruitful deeds of darkness, but instead even expose them;

"Participate" means "fellowship" or "to become a partaker together with others." Hence, the believer must not *"participate,"* "fellowship," or "become a partaker together with" individuals involved *"in the unfruitful deeds of darkness."* Such *"deeds"* are to be laid aside (Romans 13:12) due to their unprofitable (*"unfruitful"*) nature (Ephesians 5:11). Paul described some of these deeds in Ephesians 4 and the early portion of Ephesians 5.

Instead of participating in the *"unfruitful deeds of darkness,"* God's people should *"expose them"* (Ephesians 5:11). *"Expose"* is from the Greek *elegcho*, which can also be interpreted *"reprove"* (Matthew 18:15; 2Timothy 4:2; Titus 1:13; 2:15; Revelation 3:19) or *"convict"* (John 16:8 and Jude 1:15). Consequently, the behavior of the *"children of light"* (Ephesians 5:8) both silences and convicts the lost—as was the case with Paul (before he met Christ) while observing Stephen, a child of light (Acts 22:20). Yes, the Holy Spirit convicts the hearts of the disobedient (John 16:8), but He many times uses believers as the conduit through which He generates the conviction. Sometimes error is made evident through a rebuke (Matthew 18:15-17; 1Timothy 1:20; 2Timothy 4:2), while at other times a godly lifestyle generates the same result (Acts 22:20; 1Peter 3:1-2).

Ephesians 5:12—for it is disgraceful even to speak of the things which are done by them in secret.

"The things...done...in secret" (Ephesians 5:12) by the children of darkness must be exposed (reproved—Ephesians 5:11), for even speaking of such behavior brings harm to God's people (Ephesians 5:12).

Ephesians 5:13—But all things become visible when they are exposed by the light, for everything that becomes visible is light.

But all things become visible when they are exposed by the light, **(5:13a)**

Because God's Word is *"light"* (Psalm 119:105), it exposes the true character (Ephesians 5:13; Hebrews 4:12-13) of everything it makes *"visible"* (Ephesians 5:13). Thus, truth not only exposes error, but also the motive behind the error. It, as well, allows children of darkness to recognize their sin (in the midst of their depravity) and come to the light.

for everything that becomes visible is light. **(5:13b)**

Whatever *"light"* makes *"visible"* becomes *"light."* Note the following quote from Vincent:

> Therefore, whatever is revealed in its true essence by light is the nature of light. It no longer belongs to the category of darkness. (Vincent, 1985)[23]

Those content with darkness hate the light (John 3:19-20). Only when they (while depraved) allow truth's light to expose their error (Ephesians 5:13a) and follow by repenting and believing does God make them children of light. So sin, when exposed by the light, becomes light in the sense that it is revealed as destructive.

Ephesians 5:14 For this reason it says, "Awake, sleeper, And arise from the dead, And Christ will shine on you."

The origin of the quotation within verse 14 is probably (1) a combination of different Old Testament passages comprised of verses such as Isaiah 60:1 (2) a hymn from the early church. Whatever the case, a child of darkness is a *"sleeper"* in need of an awakening (Ephesians 5:14; 1Thessalonians 5:4-6). He is *"dead"* (Ephesians 5:14) due to his sin nature inherited from Adam (Ephesians 2:1-3; Romans 5:17), but not so dead that he is a spiritual corpse (reference commentary associated with Ephesians 2:1). Only through accepting Christ, *"the light of the world"* (John 8:12; 9:5), does God make him a child of light (Ephesians 5:13b, 8).

Ephesians 5:15—Therefore be careful how you walk, not as unwise men, but as wise,

Paul wrote to his readers, *"be careful how you walk"*; for the unwise *"walk"* carelessly while the wise *"walk"* sensibly. Wisdom can be defined as "the ability to view life from God's perspective," or "the correct use of knowledge." Only believers possess wisdom, receiving their first measure of wisdom at salvation (Psalm 111:10; Proverbs 9:10; 1Corinthians 1:30). Their wisdom is enlarged as they mature in the faith (Colossians 1:9)—even Jesus grew in wisdom (Luke 2:52). The value of wisdom is limitless (Proverbs 3:13-15), causing James to write:

> *But the wisdom from above is first pure, then peaceable, gentle, reasonable, full of mercy and good fruits, unwavering, without hypocrisy.* (James 3:17)

Paul encourages his readers to walk wisely (Ephesians 5:15), for to walk otherwise is to play the fool (Proverbs 17:16). What benefit is gained from retaining the behavior we exemplified before believing (Titus 3:3)?

The following verses from Proverbs contrast the fool with those who walk uprightly: 10:8, 23; 12:15; 13:16; 14:16; 15:5; 17:10; 20:3; 24:7; 28:26; 29:11. The wisdom addressed in Proverbs 2 is profound as well.

Ephesians 5:16—making the most of your time, because the days are evil.

We should be *"making the most"* of our *"time."* *"Making the most"* can also be rendered "redeeming," meaning in this case "to buy back for one's self." *"Time"* can also be interpreted "season" or "opportunity." Therefore, we are to "buy back for ourselves" every "opportunity" to be used of the Lord through a wise use of the seconds, minutes, hours, days, months, and years of our lives.

One of the greatest advantages of possessing wisdom (Ephesians 5:15) is the proper use of time (Ephesians 5:16). For example, only the wise can develop meaningful, low-maintenance relationships—where time is spent on productive activity rather than wrangling over differences. The wise can also view material possessions from God's perspective, desiring what is needed rather than what is wanted. In fact, dividing the price of an item by your hourly wage reveals the number of hours required to possess it. The wise walk away when the time investment is excessive. Wisdom also allows its possessors to determine the source of a problem rather than waste precious time on surface (superficial) concerns. Hence, the unwise consume themselves with the fruit of a matter rather than discerning and discarding its root.

"Because the days are evil" (Ephesians 5:16), to choose the *"excellent"* over the good (Philippians 1:10) is indispensable.

Wisdom is essential to detect the opportunities that cross our paths, for they are seasonal rather than continuous—confirmed vividly by Matthew 25:8-10 and John 9:4. Neither do we know the duration of our days on the earth. Thus, we should take advantage of every moment so we can say with Paul, *"I have fought the good fight, I have finished the course"* (2Timothy 4:7).

The *"days"* were *"evil"* (Ephesians 5:16) when this epistle was written, but they would worsen. The Romans severely persecuted Christians soon afterwards, many saints losing their lives. The church at Ephesus also *"left"* her *"first love"* (Revelation 2:4) and, sometime during the second century, ceased to exist. Will the church in America heed Paul's warning and live—or will she lose her first love in the face of ever-increasing evil?

Ephesians 5:17—So then do not be foolish, but understand what the will of the Lord is.

The *"foolish"* can't *"understand what the will of the Lord is."* This privilege is reserved for the wise, who alone can perceive life from God's perspective—the definition of wisdom.

While the Scriptures give God's general will for our lives, the Holy Spirit reveals His specific will—but never in violation of the written Word. Wise counsel from godly men and women is also valuable, but it too must agree with the entirety of Scripture. God's will is that we learn to walk in *"sanctification"* and holiness (1Thessalonians 4:3), for anything that would cause us to walk otherwise is sin:

> *For this is the will of God, your sanctification; that is, that you*
> *abstain from sexual immorality;* (1Thessalonians 4:3)

Our time is used wisely while walking in God's will, for the Spirit's ability to lead us to the proper place at the proper time is astounding.

Ephesians 5:18—And do not get drunk with wine, for that is dissipation, but be filled with the Spirit,

And do not get drunk with wine, for that is dissipation, **(5:18a)**

God's will does not include getting *"drunk with wine,"* for such behavior is classified as *"dissipation." "Dissipation"* means "wastefulness." Therefore, those who drink excessively waste time (which we are to *"make the most of"*—Ephesians 5:16), lose monetary resources (Proverbs 23:21), forfeit peace (Proverbs 23:29-32), abandon self-control (Proverbs 23:33-34), sacrifice reputation and cease respecting others (Proverbs 23:35), etc. These consequences result because drunkenness deceives a person into believing that his life is in order, when in essence he is playing the fool (Proverbs 20:1).

In Paul's day, drunkenness was a common practice among idol worshipers, for wine was employed to generate fleshly praise to a lifeless entity. These acts of the flesh were of no benefit to the Ephesians, especially while worshipping the true God, Jesus Christ.

Paul contrasts drunkenness (Ephesians 5:18a) with being *"filled with the Spirit"* (Ephesians 5:18b) after contrasting light with darkness (Ephesians 5:7-14) and wisdom with foolishness (Ephesians 5:15-17). Drunkenness is not to be confused with being *"filled with the Spirit"* (Ephesians 5:18), for it is counterfeit at best. It brings a false sense of peace and security while totally wasting the life of its possessor.

but be filled with the Spirit, (5:18b)

In contrasting drunkenness (Ephesians 5:18a) with being *"filled with the Spirit"* (Ephesians 5:18b), Paul was possibly thinking of the day of Pentecost, the birth of the church age—when the believers in Jerusalem were filled with the Holy Spirit, yet accused of being filled with *"sweet wine"* (Acts 2:5-13). At that time, of course, Paul was not a believer; but everyone in Jerusalem (including Paul) was very much aware of what had transpired.

At the point of salvation, New Testament believers not only receive the Holy Spirit (Romans 8:9), but are also *"baptized"* (1Corinthians 12:13) and *"sealed"* (Ephesians 1:13) in Christ through the Person of the Spirit. Thus, by writing, *"be filled with the Spirit"* (Ephesians 5:18b), Paul is not encouraging his readers to accept Christ for salvation. They were already saved. He is exhorting them, rather, to allow the Spirit to control every aspect of their being. In fact, *"be filled"* means "to influence fully, possess fully, to flood, to diffuse throughout." The use of the present passive imperative, in fact, confirms that the New Testament believer is to continually live in a state of "being filled." Consequently, to be filled with the Spirit is to be empowered by the Spirit much like a ship is enabled by the wind in its sail. Hence, saints filled with the Spirit will not carry out the deeds of *"the flesh"* (Romans 8:5-7, 12-13). They will exhibit *"the fruit of the Spirit"* (Galatians

5:22-23, 25-26) and really live (Romans 8:13).

What must we do on our part to consistently experience the Spirit's filling? The answer is found in Colossians 3:16-22, where Paul essentially covers the same topics addressed in Ephesians 5:18–6:9—that of worship, giving thanks, and submission. The one variance is that Colossians 3:16-22 begins by stating, *"Let the word of Christ richly dwell within you,"* while Ephesians 5:18–6:9 begins with, *"be filled with the Spirit."* Therefore, if we desire that the Spirit fill us to overflowing, we start by filling our minds with truth. Stephen confirms my point, for he, being *"full of the Holy Spirit"* (Acts 6:5; 7:55), spoke with breathtaking authority from the Scriptures while being condemned to death (Acts 7:1-60). God's Word generates remarkable results when etched on a mind committed to godliness and holiness. It allows the Spirit to fill such persons with *"love, joy, peace, patience, kindness, goodness, faithfulness, gentleness, self-control"* (Galatians 5:22-23), every fruit needed to endorse Whom they serve (as was the case with Stephen).

Clearly, the Spirit leads us to walk in the middle of God's *"will"* (Ephesians 5:17). The choice is ours as to whether we will do so!

Ephesians 5:19—speaking to one another in psalms and hymns and spiritual songs, singing and making melody with your heart to the Lord;

Individuals who are *"filled with"* God's Spirit (Ephesians 5:18) and walk in His *"will"* (Ephesians 5:17) behave as Paul describes in Ephesians 5:19–6:20. They find themselves with a song on their hearts (Psalm 40:3), the first characteristic addressed in Ephesians 5:19. To possess *"the fruit of the Spirit"* (*"love, joy, peace,"* etc.—Galatians 5:22-23) and refrain from *"singing"* (Acts 16:19-25) is impossible. Praise also follows those times when God delivers us from our foes (Exodus 15:1-21; Judges 5:1-31).

speaking to one another in psalms and hymns and spiritual songs, (5:19a)

"Speaking" means "to make an utterance; to babble, to talk"—sounds offered to God by the Spirit-filled believer's voice (vocal cords). These sounds are to be addressed *"to one another"* (Ephesians 5:19a)—to believers. To determine exactly what the terms *"psalms," "hymns,"* and *"spiritual songs"* meant in Paul's day is difficult. *"Psalms"* is defined as "a striking or twitching with the fingers on musical strings" and may very well point to the Old Testament Psalms, as well as New Testament Psalms (1Corinthians 14:26) put to music. *"Hymns"* are "songs of praise addressed to God." Jesus must have been greatly encouraged by the *"hymn"* of praise voiced to God (from the *"upper room"*—Mark 14:15) prior to His arrest

and crucifixion (Mark 14:26). In the case of Ephesians 5:19a, *"hymns"* could point to the songs of praise written by the early church leaders, many of which were taken directly from the Scriptures. *"Spiritual songs"* are defined by the *International Standard Bible Encyclopedia* as "songs inspired by the Holy Spirit and employed in the joyful and devotional expression of the spiritual life."[24] The songs of Revelation 5:9, 14:3, and *"the song of Moses and of the Lamb"* (Revelation 15:3) are said to be examples of *"spiritual songs."* Whatever the case, songs of praise are to be directed toward God in the presence of fellow believers (Ephesians 5:19a) for the purpose of encouragement and exhortation. In so doing, God's people experience His nearness (2 Chronicles 5:13; Psalm 22:3 KJV).

singing and making melody with your heart to the Lord; (5:19b)

"Singing" in the New Testament always points to singing with the voice (Matthew 26:30; Mark 14:26; Acts 16:25; Ephesians 5:19; Colossians 3:16). *"Making melody"* is from the Greek *psallo* from which we get "psalm," meaning "a striking or twitching with the fingers on musical strings." Therefore, the Spirit-filled *"heart"* (Ephesians 5:19b) can produce both vocal and instrumental music uplifting *"to the Lord"* and His people. Effectiveness in this case is not dependent upon musical capability. In fact, some of the most talented vocalist and musicians lack the maturity to minister effectively while leading worship. Spirit-led ministry has always been, and will continue to be, an issue of the heart.

Ephesians 5:20—always giving thanks for all things in the name of our Lord Jesus Christ to God, even the Father;

Believers filled with God's Spirit live in an attitude of thanksgiving. The converse is also true, for the Spirit doesn't fill the unthankful.

Spirit-filled saints *"always"* give *"thanks"*—regardless of the circumstance. They have no time to complain or feel slighted, for they perceive themselves as continually blessed. God is very much glorified (2Corinthians 4:7-17) through such behavior, which adds incentive to respond favorably to intense trial (Acts 16:23-25).

The Psalms are filled with praise and adoration for the Father, for He is to be approached in an attitude of *"thanksgiving"* (Psalm 100:4):

> *Enter His gates with thanksgiving, And His courts with praise.*
> *Give thanks to Him; bless His name.* (Psalm 100:4)

"Thanksgiving" and praise restore perspective, freeing us to accept God's response to our petitions as the most excellent way. Improper perspective yields inflexibility, resulting in bitterness when God's answer is "No."

We are to thank God *"for all things in the name of our Lord Jesus Christ"* (Ephesians 5:20). Because *"name"* points to character, we are to give thanks to the Father in agreement with Christ's character—Who He is in His Person, both morally and ethically. Note how He responded while suffering unjustly:

> *and while being reviled, He did not revile in return; while suffering, He uttered no threats, but kept entrusting Himself to Him who judges righteously;* (1Peter 2:23)

Jesus responded without complaint to the most horrific circumstances imaginable (Philippians 2:5-8). So can we when filled with God's Spirit!

Our thanks is to be given *"to God...the Father"* (Ephesians 5:20) because we have been *"blessed...with every spiritual blessing...in Christ"* (Ephesians 1:3), *"every good thing...and every perfect gift is from"* Him (James 1:17), and we are part of His family (John 1:12). How could we be anything but thankful!

Ephesians 5:21—and be subject to one another in the fear of Christ.

Everyone *"filled"* with God's Spirit (Ephesians 5:18) knows how to *"be subject to one another"* (Ephesians 5:21). Why? The Spirit only fills those who desire to understand, walk in, and apply the principle of submission.

Although Ephesians 5:21 is addressing submission within the church, it can apply to the family as well. Just as the members of Christ's body are to *"be subject to one another"* for the good of the whole (the entire body), submission between the husband and wife generates stability for the entire household. Husbands might say, "To submit to my wife would result in a loss of authority." Not so, for God honors the husband's submission by bestowing favor and unity, freeing him to lead according to the Divine blueprint.

True, biblical submission is to be done *"in the fear of Christ"* (Ephesians 5:21), confirming that husbands are to lead their families as Christ leads the church. This leadership on the husband's part requires personal spiritual growth, for spiritual immaturity generally yields one of the following scenarios: (1) a passive husband and dad—leaving all parties insecure within the home (2) a brutal husband and dad—generating fear and instability for the entire household (3) divorce (4) a husband and dad who abandons the home, severing all family ties. No wonder our nation is floundering so!

The power and effectiveness to *"be subject to one another"* is found only *"in the fear of Christ"* (Ephesians 5:21). *"Fear"* in this case can point to a reverential fear, a fear motivated by love for the Being Who is feared—Christ in this case. We serve Jesus because we *"love"* Jesus (2Corinthians 5:14)—not because we are afraid of Him:

> *For the love of Christ controls us,...* (2Corinthians 5:14)

God will never condemn us, for His *"kindness"* attracted us to Him in the first place:

> *Or do you think lightly of the riches of His kindness and*
> *forbearance and patience, not knowing that the kindness of God*
> *leads you to repentance?* (Romans 2:4)

> *There is therefore now no condemnation for those who are in*
> *Christ Jesus.* (Romans 8:1)

The loving, understanding husband never misuses his authority, for the very foundation of a healthy marriage is mutual submission (Ephesians 5:21; 1Corinthians 7:3-4). Jesus submitted to the Father (John 5:30) while possessing the same nature as the Father—yet retained His authority. A wife is free, therefore, to submit to her spiritual equal—her husband (Galatians 3:28). Obviously, husbands and wives play different roles within the family structure (as do leaders within the church). Thus, God ordained submission for the protection of the family, church, and society in general.

Once a couple submits to God and to one another, the supernatural kicks in. The husband suddenly finds himself submitting to Christ's presence in his wife, the wife suddenly finds herself submitting to Christ's presence in her husband—and their marriage becomes a picture of Christ's relationship with the church. The *"source of quarrels and conflicts"* (James 4:1) is suddenly eradicated, which positively affects their relationships within the church. What a meaningful way to live!

To carry this topic a step farther, the husband and wife, in carrying out their responsibilities to their children, are to *"subject"* themselves to their children's spiritual and moral wellbeing (Ephesians 6:4). Likewise, Paul encouraged masters to *"subject"* themselves to their slaves' wellbeing since *"there is no partiality with Him"* (Ephesians 6:9).

Spirit-filled Christians exemplify a lifestyle of submission because they view all believers as spiritual equals (Galatians 3:28). Yet, submission is not synonymous with passivity. Keep this fact in mind as we continue.

Ephesians 5:22—Wives, be subject to your own husbands, as to the Lord.

No institution or organization functions effectively void of submission, for submission suggests authority. In fact, insufficient submission within any area of society yields persistent chaos. Consider as well that as Genesis 2 came to a close, all of nature coexisted in a state of bliss—totally submitted to the Creator's authority. This state remained until man's rebellion (Genesis 3:6) spawned a curse upon man and creation (Genesis 3:16-18; Romans 8:19-22). But pay special attention to Genesis 3:16, where God said to Eve:

> ... *"I will greatly multiply your pain in childbirth, in pain you shall bring forth children; yet your desire shall be for your husband, and he shall rule over you."* (Genesis 3:16)

The phrase, *"yet your desire shall be for your husband,"* is not related to emotional or physical attraction, for Adam and Eve were attracted to one another before the fall. The *"desire"* alluded to here concerns Eve's craving to usurp her husband's authority and rule supreme in the relationship—a foreign mindset before the fall. This truth is confirmed by statements regarding Cain in Genesis 4:7:

> *"If you do well, will not your countenance be lifted up? And if you do not do well, sin is crouching at the door; and its desire is for you, but you must master it."* (Genesis 4:7)

Sin's *"desire"* was to control Cain (to rule over Cain). Because *"desire"* is from the same Hebrew word in both Genesis 3:16 and Genesis 4:7, these passages verify that Eve desired to rule over Adam subsequent to the fall. Yet, Eve, regardless of her level of determination, would not succeed. Why? The last phrase of Genesis 3:16 states, *"and he shall rule over you"*—*"rule"* pointing to Adam's enhanced authority over Eve not present before the fall. From this point, woman would desire to rule over man, but man would prevail (Genesis 3:16). Previously, Adam and Eve had lived in mutual submission, along with submission to the Father.

The solution to the above-mentioned dilemma is Jesus, the Father, and the Holy Spirit. Only the Triune God can instruct husbands and wives in the way of meaningful relationships—how to live together in mutual submission, doing everything for the betterment of the other person. The three Persons of the

Godhead have interacted in this fashion from eternity past? (You may want to review our discussion concerning the principle of the cross earlier in the study.)

When the chain of command is disrupted in marriage, bad things happen. For instance, a strong, unyielding wife many times produces a passive husband. Then later in life, when she realizes her need for a masculine anchor, her love turns sour due to her husband's passivity. Women were not made to dominate. When they do, they eventually despise the environment their dominance has generated.

Leadership built on truth is authoritative in nature. Leadership based on error is feeble in nature. Only God-ordained leadership can withstand the pressures accompanying a God-ordained responsibility. Hence, a domineering wife is ill equipped to function as the head of the home. True authority is attained through submission to authority, thus a wife's dominance prevents the God-ordained authority (the husband) from functioning according to design. Deficient instruction and discipline result, bringing confusion to the entire household. Homosexuality and lesbianism among the offspring can be traced to this reversal of roles among parents.

Let's attempt to put everything in perspective. Submission to authority does not mean that the submitting party is inferior to the one submitted to (Galatians 3:28). Submission is basically an acknowledgment of God's order, for individuals don't have to be alike to be equal. God didn't make another man from Adam's rib; he made a woman, a person unlike Adam. But it took Eve to make Adam complete—validating her value and significance. Consequently, when a wife functions in her God-ordained role, she completes her husband. Otherwise, she cripples him, never reaching her potential as a wife and mother. No husband or wife can parent according to design void of the submission addressed here.

If, due to the husband's disobedience, mutual submission is absent, the wife can submit knowing that God will honor her obedience. God is not as free to work in the husband's life should she respond otherwise. To submit to the husband *"as to the Lord"* (Ephesians 5:22) is key, especially during the hard times. For a superb lesson on the power of submission, read Matthew 8:5-10.

Ephesians 5:23—For the husband is the head of the wife, as Christ also is the head of the church, He Himself being the Savior of the body.

Because marriage is a picture of Christ's relationship with the church, this passage by no means grants the husband a license to mistreat his wife. For the husband to say, "I am your head, therefore bow," totally contradicts the context of Paul's statement here. This verse emphasizes submission on both Christ and the husband's part. Jesus, our *"head,"* our leader, our God, lived and died for what we (His bride) received through the cross—not for what He gained through that awesome display of selflessness (John 17:19; Ephesians 5:25-27). He, as our *"head,"* submitted to death for our sake—for the benefit of His bride-to-be. In return, the Father gave Him a bride-to-be who enjoys submitting to Him through her own choices.

No God-fearing wife regrets submitting to a husband who has adopted Christ's perception of marriage. Satisfied, fulfilled, and joyful wives dwell in homes where loving husbands lead—the same relationship that exists between Christ and the church. Christ doesn't force us to submit. He waits patiently until we choose to submit. His kindness and love, not His wrath, encourage us to walk in this sustained submission (Romans 2:4; Galatians 5:6; 2Corinthians 5:14-15).

A husband's response to his wife greatly affects his fellowship with the Father:

> *You husbands likewise, live with your wives in an understanding*
> *way, as with a weaker vessel, since she is a woman; and grant her*
> *honor as a fellow heir of the grace of life, so that your prayers may*
> *not be hindered.* (1Peter 3:7)

Thus, unity between husband and wife yields greater blessing on both parties by enhancing the husband's fellowship with the Father. His enriched prayer life and resulting spiritual growth mold him into the leader his household requires—making mom and dad's relationship amazingly intriguing to their children's watchful eye. Children raised in these environments retain what they have witnessed, seeking spouses desiring to duplicate what mom and dad displayed at home.

Some husbands refuse to lead, leaving the family vulnerable before the enemy. Our Leader, Jesus, watches over those under His care. Husbands, as the head of the home, should jump at the opportunity to do the same. Not only do the wife and children benefit, but the family, when properly led, portrays how Christ cares for His own. Men, I don't know about you, but I want my relationship with my family to make a statement. I want it to shout to the world that Christ brings fulfillment to all who believe. For this hope to come to fruition, we must love as Jesus loves—something we "catch" as we pursue Him in truth, righteousness, and holiness.

Ephesians 5:24—But as the church is subject to Christ, so also the wives ought to be to their husbands in everything.

The wife is to be subject to her husband as the church is subject to Christ. How can this be without the wife feeling slighted? Simple! The husband loves her for what she receives from the relationship (as Jesus loves the church), freeing her to willingly *"subject"* herself to the husband in *"everything."* In fact, she welcomes the opportunity to serve such a worthy and loving partner.

Wonderful things transpire in situations such as these. Selflessness rules the home, the children live in a stable environment inundated with peace, and Christ's relationship to His body, the church, is on display for all to see.

Ephesians 5:25—Husbands, love your wives, just as Christ also loved the church and gave Himself up for her;

A husband is to love his wife as Christ *"loved the church."* Notice that the wives are commanded to submit to their husbands (Ephesians 5:22-24), but the husbands are commanded to love their wives (Ephesians 5:25). This arrangement is necessary for proper family function.

"The most important thing a father can do for his children is love their mother" (Theodore Hesburgh).[25] But how can a husband properly love his wife if he misunderstands Christ's love for the church? Could this be the problem within Christian marriages today? If the typical husband within the Christian community views Jesus as unloving, just waiting to pounce on every act of disobedience with a full measure of His wrath, how can he fulfill his role as a loving, sensitive, compassionate friend to his wife? Hence, we must teach men who they are in Christ (what Christ's love has done for them through the cross). For the family to function as prescribed in these passages, we have no other option.

Wives, what if you were loved by your husband as 1Corinthians 13 prescribes? Would "submission" be an unsettling word to you? Of course not! Jesus' love for His body and bride (in dying on the cross) was not based on selfishness. It was based upon what the bride would receive through that glorious act. Therefore, if we love as Christ loves, we will love Him for what He received through the cross rather than for what we received. He received a body. Yes, Christ dying selflessly on the cross for others brought Him tremendous reward—a body and a bride. Only the spiritually mature understand this principle. Once understood, however, the believer's love and appreciation for Christ becomes the passion of his life. In fact, he is willing to face "whatever" should it please Him. This same principle (and truth) applies to the family. When the husband displays unconditional, selfless love toward his "queen," the fruit and reward will (in most cases) be a more mature wife committed to selfless living. The family unit, in turn, exemplifies the death, burial, and resurrection of Christ to the glory of the Father.

Christ died for the church. In fact, He died for everyone—even those who reject His offer of salvation. We, as husbands, must die to our plans, ideas, opinions, and agenda. When two become one flesh, they die to their singleness and are alive to a life of union with a person they long to please. Thus, when a virgin loses her virginity on the wedding night, the blood shed is a sign that a covenant has been sealed and that a death has occurred. Both marriage partners, the man and the woman, have died to their singleness and self-centeredness to live as one. In Adam's eyes, he and Eve were one (Genesis 2:23)—not two separate individuals. This union resulted in mutual submission—that is, until sin entered the picture in Genesis 3.

Ephesians 5:26—that He might sanctify her, having cleansed her by the washing of water with the word,

The Father gave up His Son for the sake of the world—every human being (John 3:16). Yet, only those who choose to repent and believe while depraved become part of His family. In the same manner, Jesus gave up His life for all of mankind, His bride (the church—which began in Acts 2) included. He will *"sanctify"* His bride (Ephesians 5:26), for New Testament believers are totally sanctified in soul and spirit at the point of salvation/justification (Hebrews 10:10)—although their behavior is being sanctified on an ongoing basis (Hebrews 10:14) as they pursue intimacy with Christ. Hence, as Christ, through the husband, leads the wife into a deeper understanding of truth, the wife's behavioral sanctification is enhanced to the glory of the Father as she chooses to respond favorably to the truth she has been taught through her husband.

Men, let's lead in our homes, for Adam's failed leadership left Eve vulnerable to sin (Genesis 3).

Ephesians 5:27—that He might present to Himself the church in all her glory, having no spot or wrinkle or any such thing; but that she should be holy and blameless.

The church will be presented to Christ *"in all her glory"* as *"holy and blameless"* saints (also read Ephesians 1:4, Hebrews 9:28, and Jude 24). We were made into a finished product (in soul and spirit) at the point of salvation/justification (Romans 5:1; Romans 8:30; 2Corinthians 5:21; etc.). We were made a saint (1Corinthians 1:2), never to be more saintly in our person. The Holy Spirit's responsibility, however, is to train us to <u>behave</u> like saints—to live in a manner (while on earth) that validates who we became the moment we accepted Christ (Romans 8:14). But consider this! If, on a scale of one to one hundred, our behavioral efficiency only reaches sixty during our stay on earth, we will still be presented to Christ as *"holy and blameless"* saints (Ephesians 5:27). God doesn't have us on a performance-based acceptance. Therefore, enjoy this day knowing that should you exit your physical body, you will be presented without *"spot or wrinkle"* before the holy Creator (Ephesians 5:27). Yet, we must remember that sins committed before and after salvation reap consequences in this life, even though forgiven (Colossians 3:25).

If Jesus desires that the church behave in a manner that agrees with who she is in soul and spirit, a husband should desire that his wife experience optimum spiritual growth. This means that the husband must mature spiritually so as to guard, not only his wife, but his entire family.

Ephesians 5:28—So husbands ought also to love their own wives as their own bodies. He who loves his own wife loves himself;

We confirmed earlier that Christ (as *"head"*) displays unconditional love toward His body, the church (Ephesians 5:2). We found likewise that the husband should love his wife in the same manner since he is *"head"* over her (Ephesians 5:23). As we will discover in Ephesians 5:31, two become one once they enter into the marriage covenant—they are no longer two separate individuals. Thus, if a husband loves his wife, he loves himself. If he does not love his wife, he does not love himself. Consequently, every husband who does not respect and love his wife does not respect and love himself!

We should love our bodies, for we are *"fearfully and wonderfully made"* (Psalm 139:14). Yet, only through knowing and trusting Christ can we properly love and accept the uniqueness of the particular "earth suit" (physical tent) that we each received. The same principle applies to the husband-wife relationship. Only through knowing and trusting Christ (and drawing his self-worth out of who God says he is) can the husband love and accept his wife as part of himself—a significant part of himself indeed.

Ephesians 5:29—for no one ever hated his own flesh, but nourishes and cherishes it, just as Christ also does the church,

Society confirms that no one hates *"his own flesh"* (body), for more resources and time are spent on conditioning and caring for the body than in any previous generation. Hence, body-worship is not uncommon. However, New Testament believers are to view their *"earthly tent"* (2Corinthians 5:1-4) as *"a temple of God"* (1Corinthians 3:16), caring for it through personal hygiene, exercise, and diet. Such disciplines yield the fruit of energy and enhanced vigor. The same is true in the husband-wife relationship, the husband reaping enormous benefit from properly caring for (and responding according to) his wife's needs. After all, they are *"one flesh"* (Ephesians 5:31).

The husband is to nourish and cherish his wife as Christ *"nourishes and cherishes"* the church (Ephesians 5:29). According to Ephesians 5:25-27, Jesus flawlessly and selflessly cares for His bride-to-be. He proved this through dying not only for her but for all mankind (John 3:16; Romans 5:6)—God bestowing salvation to individuals who repent and believe while depraved. Therefore, as the husband pursues intimacy with the Son, Christ loves the wife through the husband. Jesus alone understands how a wife is to be nourished and cherished. Since *"nourishes"* (Ephesians 5:29) means "to promote health and strength," while *"cherishes"* (Ephesians 5:29) is defined as "to impart warmth; to nurse, foster," only husbands led of God's Spirit and empowered by Christ exhibit these characteristics. In such cases the wife's physical, spiritual, and emotional needs are abundantly supplied as the husband lovingly directs the home—allowing all family members to inhabit an environment promoting optimum spiritual growth.

Ephesians 5:30—because we are members of His body.

Jesus *"nourishes and cherishes...the church"* (Ephesians 5:29) because *"we are members of His body"* (Ephesians 5:30). We are also *"one spirit with Him"* (1Corinthians 6:17), which means that we share common life—His life—making us one. (This sharing of Jesus' life does not make anyone a little Jesus.) Oh that we might comprehend the positive ramifications of being *"members of His body"* (Ephesians 5:30)!

Ephesians 5:31—For this cause a man shall leave his father and mother, and shall cleave to his wife; and the two shall become one flesh.

Verse 31, a quote from Genesis 2:24, provides wise counsel for those contemplating marriage. The husband and wife are to *"leave"* their homes, their parents no longer serving as their primary providers and counselors. The couple continues to love, care, and respect their fathers and mothers (and seek their input from time to time), but they must *"leave...and...cleave"* (Ephesians 5:31). A multitude of marriages have self-destructed due to couples failing to "cut the apron strings."

"Cleave" (Ephesians 5:31) means "to glue together," confirming that the bond between husband and wife exceeds the bond between child and parent. After all, the husband and wife are *"one flesh."* Thus, if the husband hurts his wife he hurts himself.

Ephesians 5:32—This mystery is great; but I am speaking with reference to Christ and the church.

As was determined earlier, the *"mystery"* (Ephesians 5:32) relates to Jews and Gentiles becoming one, void of racial distinction, once placed into Christ (after repenting and believing while depraved). *"This mystery is great"* because New Testament saints (believers since Acts 2) make up Christ's body, a truth that Old Testament believers failed to comprehend:

> As to this salvation, the prophets who prophesied of the grace that
> would come to you made careful search and inquiry, seeking to
> know what person or time the Spirit of Christ within them was
> indicating as He predicted the sufferings of Christ and the glories
> to follow. (1Peter 1:10-11)

We must realize that this *"mystery"* (Ephesians 5:32) is personified by the husband-wife relationship—proving that marriage is sacred indeed.

Ephesians 5:33—Nevertheless let each individual among you also love his own wife even as himself; and let the wife see to it that she respect her husband.

Because Jesus loves us (His body) as Himself, all believing husbands should love their wives as themselves. If not, they misunderstand Who Christ is, who they are, and what He desires for all who have been joined as one.

"Respect" means "to treat with reverential obedience" (*Vine's*).[26] If a believing husband loves his believing wife *"as himself,"* the wife's *"respect"* should automatically follow. Stated differently, if a husband's decisions are for the good of his wife, rather than his own benefit (by applying the principle of the cross), his wife's reverential submission should follow. Should it not, the wife needs to realize her error and appreciate, honor, and respect the selfless man inhabiting her

home.

The Master's blueprint for marriage never fails. Only when the blueprint is violated by one or both spouses does a marriage suffer harm.

Ephesians 6

Ephesians 6:1—Children, obey your parents in the Lord, for this is right.

In verses 1-4, Paul continues the theme of submission by addressing the parent-child relationship. Considering society's redefinition of right and wrong, children and parents need God's perspective concerning the matter. Pain and heartache result otherwise, validated by the turmoil overwhelming the American home today.

Scripture has much to say concerning the benefits of godly parenting. For instance, Proverbs 10:1 states:

> *...A wise son makes a father glad, but a foolish son is a grief to his mother.* (Proverbs 10:1)

Children nurtured in the things of the Lord, who respond positively to the teaching and training, bring much joy to both mother and father. Psalm 127:3-5 states:

> *Behold, children are a gift of the Lord; the fruit of the womb is a reward. Like arrows in the hand of a warrior, so are the children of one's youth. How blessed is the man whose quiver is full of them; they shall not be ashamed, when they speak with their enemies in the gate.* (Psalm 127:3-5)

Parents who view their offspring as God's precious *"gift,"* as priceless *"arrows"* that can deter a ruthless foe (warriors only get one shot per arrow while in battle, confirming that parents have one shot per child to "get it right"), these same parents will *"not be ashamed"* as those *"arrows"* are unleashed on a society opposed to truth (Psalm 127:3-5). The bold and righteous conduct of their children will validate the impact of godly instruction in the home.

Don't misunderstand. Godly parenting can't guarantee a compliant child. Trained children occasionally fail early in life yet find their way during adulthood (Proverbs 22:6). Hence, the parent is to nurture the child, trusting God that the child will be an asset in the kingdom.

"Children" (Ephesians 6:1) makes reference to offspring living under the parents' roof—not just young children. Paul states that they are to *"obey"* their *"parents in the Lord."* *"Obey"* means "to listen, attend, and submit." The phrase, *"in the Lord,"* is significant, for children of godly parents are to obey their parents' wishes.

Conversely, instruction from ungodly parents is not to be heeded should it lead to sin. Children are not required to comply in such cases, but should show respect to their parents while refusing the evil they have been encouraged to entertain.

"Children" should *"obey"* their *"parents in the Lord"* because it *"is right"* (Ephesians 6:1), *"right"* confirming that a child's obedience agrees with the God-ordained blueprint designed for healthy parent-child relationships. Since God designed the family structure for the good of parents and children alike, He knows best how it is to function. He states that children must submit to their parents' authority to reap the benefits of the family unit. These benefits will be discussed in more detail while studying Ephesians 6:3.

Power struggles between child and parent are rectified when the child understands that parents serve only as stewards of what God has entrusted to their care. The Father actually loans children to parents so parents might raise and nurture them in the things of Himself (Colossians 3:20).

Ephesians 6:2—Honor your father and mother (which is the first commandment with a promise),

Children are to *"honor"* their *"father and mother"* by treating them with the respect, courtesy, and obedience that their God-given position demands. God ordained the home as the proving ground for proper social behavior. Thus, children who *"honor"* their parents normally honor authority in general. They also learn (in most cases) to respect, reverence, and honor God—which by definition is the *"beginning of wisdom"* (Proverbs 9:10). They, in the process, discover that in losing their lives for others they find life (Matthew 16:25).

How encouraging to see young men and women develop friendships for the purpose of serving others! However, when proper instruction is lacking within the home, the child many times views relationships as a means of self-gratification, only interacting with others for what he or she might gain in the end. The result is devastating, as is evidenced by the masses who refuse to grow past their self-centeredness to pursue the principle of selfless living.

Paul states in Ephesians 6:2 that the commandment, *"honor your father and mother,"* is unique in that it *"is the first commandment with a promise."* The promise is listed in verse 3.

Ephesians 6:3—That it may be well with you, and that you may live long on

the earth.

Paul references God's original promise of Exodus 20:12, a promise assuring Israel that physical blessings would follow obedience. Paul confirms that blessings continue to follow obedience even in the church age—the age of grace. No doubt, obedient children are greatly benefited, for in lovingly submitting to the parents' authority they learn to submit to God. Even Jesus reaped the benefits and blessings associated with submission to His earthly father and mother (Luke 2:51-52), for He *"kept increasing in wisdom and stature, and in favor with God and men"* (Luke 2:52). His horizontal submission to Joseph and Mary enhanced His vertical submission to the Father, resulting *"in favor with God and men"* (Luke 2:52):

> *And He went down with them, and came to Nazareth; and He*
> *continued in subjection to them; and His mother treasured all these*
> *things in her heart. And Jesus kept increasing in wisdom and*
> *stature, and in favor with God and men.* (Luke 2:51-52)

The Proverbs are inundated with truth regarding the parent-child relationship and the need for a child's submission to parental guidance. For instance, in Proverbs 1:8 we find:

> *Hear, my son, your father's instruction, and do not forsake your*
> *mother's teaching*; (Proverbs 1:8)

Again in Proverbs 4:1 we read:

> *Hear, O sons, the instruction of a father, and give attention that*
> *you may gain understanding,* (Proverbs 4:1)

Proverbs 3:1-4 states:

> *My son, do not forget my teaching, but let your heart keep my*
> *commandments; for length of days and years of life, and peace they*
> *will add to you. Do not let kindness and truth leave you; bind them*
> *around your neck, write them on the tablet of your heart. So you*
> *will find favor and good repute in the sight of God and man.*
> (Proverbs 3:1-4)

Clearly, a child who listens to godly parental instruction finds favor with God and man (as was the case with Jesus).

God promises two things to a child who honors his parents (Ephesians 6:3). First, it will be *"well"* with him (Ephesians 6:3), meaning that his quality of life will be greatly enhanced. Instead of rebelling and reaping its consequence, an obedient child dwells in an atmosphere of peace within the home—bringing encouragement to the entire household (Proverbs 23:24-25; 15:20). After experiencing such an uplifting environment, the child desires to duplicate it with his own spouse and offspring. Thus, the cycle continues to the glory of the Creator. Second, a child who honors his father and mother will *"live long on the earth"* (Ephesians 6:2-3). Of course, not all children who honor their parents are guaranteed longevity of life. They are more apt to live longer, however, due to the exalted place submission holds in their hearts:

> *My son, do not forget my teaching, but let your heart keep my*
> *commandments; for length of days and years of life, and peace they*
> *will add to you.* (Proverbs 3:1-2)

Obedient children, who learn to respect and honor God, normally refrain from losing their lives due to the consequence of sin.

Be it friendships among believers (Ephesians 5:19-21), husband-wife relationships (Ephesians 5:22-33), or parent-child relationships (Ephesians 6:1-3), all parties must be filled with the Spirit (Ephesians 5:18) for these relationships to function according to design. Therefore, to desire that children be filled with the Spirit and walk in submission to the God-ordained authority surrounding them is normal for parents who walk in submission to Christ. Scripture is filled with young men who submitted to God at an early age (Samuel—1Samuel 2:26; David—1Samuel 17:33, 42; Josiah—2Kings 22:1-2; John the Baptist—Luke 1:15; and of course, Jesus—Luke 2:42-47; etc.) and reaped astonishing benefits from their humble, wholesome, righteous, and powerful lifestyles.

Ephesians 6:4—And, fathers, do not provoke your children to anger; but bring them up in the discipline and instruction of the Lord.

And, fathers, do not provoke your children to anger; (6:4a)

My dad, Glenn Warren, responded to me much like my heavenly Father responds to His children. In fact, when asked why I see God as a loving, compassionate, firm, uncompromising, forgiving Father, I attribute much of it to my relationship with my earthly father. Like it or not, earthly fathers affect a child's view of Father-God. Hence, many children refuse to accept Christ (and the heavenly Father) due to an unhealthy experience with "daddy." In such cases, the only solution is to allow God's Word to reshape and renew one's perspective (Romans 12:1-2). To know the Father's heart through a consistent diet of truth is vital, especially for those whose fathers failed to display God's character and disposition on a somewhat consistent basis—or maybe who were never present at all.

The full counsel of God's Word confirms that the heavenly Father does not provoke His children to anger; therefore, Paul encourages earthly fathers to follow the heavenly Father's example (Ephesians 6:4a—*"provoke"* meaning "to rouse to wrath, exasperate, anger"). God, for instance: (1) does not have His children on a performance-based acceptance (Titus 3:5; Romans 3:20) (2) sacrifices for them and makes them feel special and wanted (John 3:16) (3) never condemns their person (Romans 8:1), correcting their behavior with a tear in His eye rather than a scowl on His face (Hebrews 12:5-11) (4) never shows favoritism (Galatians 3:28) (5) always makes decisions based on how they will help rather than hinder His children (lives by the principle of the cross in other words—the theme of the 66 books of Scripture).

Obviously, earthly *"fathers"* should *"not provoke"* their *"children to anger"* (Ephesians 6:4).

but bring them up in the discipline and instruction of the Lord. (6:4b)

A father's goal should be to respond to his children as God responds to His own. Because the roadmap for proper parenting is etched in the Word of God, how can fathers expect to fulfill their responsibilities as dads without diligently applying its precepts? For this reason Paul states, *"but bring them up in the discipline and instruction of the Lord"* (Ephesians 6:4b).

The phrase, *"bring them up,"* points to more than supplying a child's physical needs. It means "to nourish to maturity, to nurture, to rear up." Thus, it includes *"discipline and instruction"* (Ephesians 6:4b). *"Discipline"* is more related to physical punishment (Proverbs 13:24) while *"instruction"* is training by word, both by encouragement and reproof. The parent must understand that discipline without instruction generally creates anger and confusion within those on whom it is directed. But discipline balanced with proper instruction should yield godliness, character, and integrity. For this reason, Paul states that all such discipline and instruction must be *"of the Lord"* (Ephesians 6:4b). Only God's Word, illuminated by the Holy Spirit, reveals the proper balance required for effective parental instruction.

Ephesians 6:5—Slaves, be obedient to those who are your masters according to

the flesh, with fear and trembling, in the sincerity of your heart, as to Christ;

The theme of submission continues throughout Ephesians 6:5-9, but we must keep in mind that only Spirit-filled believers (Ephesians 5:18) understand the benefits of submission. Someone must lead if society is to function according to design—the husband over the wife (Ephesians 5:23-24), the parent over the child (Ephesians 6:1), and the master over the *"slave"* (Ephesians 6:5)—each possessing authority for the purpose of serving those under their charge (read Ephesians 5:25 for example). Therefore, mutual submission is the goal in these relationships, not a dictatorship. As Paul relates how *"slaves"* were to respond to their masters, and masters to their slaves, what a wonderful opportunity to observe how employees and employers should interact within the workplace.

Before the birth of the church (in Acts 2), the Romans brutally mistreated slaves, in fact, treated them as animals. They used them for a variety of purposes, caring little about their person or wellbeing. Slavery remained a socially accepted practice when Ephesians was penned, but much had changed. The slave now had a healthy relationship with his master, a topic addressed in Kent Hughes' book titled *Ephesians : The Mystery of the Body of Christ.* On page 206 of this work he writes:

> The fact is, by the time of the Christian era and the writing of this Ephesians *Haustafel*, sweeping changes had been introduced which radically improved the treatment of slaves. Slaves under Roman law in the first century could generally count on eventually being set free. Very few ever reached old age as slaves. Slave owners were releasing slaves at such a rate that Augustus Caesar introduced legal restrictions to curb the trend. Despite this, inscriptions indicate that almost 50 percent of slaves were freed before the age of thirty. What is more, while the slave remained his master's possession he could own property—including other slaves!—and completely controlled his own property, so that he could invest and save to purchase his own freedom.

> We also must understand that being a slave did not indicate one's social class. Slaves regularly were accorded the social status of their owners. Regarding outward appearance, it was usually impossible to distinguish a slave from free persons. A slave could be a custodian, a salesman, or CEO. Many slaves lived separately from their owners. Finally, selling oneself into slavery was commonly used as a means of obtaining Roman citizenship and gaining an entrance into society. Roman slavery in the first century was far more humane and civilized than the

American/African slavery practiced in this country much later. This is a sobering and humbling fact! (Hughes, 1990)[27]

This insight into the treatment of slaves in Paul's day explains why slavery is nowhere condemned in New Testament Scripture. Both slaves and masters perceived it as positive and necessary. In fact, prohibiting slavery would have meant economic disaster for all. The slave/master relationship in Paul's day was very similar to the employee/employer relationship we know today. It in no way resembled American slavery (which is clearly forbidden—Exodus 21:16).

Paul states, *"Slaves, be obedient to those who are your masters according to the flesh, with fear and trembling, in the sincerity of your heart, as to Christ"* (Ephesians 6:5), because some slaves' environments were so laid back that they refused to respect their masters. Paul realized that no distinction existed between slave and free man in their standing with Christ (Galatians 3:28), but the slave was to obey his master so long as he remained a slave. Logistically this presented difficulty, especially in instances where slaves held positions of leadership over their masters in the local church (as is sometimes the case with employees and employers today). Even so, the Christian slave was to respect his Christian master, a subject Paul also addresses in 1Timothy 6:1-2.

The phrase, *"with fear and trembling"* (Ephesians 6:5), is rendered *"with a proper sense of respect and responsibility"* in the J.B. Phillips translation (Modern English New Testament).[28] Paul was not encouraging the slave of his day to be terror-stricken when in his master's presence. The slave was, however, to respect his master as he carried out his master's wishes. He was also to respond *"in...sincerity of...heart."* *"Sincerity"* in this case means "singleness, purity, or uprightness." Hence, the slave's motives were to be proper and upright by viewing his response to his master as a response to Christ—*"as to Christ"* (Ephesians 6:5). Employees today should adopt this same mindset as they fulfill their responsibilities to their employers.

Ephesians 6:6—not by way of eyeservice, as men-pleasers, but as slaves of Christ, doing the will of God from the heart.

By implementing the phrase, *"not by way of eyeservice,"* Paul is communicating that slaves (employees) should never "appear overly busy" while in the employer's presence for the sake of personal gain. The employee should perform all tasks with utmost integrity and faithfulness, never doing the minimal just to get by. Such a slave/employee goes the second mile to make certain that his master/employer receives maximum benefit from his time and labor (Matthew 25:14-30, the *Parable of the Talents*, serves as a good example). Neither are slaves/employees to labor faithfully for the sake of impressing bystanders (they are not to be *"men-pleasers"*—Ephesians 6:6). Rather, they are to be *"slaves of Christ, doing the will of God from the heart."* They are to work for what their employer receives (and what Christ receives) through their efforts, for the principle of the cross applies to the workplace like everywhere else.

Ephesians 6:7—With good will render service, as to the Lord, and not to men,

A slave/employee should work as though the Lord were his master/employer (Ephesians 6:7; Colossians 3:23), even in situations where the master/employer is less than fair. The slave/employee must *"render service, as to the Lord, and not to men"* (Ephesians 6:7) in such cases. This principle applies in ministry as well, for obedience (not results) should be the motivating factor as we serve others for their good.

Ephesians 6:8—knowing that whatever good thing each one does, this he will receive back from the Lord, whether slave or free.

Paul desired that the slaves who read this epistle would understand an important principle: that God rewards those who do their work as unto Him. Thus, the slave/employee can rest assured that God notices and rewards deeds done in faith. Hence, if the employer fails to reward the hardworking employee for his good service, God fills the gap. What comforting words for a day such as ours!

Ephesians 6:9—And, masters, do the same things to them, and give up threatening, knowing that both their Master and yours is in heaven, and there is no partiality with Him.

As the Christian masters of Paul's day interacted with their slaves, they were to display the same respect they expected in return. This principle applies to our day as well. Only those employers who respect their employees' physical, emotional, and spiritual needs are in a position of pleasing God. Therefore, in God's economy, *"threatening"* is out and sensitivity and respect for the employee are in. How could an employer threaten an employee and at the same time live by the principle of the cross—the principle that has controlled the relationships in the Godhead from eternity past? It would be totally impossible! As a result, the master/employer is to concern himself with creating a healthy work environment, paying fair wages, providing proper benefits, not requiring excessive hours on the job (keeping the wellbeing of the family in mind), and doing everything possible to fulfill his role as a godly master/employer.

The *"Master"* of both the slave/employee and master/employer *"is in heaven, and there is no partiality with Him"* (Ephesians 6:9)—for neither *"slave nor free man"* (Galatians 3:28) exists in God's economy. Why then would a Christian master/employer treat a slave/employee with anything but respect?

Ephesians 6:10—Finally, be strong in the Lord, and in the strength of His might.

All believers who know their worth in the Lord (Ephesians 1-3), who walk in humility, unity, maturity, truth, love, light, wisdom, the filling of the Spirit, and mutual submission (Ephesians 4:1–6:9), must learn to do war in God's strength against the master of deceit, Satan himself (2Corinthians 11:14; Revelation 20:3). All saints are attacked by *"the accuser of"* the *"brethren"* (Revelation 12:10). But just as God used Israel's wilderness wanderings to teach her to war (she was inexperienced in spiritual warfare as she exited Egypt—Exodus 13:17), He likewise uses our enemy (Satan) to train us for battle. God's goal is to teach us to fight spiritual battles with spiritual weaponry—never spiritual battles with physical weaponry (2Corinthians 10:4). We must learn that He alone is capable of defeating our enemy—never us.

Interestingly, *"be strong"* (Ephesians 6:10) can be translated *"be strengthened"* or *"be ye empowered"* (Greek Interlinear), pointing to God's empowering—never our own. Paul was well aware of this truth (2Corinthians 12:9-10), along with King David (Psalm 124:1-8) and King Jehoshaphat (2Chronicles 20:12), all of whom displayed incredible faith during times of adversity. Ephesians 6:10 and Ephesians 1:19 are in agreement:

> *and what is the surpassing greatness of His power toward us who believe. These are in accordance with the working of the strength of His might* (Ephesians 1:19)

We must never be caught off guard by the intensity of the battle (1Peter 4:12-16). Only the compromised believer meets with little opposition. Jesus began His public ministry with opposition from the enemy (Matthew 4:1-11) and ended it by defeating him on the cross (John 12:31). This same Jesus promised *"tribulation"* (John 16:33) for his followers and that *"friendship with the world"* was to end (James 4:4). Paul's trials are well documented, for while at Ephesus he wrote to the church at Corinth:

> *But I shall remain in Ephesus until Pentecost; for a wide door for*
> *effective service has opened to me, and there are many*
> *adversaries.* (1Corinthians 16:8-9)

Through living by the strength of Another, both Jesus (John 14:10) and Paul (Philippians 4:13) experienced the will of the Father fulfilled in their lives. So can we! We are in Jesus (2Corinthians 5:17), and He is in the Father (John 14:20)— meaning that we are in the Father as well. Jesus is in us (Galatians 2:20), along with the Spirit (John 14:17) and the Father (John 14:23), confirming that the Godhead's strength is continually accessible. Only a small portion of God's power is sufficient to overcome the enemy's fiercest assault, so Paul penned:

> *Finally, be strong in the Lord, and in the strength of His might.*
> (Ephesians 6:10)

God's *"might"* is our might when appropriated through faith.

Ephesians 6:11—Put on the full armor of God, that you may be able to stand firm against the schemes of the devil.

Put on the full armor of God, (6:11a)

Paul, a Roman citizen (Acts 22:27-28), had to be considering the Roman soldier as this God-inspired passage was penned. The apostle understood that no soldier entered battle without proper *"armor"* (that is, if he desired to see another day). *"Put on"* can actually be interpreted *"to envelop in,"* meaning that God's *"armor"* encases the believer. Thus, the saint is safe. *"Put on"* (in the Greek) also communicates that God's *"armor"* is never to be removed. Once the *"whole"* is in place, both offensive and defensive (helmet, breastplate, shield, sword, etc., as is described in verses 14-17), it remains. This *"armor of light"* (Romans 13:12) will be discussed in depth shortly.

that you may be able to stand firm against the schemes of the devil.(6:11b)

In military terms, *"stand firm"* meant "to hold your ground while under attack" as opposed to cowardly fleeing in a state of fright. Paul realized that the properly equipped saint could stand firm while facing *"the schemes of the devil."* *"Schemes"* is from the Greek *methodeia,* meaning "wiles (KJV), craftiness, trickery, cunning, or deception." Therefore, Satan, having mapped out his strategy, stalks believers as a lion stalks his prey, waiting for the proper moment to attack and *"devour"* (1Peter 5:8). Even Jesus was attacked by Satan at *"opportune"* times (Luke 4:13).

How good is Satan at his game? Very good! He has for centuries convinced lost mankind that God is something He isn't—a tyrant rather than a God of *"love"* (1John 4:8, 16). Satan has also persuaded believers to settle for much less than what Christ did for the saints the moment they were saved. As a result, deceived believers expend vast amounts of energy hoping to obtain what they already possess—a righteousness granted to them the moment they repented and believed while depraved (2Corinthians 5:21). God saved us to enjoy Him—not to work for Him. We were made *"holy and blameless"* (Ephesians 1:4) *"saints"* (1Corinthians 1:2), the apple of God's eye in fact, the instant we repented and believed. No need exists to work for what is already ours.

Salvation is neither obtained nor maintained through good works (Romans 3:20; Romans 5:20; Ephesians 2:8-9; Titus 3:5; Hebrews 7:25), for we were *"saved"* (Ephesians 2:8-9) by grace and are being *"kept"* (Jude 1) by grace. God's grace in offering His Son did it all, having saved us from our condemned state through Jesus' death (once we repented and believed) while saving us daily from the power of sin as we yield to His indwelling *"life"* (Romans 5:10; Colossians 3:4). Such knowledge should motivate us to (1) pursue holiness in all areas of our behavior (1Peter 1:16) (2) make our *"bodies a living and holy sacrifice"* (Romans 12:1) (3) understand fully that faith is to work *"by love"* (2Corinthians 5:14-15; Galatians 5:6) (4) realize that every good thing done for the cause of Christ is done by God as He sovereignly works through our personal choices (Philippians 2:13). In other words, He never needs our help!

The devil reels when a New Testament believer embraces his true identity in Christ. Only those equipped in God's armor, through basking in His truth, know how to war against such a devious foe. Paul speaks of this armor in more detail in verses 13-17.

Ephesians 6:12—For our struggle is not against flesh and blood, but against the rulers, against the powers, against the world forces of this darkness, against the spiritual forces of wickedness in the heavenly places.

"Struggle" can also be interpreted "wrestling," pointing to hand-to-hand combat rather than warring with bows and arrows, guns, etc. Believers enter this *"struggle"* the moment they submit to Christ, a *"struggle...not against flesh and blood."* Hoping to deceive believers into warring on the wrong front, our foe (Satan) attempts to convince man that he (Satan) isn't real.

The body of Christ faces a battle in the spiritual realm—not the physical. Therefore, so long as believers enter into spiritual battles with physical weaponry, their enemy makes a mockery out of their every move. Paul wisely reminded his readers that their battle was to be fought in the invisible realm against a highly organized foe. Satan and his demons, skilled in deception and trickery, coordinate all activity toward one well-defined goal—to come against God by coming against His people. Thus, our battle is *"against the rulers, against the powers, against the world forces of this darkness, against the spiritual forces of wickedness in the heavenly places"* (Ephesians 6:12), who desire that believers consider them non-existent.

Paul longed that his readers understand the reality of the demonic realm—not make it their main topic of study. Satan is never overcome through comprehending the details of his person and kingdom. Only God overcomes Satan, for He defeated him through the cross and Jesus' subsequent resurrection. God will cast Satan into *"the lake of fire"* at the end of the Millennium, the one-thousand-year reign of Christ on the earth (Revelation 20:7-10).

"Rulers" (Ephesians 6:12) is from the Greek *arche* and probably points to high-ranking demons (also rendered *"principalities"* in Romans 8:38 and *"rulers"* in Colossians 2:15). *"Powers"* (Ephesians 6:12) probably refers to a different rank of demons (also rendered *"power"* in Ephesians 2:2, *"authorities"* in Colossians 2:15, and *"authorities"* in 1Peter 3:22), the demons who dwell in the atmospheric heavens and make up Satan's kingdom *"of the air"* (Ephesians 2:2). The phrase, *"the world forces of this darkness"* (Ephesians 6:12), could point to those demons who rule over the individual nations, demons such as *"the prince of the kingdom of Persia"* in Daniel's day (Daniel 10:13). This scenario is reasonable considering that Satan remains the small "g" *"god of this world"* (2Corinthians 4:4). And finally, *"the spiritual forces of wickedness in the heavenly places"* (Ephesians 6:12) may point to the combination of Satan's activities, for his present abode is in the atmospheric heavens (Ephesians 2:2; 6:12; Revelation 12:7-12). From this location he periodically descends to earth in the form of *"a roaring lion"* (1Peter 5:8) or *"an angel of light"* (2Corinthians 11:14). He also enters into the highest heavens (into God's presence) for the purpose of accusing the *"brethren"* (Job 1:6; 2:1; Revelation 12:10). But note that although Satan has access to the highest heavens (where God dwells), his abode is in the atmospheric heavens, beneath where we dwell *"in Christ"* (Ephesians 2:6) and Christ dwells in God (John 14:20). He is a defeated foe (Colossians 2:15). This means that we can take authority over anything he and his demons send our way so long as it is done in God's strength, grace, and power. But we must continually be reminded that the conflict with these authorities and powers increases, rather than decreases, as the world progresses in sin (Revelation 12:12).

Ephesians 6:13—Therefore, take up the full armor of God, that you may be able to resist in the evil day, and having done everything, to stand firm.

Because Paul begins this verse with *"therefore,"* he desires that his readers take everything stated earlier and apply it to what follows. Consequently, Paul exhorts his readers to *"take up"* the *"armor"* he has encouraged them to *"put on"* in Ephesians 6:11. Since the verb *"take up"* is an aorist imperative, this armor is to be taken up with suddenness and intensity, put on, and never removed. Only our *"love"* for Christ and His Word (2Corinthians 5:14; Galatians 5:6) prevents us from discarding this protective attire. In Ephesians 6:14 we will begin to discuss the details of this armor and how it is to be taken up.

"Resist" (Ephesians 6:13) means "to oppose or stand against." We are to *"resist the devil"* (James 4:7) through standing *"firm"* in our *"faith"* (1Peter 5:9). The phrase, *"in the evil day"* (Ephesians 6:13), is perceived by Wuest as follows:

> the definite article before "day," marks it out as a particular day, probably, as Expositors says, "the day of violent temptation and assault, whenever that may come to us during the present time." (Wuest, 1989)[29]

We are to *"take up the full armor of God"* so we might "oppose" or "stand against" (in God's strength, of course) the evil one whenever he comes our way.

Believers who have *"done everything"* required to *"take up"* God's *"armor"* will *"stand firm"* (Ephesians 6:13), for properly equipped saints never wilt in battle. The converse is true as well, for defeated saints have committed one common error—they have removed their spiritual armor.

Even Christ wears armor while battling the enemy (Isaiah 59:17). Thus we, as Christ's body (Ephesians 4:12), are to *"take up the full armor of God"* (Ephesians 6:13). This armor, which fits perfectly in every way, prepares the warrior for spiritual confrontation. Hence, David rejected Saul's armor prior to facing Goliath (1Samuel 17:38-39).

Ephesians 6:14—Stand firm therefore, having girded your loins with truth, and having put on the breastplate of righteousness,

Stand firm therefore, having girded your loins with truth, (6:14a)

To *"stand firm"* against the enemy, a saint's *"loins"* must be *"girded with truth."*

"Having girded" is in the middle voice, confirming that the New Testament believer girds himself—God does not do the girding. To be *"girded"* basically means to prepare one's self, as confirmed by *"dressed in readiness"* in Luke 12:35:

> *"Be dressed in readiness, and keep your lamps alight.* (Luke 12:35)

Peter penned, *"Gird up your minds for action"* (1Peter 1:13). He did so realizing that truth written on the mind, and energized by the Holy Spirit, equips the soldier for battle.

Readily accessible weapons are essential for the victorious warrior. No soldier is prepared for battle without first tightening his belt around his *"loins"* (around his waist—Matthew 3:4; Mark 1:6). The belt holds crucial armor in place while allowing unrestricted movement. Therefore, the belt of *"truth"* (Ephesians 6:14) readies the soldier for action by providing freedom of movement. Clearly, Jesus set us free (John 8:32) so we might respond to the need of the moment.

The belt of *"truth"* consists of more than Bible knowledge, for revealed truth alone brings victory. Sin both blinds (1John 1:6) and deceives; thus the world's mindset, when accepted as truth, short-circuits our ability to stand in battle (2Timothy 2:4). (Elijah's fear of Jezebel robbed him of his spiritual strength—1Kings 19:1-4). Consequently, the belt of truth consists of truth learned plus truth applied.

and having put on the breastplate of righteousness, (6:14b)

The phrase, *"having put on,"* being in the middle voice, confirms that the believer clothes himself with the *"breastplate of righteousness."* Someone might ask, "Why put on a breastplate of righteousness when 1Corinthians 1:30 and 2Corinthians 5:21 confirm that New Testament believers have already been made righteous?" Yes, we were made righteous in our person (in our souls and spirits) the moment we accepted Christ (1Corinthians 1:30; 2Corinthians 5:21)—a righteousness not attained through good works or deeds (Romans 3:20; Ephesians 2:8-9; Titus 3:5). However, a difference exists between possessing righteousness versus implementing that righteousness while combating the enemy. God's people are to *"put on the breastplate of righteousness"* (Ephesians 6:14b) by appropriating (through faith) the fact that they are already righteous. Thus, rule number one when facing the enemy is to remember that he first attacks our person, our identity, by attempting to convince us that we are something we are not—confirmed by Satan's initial attack against the Son of God:

And the devil said to Him, "If You are the Son of God, tell this stone to become bread." (Luke 4:3)

Satan's goal was to convince Jesus that He was not the Father's Son. His mission, therefore, is to convince us that we are lowly sinners saved by grace rather than righteous saints of God. Why? Believers who view themselves as sinners saved by grace act like sinners saved by grace by accepting sin as a natural response. Believers who view themselves as righteous saints perceive sin as totally unnatural, avoiding sin at all costs by rejecting the enemy's schemes.

Believers who fail to understand who they are in Christ are incapable of using *"the breastplate of righteousness"* as protective armor (Ephesians 6:14a). Countless believers struggle with their identity, viewing themselves as worthless sinners when they are righteous saints (1Corinthians 1:2; 2Corinthians 5:21). So long as *"the accuser of the brethren"* (Revelation 12:10) can convince God's people that they are second-class citizens of the Kingdom, and thus partially unrighteous, the church cannot stand in battle. As the breastplate of righteousness protected the heart of the Roman soldier, it, in the spiritual sense, covers the heart of the saint—which includes his mind, will, and emotions. Only as we appropriate our true identity do we protect our minds from Satan's onslaught. We were made the *"righteousness of God"* (2Corinthians 5:21) the moment we accepted Christ. Because we received such a standing, God will never condemn us (Romans 8:1). In fact, He will present us *"blameless with great joy"* (Jude 24) before Him. The enemy cringes when we begin to realize this truth. Consequently, one of the prerequisites for wearing the *"breastplate of righteousness"* is realizing that our person (being soul and spirit) has been made totally righteous—that only our behavior improves in righteousness as we mature in the faith. What wonderful news! This truth extinguishes the false accusations directed our way by *"the father of lies"* (John 8:44), *"the accuser of the brethren"* (Revelation 12:10).

Believers unconcerned with righteous living are incapable of putting on the breastplate. Sin handicaps, making us weak-kneed and feeble before our enemy. It gives Satan *"an opportunity"* to defeat us (Ephesians 4:25-27) by robbing us of our authority and joy.

Conclusion: Understanding our righteous standing before God, along with a passion to walk in righteousness, is required before we can *"put on the breastplate of righteousness"* (Ephesians 6:14).

Ephesians 6:15—and having shod your feet with the preparation of the gospel of peace;

In Paul's day, Roman soldiers wore boots that provided ample traction. These boots were essential, for to lose footing while engaging in hand-to-hand combat normally meant death. Paul equates the *"gospel of peace"* with such attire. He realized that none of God's children could stand without being *"shod...with the preparation of the gospel of peace."* Again the middle voice is implemented, confirming that the believer is to perform this action on himself.

"The gospel of peace" can be defined in two statements. First, the New Testament believer has *"peace with God"* once *"justified by God"*—subsequent to exercising *"faith"* in Christ (Romans 5:1). Second, the New Testament saint walks in *"the peace of God"* (Philippians 4:7; John 16:33; 14:27) as he allows the Holy Spirit to fill (Ephesians 5:18; Galatians 5:22) and empower (Acts 1:8; Romans 15:13) him for daily living. Therefore, the *"gospel of peace"* not only establishes peace between God and the saints but also brings peace to the souls of saints who properly apply it (the gospel) in principle and practice.

Scripture validates that peace "with" God must be established before one walks in the peace "of" God. Peace "with" God is gained at the point of salvation/justification and cannot be undone, while the peace "of" God is dependent on the believer's thought life and conduct. The saint who chooses disobedience instantaneously loses the peace "of" God, regaining it only after repenting of his misdeeds.

We must be equipped with these truths if we are to withstand the enemy's onslaught. As the serpent falsely accused God while addressing Eve (Genesis 3:4-5), he continues placing lies about God's Person in the minds of the saints. He desires that we view God as an unjust, unfair, vicious tyrant who is out to destroy us. Nothing, not even a cross, could allow such a God to enter into a peaceful relationship with the redeemed. Only one weapon extinguishes Satan's falsities: A contextual interpretation and application of God's Word. We, without hesitation, are to replace his lies with truth. We have *"peace"* with the God of the universe (Romans 5:1), Who loves us (John 3:16), is for us (Romans 8:31), and views us as part of his glorious family (John 1:12). No believer can stand void of these truths.

Neither can the believer stand unless he walks in the peace "of" God, the peace that results from a godly lifestyle. This peace is a *"fruit of the Spirit"* (Galatians 5:22) which can be instantaneously squelched through disobedience, leaving us powerless against the enemy. Satan has purpose in making sin so extraordinarily enticing. He knows we will retreat in battle if we will but take a bite.

"Preparation" (Ephesians 6:15) can be rendered "readiness," meaning that *"the gospel of peace,"* once understood (in context), "readies" the saint for Satan's

202

fiercest attack. The converse is true as well, for believers whose understanding of the gospel is lacking retreat at the slightest sign of conflict.

Ephesians 6:16—in addition to all, taking up the shield of faith with which you will be able to extinguish all the flaming missiles of the evil one.

Three pieces of equipment are mentioned in verses 16 and 17—*"the shield of faith"* (Ephesians 6:16), *"the helmet of salvation"* (Ephesians 6:17), and *"the sword of the Spirit"* (Ephesians 6:17). They will be examined at this time.

The Roman soldier possessed two shields: (1) a small shield worn on the forearm (2) a large shield measuring approximately four feet by two and one half feet. Paul addresses the second shield in verse 16.

The root word for *"shield"* (Ephesians 6:16) is rendered *"door"* in Matthew 6:6. Thus, the soldier's shield was similar to a door in that it was large enough to hide behind (the Roman soldier was smaller in stature than the average man today). Made of thick wood and covered with leather, it could intercept the enemy's fiery arrows (*"flaming missiles"*) and, in many cases, *"extinguish"* them. (Several of these arrows were covered with pitch and ignited before being launched.) Can you imagine the appearance of the shield after battle? Its exterior might have been peppered with arrows and charred beyond recognition, but the shield would have functioned according to design.

Paul's message is clear. The believer's shield is capable of intercepting and extinguishing all the *"flaming missiles of the evil one"* (Ephesians 6:16). This shield consists of *"faith"* (Ephesians 6:16), the *"victory"* that overcomes anything the enemy sends our way (1John 5:4). Hence, all of the enemy's sinful thoughts (flaming missiles) are intercepted and squelched by *"the shield of faith."*

"Faith" in this instance points to simple trust in God and His Word, a faith that grows as the believer matures (2Thessalonians 1:3). Without it we cannot please God (Hebrews 11:6) or prevail in battle (Romans 5:2; 1Corinthians 16:13; 2Corinthians 1:24; 1Peter 5:9; 1John 5:4), for faith extinguishes the enemies lies so we can live victoriously! Regardless of the magnitude, type, or timing of the temptation, we can triumph through faith—faith in God's ability to see us through!

Ephesians 6:17—And take the helmet of salvation, and the sword of the Spirit, which is the word of God.

And take the helmet of salvation, (6:17a)

As the Roman soldier dressed for battle, he made certain that the *"helmet"* was in place. This piece of armor, made of leather or metal, shielded the crown of the head, the forehead, cheeks, and neck. It protected him against weaponry designed for decapitation.

This particular piece of armor reminds me of an event that occurred during my stint in the army. My drill instructor directed our platoon members to fight each other (two at a time and toe-to-toe) with long sticks padded on both ends. This arrangement would have been quite intimidating had it not been for the equipment issued beforehand. We each received a football helmet as the sole source of protection and were told that the last man standing was the winner. Since I appreciated the health the Lord had given me and desired to live a long and fruitful life, I was, to say the least, concerned about the outcome. However, the moment my head entered that football helmet I changed into a different creature. I could not believe my bolstered confidence; the helmet made me feel as if I could conquer the world. I was ready to go, so fight I did—with fervor and authority!

The *"helmet of salvation"* (Ephesians 6:17a) emboldens the believer. It supplies the hope and confidence necessary to stand poised in battle—the posture feared most by Satan and his henchmen. No soldier donning this helmet goes limp or turns passive while confronting the enemy. Yet, we must be careful. Such confidence must rest in God's abilities—never our own. Only the omnipotent, Triune God is capable of standing toe-to-toe with a foe so fierce and deceitful.

Believers void of *"the helmet of salvation"* (Ephesians 6:17) cannot stand, for one stroke from the enemy's sword of deception results in immediate decapitation (incapacitation). We best understand, therefore, how to secure our headgear.

"Helmet of salvation" is not necessarily referencing our salvation (born again) experience, but the assurance of that salvation. Only believers who understand their security in Christ can properly don this headgear. Once mounted and adjusted, it grants the hope and confidence necessary for victory (1Thessalonians 5:8-9). The opposite is also true. The saint who views himself as saved today, lost tomorrow, and saved the next, opens himself to incredible deception. In fact, he is incapable of looking Satan in the eye and, in God's authority and strength, demanding that he flee. Thus, the helmet of salvation grants boldness and courage as Satan questions the stability of our relationship with the Father—one of Satan's most treasured and frequently employed weapons. No saint of God lives abundantly who allows this matter to remain unsettled.

The enemy also desires that we perceive salvation as our responsibility to maintain. This lie is refuted by Hebrews 7:25:

> *Hence, also, He is able to save forever those who draw near to God through Him, since He always lives to make intercession for them .* (Hebrews 7:25)

Jesus' duty, obligation, and mandate, as high priest, is to *"save forever"* those who are His. We could lose our salvation only if Jesus died a second time—an impossibility according to Hebrews 10:10:

> *By this will we have been sanctified through the offering of the body of Jesus Christ <u>once</u> for all.* (Hebrews 10:10)

We are *"sealed"* in Christ (Ephesians 1:13), *"kept for Christ"* (Jude 1), and nothing can snatch us *"out of the Father's hand"* (John 10:28-29):

> *In Him, you also, after listening to the message of truth, the gospel of your salvation — having also believed, you were sealed in Him with the Holy Spirit of promise,* (Ephesians 1:13)

> *...to those who are the called, beloved in God the Father, and kept for Jesus Christ:* (Jude 1)

> *and I give eternal life to them, and they shall never perish; and no one shall snatch them out of My hand. "My Father, who has given them to Me, is greater than all; and no one is able to snatch them out of the Father's hand.* (John 10:28-29)

and the sword of the Spirit, which is the word of God. (6:17b)

The Roman soldier's double-edged sword, ranging from six to eighteen inches in length, was carried in a sheath attached to his belt for easy accessibility. In hand-to-hand combat it assisted him both defensively and offensively, so no soldier entered battle without it. Defensively it intercepted the enemy's blows, while offensively it drew the enemy's blood.

The believer's sword, *"the sword of the Spirit"* (Ephesians 6:17b), is *"the word of God"* (Ephesians 6:17b). Interestingly, *"inspired"* in 2Timothy 3:16 can actually be translated "God-breathed":

> *All Scripture is <u>inspired</u> by God and profitable for teaching, for reproof, for correction, for training in righteousness; that the man of God may be adequate, equipped for every good work.*
> (2Timothy 3:16-17)

Therefore, when Paul writes that *"all Scripture is inspired by God"* (2Timothy 3:16), he is actually communicating that all Scripture is God-breathed. If Scripture truly is the "breath of God," then Isaiah 11:4 adds intriguing insight by stating:

> *...And He will strike the earth with the rod of His mouth, and with <u>the breath of His lips</u> He will slay the wicked.* (Isaiah 11:4)

In Revelation 19:15 we also read:

> *And from His mouth comes a sharp sword, so that with it He may smite the nations;...* (Revelation 19:15)

Christ's weapon is the truth that He speaks. Thus, our *"sword," "the word of God"* (Ephesians 6:17b), is *"two-edged"* (Hebrews 4:12) in that it feeds and encourages us and, at the same time, defeats the enemy. Satan, a liar (John 8:44), cannot stand against truth; for truth exposes him for who he is (John 3:19-20). Consequently, when Christ returns with His church at His Second Coming, the *"lawless one"* (the Antichrist) will be slain *"with the breath of His* (Jesus') *mouth"*:

> *And then that lawless one will be revealed whom the Lord will slay with the breath of His mouth and bring to an end by the appearance of His coming;* (2Thessalonians 2:8)

Clearly, the *"sword...,which is the word of God"* (Ephesians 6:17b), functions both defensively and offensively. But to appreciate its value, one must understand the difference between knowing Scripture in the form of general information (*logos*) and applying it to daily living (*rhema*). Because *"word"* (Ephesians 6:17b) is *rhema* in the Greek, *Vine's Dictionary* states:

> Here the reference is not to the whole Bible as such, but to the individual Scripture which the Spirit brings to our remembrance for use in time of need, a prerequisite being the regular storing of the mind with Scripture. (Vine, 1996)[30]

Only as the believer saturates his mind with truth does the Spirit bring remembrance (in the form of *rhema*) regarding the specific verses that counter the enemy's schemes (John 14:26; 16:13; Galatians 5:16)—as was the case with Jesus in Matthew 4:1-22. So Paul uses the Greek *rhema* in Romans 10:17:

> *So faith comes from hearing, and hearing by the word* [rhema] *of Christ.* (Romans 10:17)

Active faith that can withstand the enemy's onslaught is bolstered as the Holy Spirit brings revelation (*rhema*) to the mind saturated with the written Word of God (*logos*). Hence, God's children are to familiarize themselves with truth (Psalm 1; 2Timothy 2:15; 3:15-16; Hebrews 5:12-14) if they desire the Spirit to work mightily in their daily experiences.

One final thought and we will exit this powerful passage. Because we so easily forget God's Word (Hebrews 2:1), meditating on truth must become a lifestyle. God longs that we permeate our minds with His Word (Psalm 1:1-3; 119:9-11; 2Timothy 2:15; 3:15-17; Hebrews 5:12-14; etc.), for continued growth is necessary for abundant living. Satan's hobby is snatching truth from the mind of man (Matthew 13:19-22; Hebrews 5:12). He masterfully convinces the unwise and immature that God's Word is irrelevant to the need of the day. When his lies are allowed to take root, the warrior stands helpless as his sword remains fixed in its sheath.

Ephesians 6:18—With all prayer and petition pray at all times in the Spirit, and with this in view, be on the alert with all perseverance and petition for all the saints,

The armor of God functions remarkably once fixed in place. It prepares the saint for spiritual battles he can't win. Only God overcomes the forces of darkness (Romans 16:20; 1John 4:4; Revelation 19:11-21). Therefore, the armor of verses 10-17 equips the saint to pray—the prerequisite for victory. Only saints who have *"girded"* their *"loins with truth"* (Ephesians 6:14), wear *"the breastplate of righteousness"* (Ephesians 6:14), have *"shod"* their *"feet with the...gospel"* (Ephesians 6:15), carry *"the shield of faith"* (Ephesians 6:16), don *"the helmet of salvation"* (Ephesians 6:17), and wield *"the sword of the Spirit"* (Ephesians 6:17) are equipped to do battle in prayer.

Scripture confirms that God honors prayer. Through prayer the nation of Israel overcame the Amalekites (Exodus 17:8-13), Hannah conceived and bore Samuel (1Samuel 1:9-20), Nehemiah was shown favor before King Artaxerxes and allowed to rebuild the wall in Jerusalem (Nehemiah 1:11–2:8), Satan's forces were overthrown (Daniel 10:1-21), Cornelius and the Gentiles heard the gospel (Acts

10:1-48), Peter was delivered from prison (Acts 12:1-17), etc. Prayer works! In fact, know all about the blessings bestowed to the New Testament believer (the subject matter of Ephesians 1-3), yet neglect prayer, and life becomes astonishingly fruitless. God imparted truth to teach us the necessity of dependence upon Him, a dependence confirmed and substantiated by a lifestyle of prayer. How we are to pray is the subject matter of Ephesians 6:18.

With all prayer and petition pray at all times in the Spirit, (6:18a)

"Prayer" (*proseuche*) makes reference to prayer in general, while *"petition"* (*deeseos*) points to specific requests. By writing, *"all prayer and petition,"* Paul confirms that believers are to pray all types of prayers as needs arise. Sometimes we pray for others (intercessory prayer). Sometimes we pray for ourselves. We can ask for God's blessings (Numbers 6:23-27), confess sin (Psalm 32:1-5), and pray when emergencies arise (Matthew 14:30). We can pray silently or out loud, in all types of postures, and in all types of places—in fact, *"in every place"* (1Timothy 2:8). We are to pray *"at all times"* (Luke 18:1; Ephesians 6:18a); in fact, we are to pray *"without ceasing"* (1Thessalonians 5:17). Saints are to devote themselves to prayer (Acts 1:14; Romans 12:12; Colossians 4:2), persevere in prayer (Daniel 10:12-13), and live in an attitude of prayer (Psalm 5:3; 55:17; Psalm 119:55, 62, 147; Daniel 6:10; Mark 1:35; Luke 2:37; 6:12; 18:1; Acts 10:2; 16:25; 1Thessalonians 3:10). Our lives should be characterized by uninterrupted communion with the Father.

To *"pray at all times"* (Ephesians 6:18a) doesn't mean to pray out loud (or even silently) every moment of the day. No one addressed in Scripture lived as such, not even Paul. What is being encouraged is an attitude of prayer. Consequently, when we are blessed, we thank God immediately for His blessings. When we meet someone in need, we ask God to meet that need. When we see a flower in bloom or a bird in flight, we praise Him that instant for His creativity and power. When we are tempted, we approach Him for grace to overcome. Through living in an attitude of prayer, we are *"saved by His life"* (Romans 5:10), the natural byproduct of living in uninterrupted fellowship with the Creator (John 17:3; 1John 1:3).

To *"pray...in the Spirit"* (Ephesians 6:18) means to pray in harmony with the Holy Spirit—Who approaches the Father on our behalf (Romans 8:26-27). Because the Person of the Spirit intercedes for us *"with groanings too deep for words"* (Romans 8:26) and *"according to the will of God"* (Romans 8:27), to *"pray...in the Spirit"* (Ephesians 6:18) simply means to pray in agreement with what the Spirit is already praying. Any prayer offered in this manner will agree with the full counsel of God's Word, for the Spirit never leads us to violate truth. Only as saints are *"filled with the Spirit"* (Ephesians 5:18) can they experience the prayer life described in these powerful passages.

and with this in view, be on the alert with all perseverance and petition for all the saints, (6:18b)

As we *"pray at all times in the Spirit"* (Ephesians 6:18a), we are to *"be on the alert with all perseverance and petition for all the saints"* (Ephesians 6:18b). The Greek *agrupeno*, from which we get *"be on the alert"* (Ephesians 6:18b), is also translated *"keep watch"* in Hebrews 13:17. It means "to be wakeful or sleepless." This same word is used in association with prayer in Luke 21:36:

> *"But keep on the alert at all times, praying in order that you may have strength to escape all these things that are about to take place, and to stand before the Son of Man."* (Luke 21:36)

The believer is to remain alert in prayer by thanking God for His Person and provision:

> *Devote yourselves to prayer, keeping alert in it with an attitude of thanksgiving;* (Colossians 4:2)

> *Be anxious for nothing, but in everything by prayer and supplication with thanksgiving let your requests be made known to God.* (Philippians 4:6)

Thanking and praising God serves to restore perspective in any and all circumstances. Hence, prayer is essential if the outfitted warrior is to stand!

When we pray we are to *"be on the alert with all perseverance and petition for all the saints"* (Ephesians 6:18b). *"Perseverance"* is from a Greek word that can also be interpreted "to be intently engaged in, to attend to constantly." A close relative of this word is employed in Colossians 4:2 and interpreted *"devote"*:

> *Devote yourselves to prayer, keeping alert in it with an attitude of thanksgiving;* (Colossians 4:2)

As we learned in Ephesians 6:18a, *"petition"* (Ephesians 6:18b) points to specific requests. Coupling this fact with *"for all the saints"* (Ephesians 6:18b), we can conclude that believers are to pray specific requests on behalf of all of Christ's body. Should this possibility become a reality, God would work amazingly through and for His people regardless of what Satan sent their way! Thus, Paul practiced and promoted intercessory prayer (Romans 1:9; 2Corinthians 9:14; Ephesians 1:15-

19a; 3:14-19; Colossians 4:3; 12; 1Timothy 2:1-2; Philemon 1:22).

I am realizing, as Samuel discovered years ago, that to cease praying for others is sin (1Samuel 12:23). In fact, when I am negligent in praying for my family, friends, and specific needs of others, I sense I am by-passing and short-circuiting God's best for all concerned. Prayer is sometimes exhausting (Exodus 17:8-13; Colossians 4:12), for it is warfare fought on our knees. What a wonderful opportunity to apply the principle of the cross! To pray for what others might receive through God honoring our petitions is one of the greatest acts of selflessness accessible to man.

Ephesians 6:19—and pray on my behalf, that utterance may be given to me in the opening of my mouth, to make known with boldness the mystery of the gospel,

Paul, recognizing that God honors the prayers of the intercessor, encouraged the Ephesians to intercede on his behalf. He had only one request: *"that utterance may be given to me in the opening of my mouth, to make known with boldness the mystery of the gospel"* (Ephesians 6:19). As far as ministry was concerned, Paul's chief desire was to speak boldly as he shared *"the mystery of the gospel"* (for more input concerning *"the mystery,"* review Ephesians 3:3). To make certain that Satan's assault did nothing to cloud his focus or thwart his vision, he requested that the church at Ephesus stand in the gap through prayer.

Ephesians 6:20—for which I am an ambassador in chains; that in proclaiming it I may speak boldly, as I ought to speak.

The words, *"in chains"* (Ephesians 6:20), confirm that *Ephesians* is one of Paul's prison epistles. Even though imprisoned, his greatest concern ministry-wise was that he speak truth with boldness. *"Boldly"* (*parresia*) means "freedom, confidence, clarity, openness, and frankness." Only speech of this sort could captivate the audience addressed in Paul's environment.

Ephesians 6:21—But that you also may know about my circumstances, how I am doing, Tychicus, the beloved brother and faithful minister in the Lord, will make everything known to you.

Paul desired that the Ephesians *"know about"* his *"circumstances"* and how he was *"doing"* (Ephesians 6:21), so he sent *"Tychicus"* to *"make everything known to"* them. It would stand to reason that Tychicus, an Asian (Acts 20:4), would carry Paul's letter to Ephesus, a seaport city of the Roman province of Asia. Not only would the epistle bring encouragement to the church, but Tychicus could provide additional input concerning Paul's wellbeing. Tychicus had delivered other Pauline epistles such as the letter to Colosse (Colossians 4:7-9). Based on 2Timothy 4:12 and Titus 3:12, he often functioned as Paul's messenger. He was a *"beloved brother and faithful minister in the Lord"* (Ephesians 6:21) who could be trusted.

Paul must have been comforted that a man of such caliber would deliver this epistle. Tychicus knew Paul's heart and soul; so in a sense, Paul was sending his very heart through him (as was the case with Onesimus in Philemon 1:10-12). Friends of this caliber are hard to find; but once found, their value and worth are immeasurable.

Ephesians 6:22—And I have sent him to you for this very purpose, so that you may know about us, and that he may comfort your hearts.

Paul's purpose in sending Tychicus was that the Ephesians might be comforted, so again the apostle makes a decision based on the needs of others rather than his own. Evidently the church had become burdened over Paul's imprisonment in Rome.

Ephesians 6:23—Peace be to the brethren, and love with faith, from God the Father and the Lord Jesus Christ.

Verses 23-24 make up Paul's benediction. In using the phrase, *"peace be to the brethren,"* Paul evidently references the believer's *peace with God* (Romans 5:1) as well as *the peace of God* experienced by the Spirit-filled saint (Galatians 5:22; Ephesians 5:18)—both of which combine to establish relational *"peace"* among *"the brethren"* (Ephesians 6:23). Paul has addressed these subjects previously in this epistle, so his saying *"Peace be to the brethren"* in his benediction would likely have been well received.

"Love" (Ephesians 6:23), a *"fruit of the Spirit"* (Galatians 5:22), has also been a recurring theme. The Ephesians could walk in God's *"love"* (1John 4:8, 16) because it had been poured into their hearts through the Holy Spirit (Romans 5:5). They could love because God first loved them (1John 4:19) and so prove to be Jesus' disciples (John 13:34-35).

"Faith" (Ephesians 6:23), which grows as we absorb truth (2Thessalonians 1:3), is more than believing that God exists. True *"faith"* applies God's Word in the daily

affairs of life, so Paul made sure to mention it in his benediction.

Ephesians 6:24—Grace be with all those who love our Lord Jesus Christ with a love incorruptible.

In closing, Paul prays that his readers walk in God's *"grace."* As we discovered earlier, *"grace"* is *"unmerited favor."* God's *"grace"* also empowers His people (1Corinthians 15:10). Thus, Paul prayed this prayer realizing that saints are saved by grace (Ephesians 2:8-9) and kept by grace (Acts 20:32; Romans 5:2; 1Corinthians 15:10; 2Corinthians 12:9; Hebrews 4:16; James 4:6; 1Peter 5:10). Such grace, however, is not supplied to everyone. Only individuals who *"love our Lord Jesus Christ with a love incorruptible"* (Ephesians 6:24) receive and display it. May we never forget that loving God with all our heart and soul is the essence, substance, and core of a life worth living.

Having now finished this remarkable epistle, may we love and enjoy Jesus as never before. May we, through the power of the Holy Spirit, live by His life for the good of others!

Diagram 1

Eternity
No Beginning And No End

∞   ∞

Diagram 2   ## Why God's Foreknowledge Cannot Precede His Eternal Decrees

Calvinism and Arminianism adhere to the idea that the elect were elected (chosen) and predestined <u>to salvation</u> from eternity past by means of an eternal decree. This arrangement is impossible, and the following explains why.

Scripture teaches that God's decrees are eternal (Jeremiah 5:22), having always existed in His heart.

> *'Do you not fear Me?' declares the LORD. 'Do you not tremble in My presence? For I have placed the sand as a boundary for the sea, An eternal decree, so it cannot cross over it. Though the waves toss, yet they cannot prevail; Though they roar, yet they cannot cross over it.* (Jeremiah 5:22)

Scripture also requires God's foreknowledge (which means to know beforehand) to precede the predestination and election (choosing) of a New Testament believer.

> *For those <u>whom He foreknew, He also predestined</u> to become conformed to the image of His Son, so that He would be the firstborn among many brethren;* (Romans 8:29)

> *Peter, an apostle of Jesus Christ, To those who reside as aliens, scattered throughout Pontus, Galatia, Cappadocia, Asia, and Bithynia, who are <u>chosen according to the foreknowledge of God the Father,</u> by the sanctifying work of the Spirit, to obey Jesus Christ and be sprinkled with His blood : May grace and peace be yours in the fullest measure.* (1Peter 1:1-2)

Should God's foreknowledge, meaning "to know beforehand," precede His eternal decrees, eternity would have a beginning (a starting point)—a total impossibility.

Because God's decrees are eternal (Jeremiah 5:22), and foreknowledge is required to precede the predestination and election (choosing) of the New Testament believer (Romans 8:29; 1Peter 1:1-2), for God to have predestined or elected (chosen) New Testament believers to salvation from eternity past by means of an eternal decree is impossible.

The Scriptures teach that New Testament believers are elected and predestined to blessings (rather than to salvation), a predestination and election that occur when they are placed in Christ subsequent to their exercising personal repentance and faith while depraved. This truth allows God's foreknowledge to precede the predestination and election of a New Testament believer, as displayed below.

FOREKNOWLEDGE | Predestination of New Testament Believers when they are spiritually regenerated (saved). Election/Chosenness of New Testament Believers when they are spiritually regenerated (saved).

∞

213

Diagram 3

God, The Eternal I AM

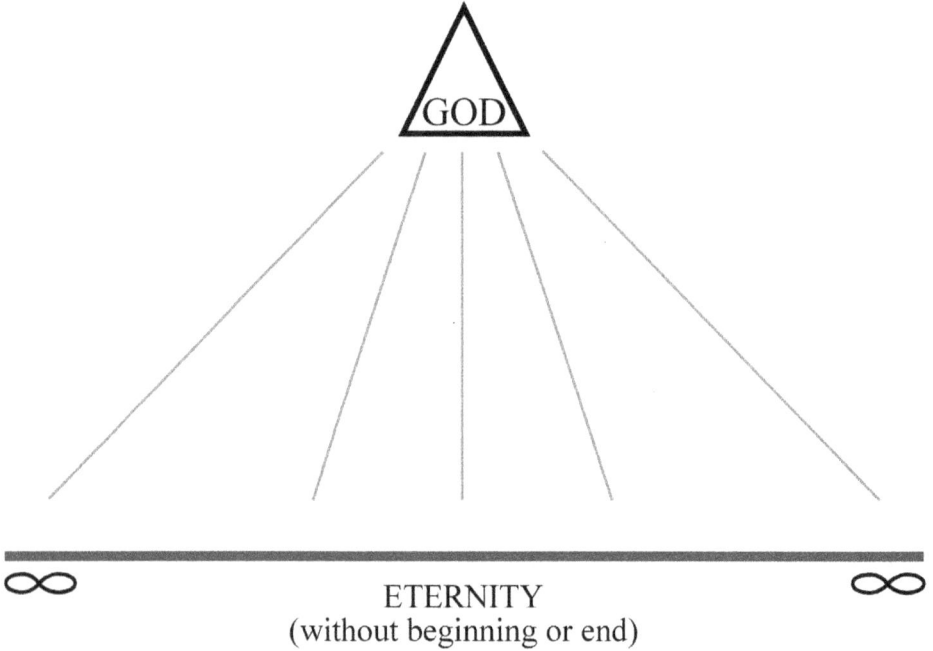

∞   ETERNITY   ∞
(without beginning or end)

God sees all events, from eternity past through eternity future, throughout His eternal existence. In other words, He possesses the ability to see all things at once. He therefore, is never caught off guard since He possesses knowledge of all past, present, and future events. God is not required to cause events to foreknow them.

Diagram 4

Arminius' Beliefs

Election
Predestination

| FOREKNOWLEDGE |

∞

Arminius' belief regarding foreknowledge affected his view of salvation. He believed that God looked into the future and, by means of His eternal foreknowledge, saw who would choose to repent and believe while depraved. God then, based on Arminius' theology, elected (chose) and predestined these future believers to salvation from eternity past by means of an eternal decree.

Diagram 5

What Arminius' Belief System Actually Communicates

Election
Predestination
God's Foreknowledge

∞   ∞

Arminius believed that God's decrees, as well as His foreknowledge, are eternal. He also believed that certain individuals were elected (chosen) and predestined to salvation by means of an eternal decree. This order, however, leaves no room for God's foreknowledge to precede the New Testament believer's election and predestination. Arminius' theological chronology actually stacked election, predestination, and God's foreknowledge on top of each other, when Romans 8:29 and 1Peter 1:1-2 require God's foreknowledge to precede the election and predestination of a New Testament believer. Arminius arrived at this contradiction due to equating the blessings associated with salvation with salvation itself.

Diagram 6

Calvin's Beliefs

Election
Predestination
(God's Foreknowledge = Foreordination or Predestination)

∞   ∞

Calvin believed that God, from eternity past and by means of an eternal decree, elected (chose) and predestined the elect to salvation. This view contradicts Romans 8:29 and 1Peter 1:1-2, both of which require God's foreknowledge to precede the election (chosenness) and predestination of a New Testament believer. Thus, Calvin's theology fails to provide room for foreknowledge to precede the election (chosenness) and predestination of a New Testament believer. Therefore, Calvin deemed foreknowledge as synonymous with foreordination or predestination. In other words Calvin redefined foreknowledge as foreordination or predestination, which required the writing of volumes of materials in an effort to remedy such contradiction. Calvin arrived at this error due to equating the blessings associated with salvation with salvation itself.

Diagram 7

The Remedy to Calvin's and Arminius' Error

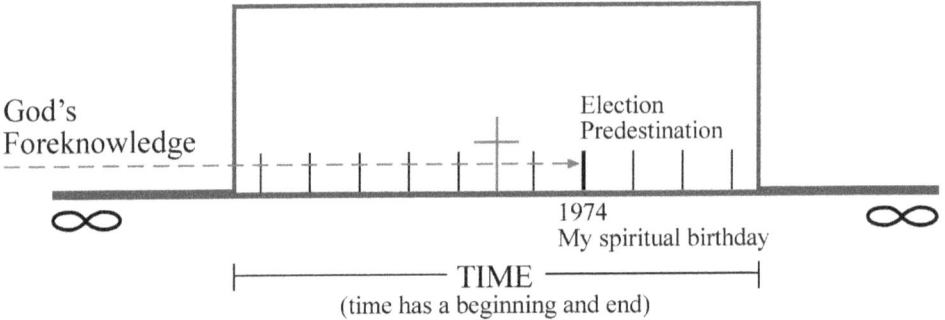

God's
Foreknowledge

Election
Predestination

∞   1974
My spiritual birthday   ∞

TIME
(time has a beginning and end)

The remedy to Calvin's and Arminius' error is found in allowing God's foreknowledge in this case to point to His foreknowledge of the thoughts, actions, and decisions of those who choose to repent and believe during the church age. Once they exercise repentance and faith while depraved, they are placed in Christ. God then predestines them to one day receive a glorified body (Romans 8:23; Ephesians 1:5). He also elects (chooses) them in Christ (Ephesians 1:4), after they repent and believe while depraved, bestowing upon them the office (gifting--1Peter 4:10) to which he elects them.

New Testament believers are placed in Christ, subsequent to repenting and believing while depraved, and only then are elected (chosen) and predestined. At that point they receive eternal life, life with no beginning and no end, and are viewed by the Father as having always been in Christ (Ephesians 1:4).

216

Diagram 8

Scriptural Election/Chosenness and Predestination

The Father sees all New Testament believers, subsequent to their exercising personal repentance and faith while depraved and being made new, as having always been in Christ due to the type of life they receive at the point of salvation - eternal life.

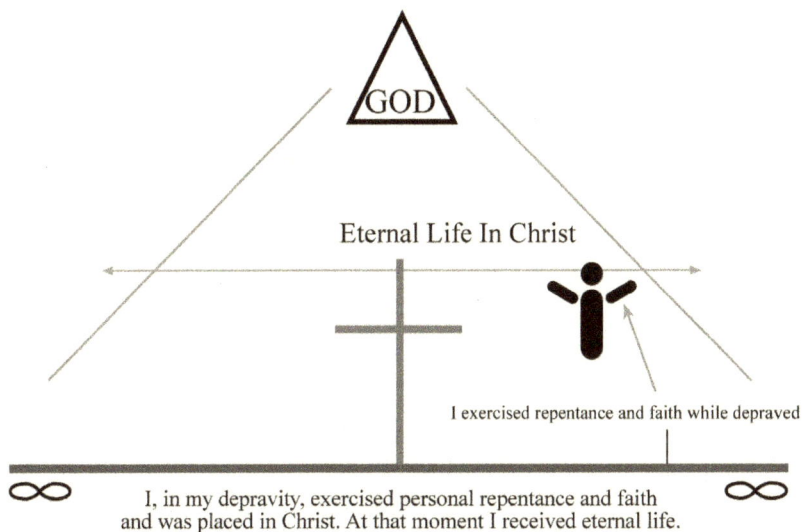

I, in my depravity, exercised personal repentance and faith and was placed in Christ. At that moment I received eternal life.

The Holy Spirit places those seeking salvation during the church age into Christ when they repent and exercise faith while depraved (1Corinthians 12:13). Once this occurs, God makes them new (2Corinthians 5:17). He also predestines them (at that time) to receive glorified bodies at the Rapture of the church (Ephesians 1:5; Romans 8:23; 1Corinthians 15:35-58; 1Thessalonians 4:13-18). They are also elected/chosen (at that time) to office due to having been placed into Christ, the Father's elect/chosen one (Luke 9:35; Isaiah 42:1), Who was elected/chosen to the office of Messiah. The office to which New Testament believers are elected/chosen is the special office or position (gift) they receive (1Peter 4:10) in conjunction with being placed in Christ and made new. Therefore, New Testament believers were not predestined and elected/chosen to salvation from eternity past by means of an eternal decree. They are predestined the moment they are made new in Christ subsequent to repenting and believing while depraved; predestined to receive a new body (Ephesians 1:5; Romans 8:23) at the Rapture of the church. They are also elected/chosen to office when placed in Christ, subsequent to repenting and believing while depraved, Christ having been elected/chosen to office, the office of Messiah. Ephesians 1:4 states:

> just as He chose us in Him before the foundation of the world, that we should be holy
> and blameless before Him. (Ephesians 1:4)

Once New Testament believers are placed in Christ, they receive His kind of life, eternal life (Romans 6:23; Colossians 3:4), life with no beginning and no end. As a result, the Father sees them as having always been in Christ, even "*before the foundation of the world*" (Ephesians 1:4). Consequently, their point of entry into Christ is when they repent and believe while depraved; but once they are placed in Him through the power of the Holy Spirit (1Corinthians 12:13), the Father sees them as having always been in His holy Son. He will continue to view New Testament believers in this manner throughout eternity.

217

Diagram 9

The Predestination of Jesus' Death and the Hidden Wisdom

Acts 4:27-28; 1Corinthians 2:7

For truly in this city there were gathered together against Your holy servant Jesus, whom You annointed, both Herod and Pontius Pilate, along with the Gentiles and the peoples of Israel, to do whatever Your hand and Your purpose predestined to occur. (Acts 4:27-28)

but we speak God's wisdom in a mystery, the hidden wisdom which God predestined before the ages to our glory; (1Corinthians 2:7)

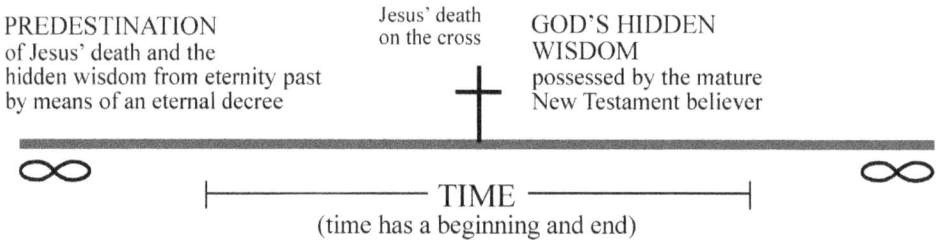

PREDESTINATION
of Jesus' death and the
hidden wisdom from eternity past
by means of an eternal decree

Jesus' death
on the cross

GOD'S HIDDEN
WISDOM
possessed by the mature
New Testament believer

∞   ——— TIME ———   ∞

(time has a beginning and end)

The Scriptures do not require that the predestination of the cross (Acts 4:27-28) and the hidden wisdom of God (1Corinthians 2:7) be preceded by God's foreknowledge. This difference leaves room for God to have predestined the cross and the hidden wisdom from eternity past by means of an eternal decree. Such an arrangement is unlike the predestination of the New Testament believer, which occurs in time, and requires God's foreknowledge to precede it.

218

Diagram 10

Reformed Theology (Extreme and Hyper-Calvinism)

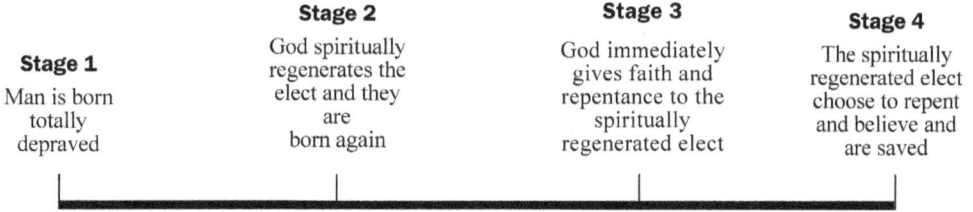

	Stage 2	Stage 3	Stage 4
Stage 1	God spiritually regenerates the elect and they are born again	God immediately gives faith and repentance to the spiritually regenerated elect	The spiritually regenerated elect choose to repent and believe and are saved
Man is born totally depraved			

This view is contradictory because Scripture equates spiritual regeneration and being born again with salvation. With Reformed Theology's configuration, believers would be saved twice--a total impossibility.

The Scriptual View

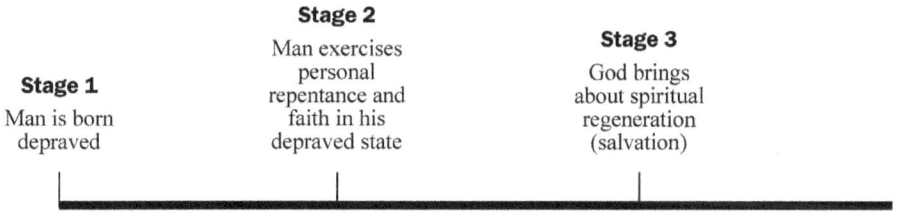

	Stage 2	Stage 3
Stage 1	Man exercises personal repentance and faith in his depraved state	God brings about spiritual regeneration (salvation)
Man is born depraved		

Be aware that man is brought out of his state of depravity and into the kingdom in a flash, in fact, less than a flash. Therefore, the brevity of time between man's choice to repent and believe while depraved and God's act of spiritual regeneration (salvation) is impossible to imagine.

Diagram 11

Hyper-Calvinism (One Brand of Reformed Theology)

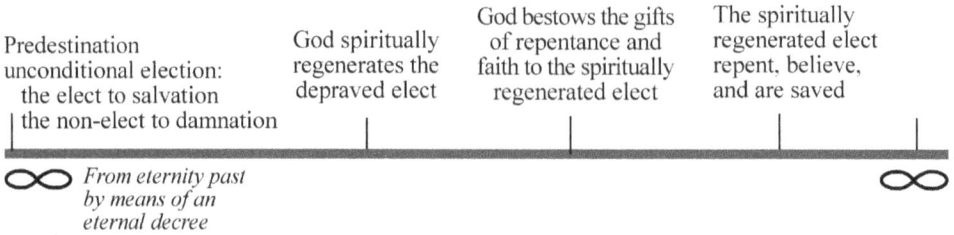

Predestination unconditional election: the elect to salvation the non-elect to damnation

God spiritually regenerates the depraved elect

God bestows the gifts of repentance and faith to the spiritually regenerated elect

The spiritually regenerated elect repent, believe, and are saved

∞ *From eternity past by means of an eternal decree*

∞

Strong (Extreme) Calvinism (A Second Brand of Reformed Theology)

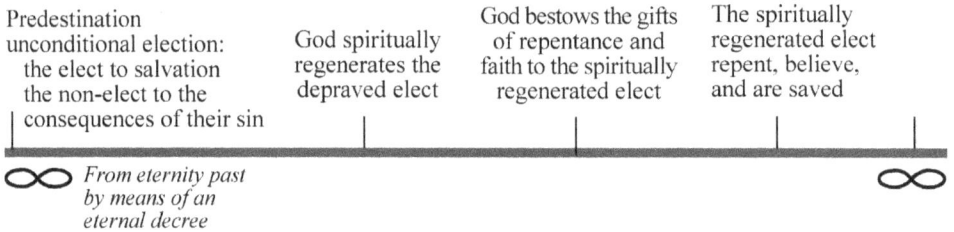

Predestination unconditional election: the elect to salvation the non-elect to the consequences of their sin

God spiritually regenerates the depraved elect

God bestows the gifts of repentance and faith to the spiritually regenerated elect

The spiritually regenerated elect repent, believe, and are saved

∞ *From eternity past by means of an eternal decree*

∞

Moderate Calvinism

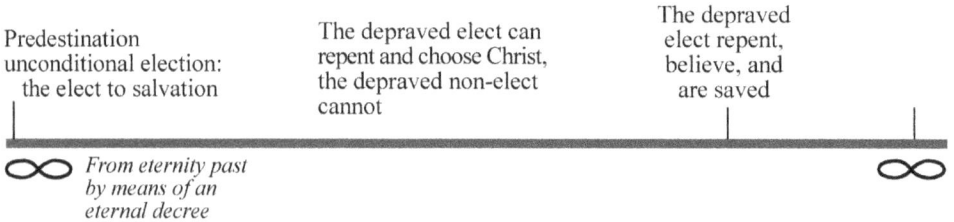

Predestination unconditional election: the elect to salvation

The depraved elect can repent and choose Christ, the depraved non-elect cannot

The depraved elect repent, believe, and are saved

∞ *From eternity past by means of an eternal decree*

∞

Arminianism

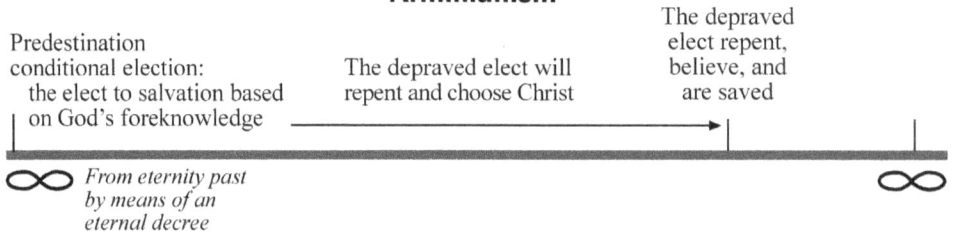

Predestination conditional election: the elect to salvation based on God's foreknowledge

The depraved elect will repent and choose Christ

The depraved elect repent, believe, and are saved

∞ *From eternity past by means of an eternal decree*

∞

220

226

Romans (cont.)
16:25-26—103

1Corinthians
1:2—14, 27, 122, 150, 182, 197
1:3—8
1:4—14
1:5—14, 107
1:9—26, 121
1:24—36
1:30—39, 84, 171, 200, 201
2:4—119
2:4-5—47
2:5—82
2:6-12—35
2:7—21, 36
2:8—29
2:10—155
2:12—57
2:13—155
2:16—11, 35
3:16—115, 125, 127, 184
3:23—107
4:16-17—161
4:19—47
6:9—164
6:9-12—153
6:11—155
6:17—184
6:19—115, 125
6:20—47
7:2-5—164
7:3-4—177
8:4-6—126
8:6—11, 108, 113
9:1—7, 133
9:16-17—100
9:27—106, 119
10:1-2—75

10:17—11
11:1—86, 161
11:3-16—110
11:10—110
11:23-24—101
12—134
12:4-30—131
12:6—43
12:10—134
12:11—131, 153
12:12-13—102, 104
12:12-27—11, 84, 142
12:13—14-17, 19, 22, 27, 26, 31, 36, 46, 74, 96, 125, 126, 147, 155, 173
12:14-27—152
12:28—132, 134
13—181
14:3—134
14:20—156
14:26—174
14:37—133, 134
15:8—7
15:9—106
15:10—31, 74, 105, 161, 212
15:25—40
15:26—40, 132
15:26-28—131
15:28—40, 41, 58
15:35-38—22
15:35-58—27
15:42-55—155
15:45—160
15:51-53—23
15:53—24
16:8-9—196
16:13—203

2Corinthians
1:2—8
1:21-22—47
1:22—48
1:24—203
2:10-11—153
2:14—14
2:14-15—147
2:14-16—141
3:6—117, 155
3:12—53
3:16—74
3:18—12, 24, 38, 111, 114, 125, 141, 161
4:4—37, 48, 68, 69, 88, 91, 146, 198
4:7-17—175
4:11—41
4:12—42
4:16—114
4:17—30, 55, 112
5:1-4—184
5:1-8—84
5:5—48
5:8—130
5:13—41
5:14—10, 28, 116, 177, 199
5:14-15—162, 180, 197
5:17—14-16, 20-22, 27, 31, 36, 39, 46, 74, 84, 85, 90, 93, 94, 102, 107, 111, 114, 117, 146-148, 150, 151, 167, 196
5:21—14, 20, 24, 83, 107, 112, 150, 168, 182, 197, 200, 201
7:6—115
8:1-5—154
8:23—133

Ephesians (cont.)
1:15—49
1:15-19—35, 209,
  210
1:18—7, 28, 42, 52,
  53, 55
1:20—58, 75
1:21—58, 59, 109,
  117
1:22—59
1:22-23—58
1:23—132
2—103
2:1—167, 170
2:1-2—44
2:1-3—167, 170
2:2—71, 163, 198
2:3—12, 25, 26, 94,
  145, 146
2:4—73
2:5—75
2:6—14, 57, 97, 111,
  117, 147, 198
2:8-9—8, 76, 83, 197,
  200, 212
2:8-10—77
2:9—78
2:10—98, 160, 161
2:11-22—101, 102,
  104, 124
2:13—14, 92
2:14-15—93, 94
2:16—151
2:18-22—125
2:19-22—11, 85
2:20—103, 133, 134
2:20-22—11
2:21—133
2:22—113
3:1—7, 121
3:2-12—100
3:3—36, 118, 210

3:3-4—105
3:4-6—124
3:5—155
3:10—75
3:12—109
3:13—113-115
3:13-15—117
3:14-15—113
3:14-19—210
3:16—115, 116, 155
3:17—118, 119, 140
3:18—124
3:19—60, 119, 132,
  139, 140
4—134, 169
4:1—26, 27, 124, 143,
  144, 163
4:1-16—26, 122, 151
4:1-6:9—195
4:1-6:24—163
4:2—124
4:2-3—124
4:3—128, 139
4:4—128
4:4-6—127
4:10—60, 117
4:11—97, 131, 141
4:11-13—117, 131,
  140
4:12—199
4:12-13—131, 134
4:13—60, 118
4:14—141
4:15—142
4:15-16—141
4:17—145
4:17-19—147
4:17-24—151
4:19—164
4:21—144
4:22—114, 150, 151
4:24—114, 151

4:25—150
4:25-27—201
4:25-32—151
4:26—123, 153
4:30—47, 162
4:32—14, 20, 24, 33,
  34, 150, 159
5—169
5:1—86
5:1-2—162-164
5:2—183
5:3—165
5:4—165
5:5—42
5:7-14—173
5:8—168-170
5:11—170
5:15—170
5:15-17—173
5:16—173
5:17—174
5:18—118, 155, 176,
  190, 192, 202, 208,
  211
5:18-6:9—174
5:19-21—190
5:22-24—181
5:22-33—97, 190
5:23—11, 48, 120,
  183
5:23-24—192
5:25—192
5:25-27—180, 184
5:27—84
5:29-30—11
5:30—29
5:31—183, 184
6—69
6:1—192
6:1-3—190
6:2-3—190
6:3—187

Ephesians (cont.)
6:4—177
6:5-9—192
6:9—177
6:10—14
6:11—14, 140, 199
6:11-12—75
6:12—57, 58, 69, 109,
 130, 167, 198
6:13—11
6:14—207
6:15—207
6:16—207
6:17—207
6:21-22—7
6:24—163

Philippians
1:1—7
1:2—8
1:6—8, 47
1:10—172
1:12—112
1:21—51, 86
1:23—130
1:29—38
2:3—122
2:5-8—176
2:10—37, 40
2:13—43, 85, 127,
 161, 197
2:20—59
3:7—105
3:9—75, 168
3:10—12, 51, 56, 105,
 118, 119, 139, 161
3:20—97
4:6—209
4:7—202
4:11-13—38
4:13—57, 161, 196
4:18—162

4:19—10, 14

Colossians
1:2—8
1:4—82
1:9—49, 171
1:10—169
1:12—42
1:13—31, 167
1:15—29, 59
1:15-16—48, 108
1:16—40, 106, 107,
 109
1:18—25, 48
1:19—39, 59, 118,
 139
1:20—40
1:25—100
1:26-27—36, 105
1:27—14, 30, 50, 57,
 83, 103
1:28—14
1:29—43, 57, 106
2:2—36, 105, 111
2:3—105
2:8—140
2:9—9, 39, 59, 60,
 118, 139
2:10—14, 20, 24, 27,
 107, 150
2:11—14
2:12—74
2:12-13—74
2:13—20, 24, 33, 34,
 150
2:13-14—32
2:15—130, 198
2:18-19—141
2:19—142
2:20-23—159, 160,
168
3:1—57

3:4—19, 29, 30, 42,
 51, 56, 59, 86, 104,
 115, 117, 161, 197
3:5—165, 166
3:8—154
3:9—114, 148, 151
3:9-10—151
3:10—114, 149-151
3:14—124
3:15—26
3:16—175
3:16-22—174
3:20—188
3:23—194
3:23-24—42
3:25--183
4:2—208, 209
4:3—36, 210
4:6—154
4:7-9—211
4:12—210

1Thessalonians
1:1—8, 133
1:6—161
1:8—82
2:3—164
2:6—133
2:14—161
3:10—208
4:3—172
4:5—144
4:12—121
4:13—53
4:13-18—22, 23, 48,
 55, 84, 132
5:4-6—170
5:8-9—204
5:11—154
5:14—114
5:15—37, 168
5:17—113, 208

[1] Wuest, Kenneth S. (1989). *Word Studies in the Greek New Testament,* Page 20. Wm. B. Eerdmans Publishing Co. Grand Rapids, MI. www.eerdmans.com. Used by permission.

[2] Phillips, J.B. (1996). *The New Testament In Modern Language.* Touchstone Books, a division of Simon & Schuster. Used by permission.

[3] Vine, W.E.; Unger, Merrill F., White, William Jr. (1996). *Vine's Expository Dictionary.* Thomas Nelson. Nashville, TN. Used by permission. All rights reserved.

[4] Wuest, Kenneth S. (1983). *Ephesians and Colossians.* Wm. B. Eerdmans Publishing Co. Grand Rapids, MI. www.eerdmans.com. Used by permission.

[5] Ibid.

[6] Stedman, Ray C. (1972). *Turned On By Prayer* from the *Riches In Christ* series. http://www.raystedman.org/new-testament/ephesians/turned-on-by-prayer

[7] Wuest, Kenneth S. (1983). *Ephesians and Colossians.* Wm. B. Eerdmans Publishing Co. Grand Rapids, MI. www.eerdmans.com. Used by permission.

[8] Hunt, Dave. (2006). *What Love Is This?*, Third Edition, pages 452-453. The Berean Call. Bend, OR. Used by permission.

[9] Calvin, John. *Commentary on the Epistle to the Ephesians,* from *The Comprehensive John Calvin Collection* Ages Digital Library. ©1998.

[10] Anderson, Sir Robert. (1978). *The Gospel and Its Ministry*, page 54. Kregel Publications, Grand Rapids, MI. Used by permission of the publisher. All rights reserved.

[11] Orr, James, M.A., D.D. General Editor. (1915). Entry for 'Gentiles, Court of the'. *International Standard Bible Encyclopedia.* http://www.studylight.org/encyclopedias/isb/view.cgi?n=6655.

[12] Vine, W.E.; Unger, Merrill F., White, William Jr. (1996). *Vine's Expository Dictionary.* Thomas Nelson. Nashville, TN. Used by permission. All rights reserved.

[13] Wuest, Kenneth S. (1983). *Ephesians and Colossians.* Wm. B. Eerdmans Publishing Co. Grand Rapids, MI. www.eerdmans.com. Used by permission.

[14] Phillips, J.B. (1996). *The New Testament In Modern Language.* Touchstone Books, a division of Simon & Schuster. Used by permission.

[15] Ibid., Page 132.

[16] Wuest, Kenneth S. (1989). *Word Studies in the Greek New Testament.* Wm. B. Eerdmans Publishing Co. Grand Rapids, MI. www.eerdmans.com. Used by permission.

[17] Guthrie, D., Motyer, J. A., Stibbs, A. M., and Wiseman, D. J. (Eds.) (1984). *The New Bible Commentary: Revised.* Wm. B. Eerdmans Publishing Co., Grand Rapids, MI. www.eerdmans.com. Used by permission.

[18] Sanders, J. Oswald. (2007). *The Search For Leaders.* (Excerpted from *Spiritual Leadership.* Moody Publishing, Chicago). Cru Press, Campus Crusade For Christ, Inc. http://crupressgreen.com/wp-content/uploads/2012/04/sandersthesearchforleaders.pdf. Used by permission.

[19] Murray, John. (1957). *Principles Of Conduct, Aspects Of Biblical Ethics.* Wm. B. Eerdmans Publishing Co. Grand Rapids, MI. www.eerdmans.com. Used by permission.

[20] Wuest, Kenneth S. (1989). *Word Studies in the Greek New Testament.* Wm. B. Eerdmans Publishing Co. Grand Rapids, MI. www.eerdmans.com. Used by permission.

[21] Vine, W.E.; Unger, Merrill F., White, William Jr. (1996). *Vine's Expository Dictionary.* Thomas Nelson. Nashville, TN. Used by permission. All rights reserved.

[22] Ibid.

[23] Vincent, Marvin R. (1985). *Word Studies in the New Testament*, Hendrickson Publishers, Peabody, MA. Used by permission.

[24] Orr, James, M.A., D.D. General Editor. (1915). Entry for 'Spiritual Songs'. *International Standard Bible Encyclopedia.*
http://www.studylight.org/encyclopedias/isb/view.cgi?n=8278.

[25] Hesburgh, Theodore. "Quotable Quotes," *Reader's Digest,* Jan. 1963, pp. 25; see also *Richard Evans' Quote Book* (1971) pp. 11.

[26] Vine, W.E.; Unger, Merrill F., White, William Jr. (1996). *Vine's Expository Dictionary.* Thomas Nelson. Nashville, TN. Used by permission. All rights reserved.

[27] Hughes, R. K. *Ephesians: The Mystery of the Body of Christ.* ©1990. pp. 206. Used by permission of Crossway, a publishing ministry of Good News Publishers, Wheaton, IL 60187, www.crossway.org.

[28] Phillips, J.B. (1996). *The New Testament In Modern Language.* Touchstone Books, a division of Simon & Schuster. Used by permission.

[29] Wuest, Kenneth S. (1989). *Word Studies in the Greek New Testament.* Wm. B. Eerdmans Publishing Co. Grand Rapids, MI. www.eerdmans.com. Used by permission.

[30] Vine, W.E.; Unger, Merrill F., White, William Jr. (1996). *Vine's Expository Dictionary.* Thomas Nelson. Nashville, TN. Used by permission. All rights reserved.

www.ingramcontent.com/pod-product-compliance
Lightning Source LLC
Chambersburg PA
CBHW021503090426
42739CB00007B/439